W. Tölle   J. Yasner   M. Pieper

Study and Research Guide in

Computer Science

Profiles of Universities in the USA

Springer-Verlag

Berlin Heidelberg New York
London Paris Tokyo
Hong Kong Barcelona
Budapest

Wolfgang Tölle
Jason Yasner
Michael Pieper

National Research Center for Computer Science (GMD)
Department of International Affairs
Schloss Birlinghoven
W-5205 Sankt Augustin 1
Federal Republic of Germany

CR Classification (1991): A.2, K.3

ISBN-13: 978-3-540-55319-9   e-ISBN-13: 978-3-642-77393-8
DOI: 10.1007/978-3-642-77393-8

Library of Congress Cataloging-in-Publication Data.
Tölle, W. (Wolfgang), 1961–. Study and research guide in Computer Science : profiles of
universities in the USA / W. Tölle, J. Yasner, M. Pieper ; [National Research Center for
Computer Science]. p. cm. Includes bibliographical references and index.
ISBN-13:978-3-540-55319-9
1. Computer science – Study and teaching (Higher) –United States-Directories. I. Yasner, J.
(Jason), 1966– . II. Pieper, M. (Michael), 1953– . III. Gesellschaft für Mathematik und
Datenverarbeitung. IV. Title.
QA76.27.T64   1993   004'.071'173–dc20   92-39481

This work is subject to copyright. All rights are reserved, whether the whole or part of the
material is concerned, specifically the rights of translation, reprinting, reuse of illustrations,
recitation, broadcasting, reproduction on microfilm or in any other way, and storage in data
banks. Duplication of this publication or parts thereof is permitted only under the provisions
of the German Copyright Law of September 9, 1965, in its current version, and permission for
use must always be obtained from Springer-Verlag. Violations are liable for prosecution under
the German Copyright Law.

© Springer-Verlag Berlin Heidelberg 1993

The use of general descriptive names, registered names, trademarks, etc. in this publication
does not imply, even in the absence of a specific statement, that such names are exempt from
the relevant protective laws and regulations and therefore free for general use.

Typesetting: Camera ready by authors
45/3140 - 5 4 3 2 1 0 – Printed on acid-free paper

Table of Contents

Preface

This guide developed from an internal project initiated by the International Department and directed by the Washington, D.C. office of the German National Research Center for Computer Science (GMD = Gesellschaft für Mathematik und Datenverarbeitung). It aims at describing **computer science departments at universities in the United States of America in several ways**. The reasons for starting this project were manifold and included the following:

* GMD is a national research center which is pursuing research in many areas of computer science and information technology. At the same time, GMD has close ties to computer science departments at German universities. For the researchers as well as for the management at GMD, it was (and is) of much value to have (at least) a brief description of computer science departments at universities in the United States of America. Especially valuable is information about faculty with their research interests (Where are researchers pursuing research in similar areas?), information about projects (Are there similiar projects?), and collaborations (Can and should we cooperate?).

* In the Federal Republic of Germany a book entitled *Studien- und Forschungsführer Informatik* (Study and Research Guide for Computer Science) has been published for many years and updated annually. This guide describes all German universities offering graduate programs for computer science as well as the overall "computer science landscape" in detail. It includes general rules for studying in Germany, and information on the curricula at the departments, the faculty with research interests, specific research projects, cooperation with industry, etc. It is a useful guide for anyone interested in research and education in the field of computer science in Germany.

Since nothing comparable existed thus far, we began to think about assembling a similar guide for the United States. Initially, this guide only was supposed to be published internally within our own organization. But as soon as we began to develop a detailed plan of how to assemble the profiles of the universities, it became clear that a much broader description of the departments would be very valuable. At the same time – by discussing the project with many people – we realized that the guide was not only very interesting for GMD, but also for many other groups. Among those who might be interested in the profiles are researchers, faculty and students at any computer science department, research laboratory, government agency, industry, etc. in the world.

There are about 130 Ph.D.-granting Computer Science Departments in the U.S. and Canada, and for the first edition of this guide we started with about 40 of the best known in the U.S. Not mentioning any other department in this edition does not mean that they are not highly ranked.

This guide is only aimed at describing the departments and includes information up to August 1991. We were not aiming at advertising any department and we did our best to be as objective as we could be. We never hid the purpose of our inquiry to the departments, and always explained the project to them in detail. Furthermore, we tried very hard to only include the latest available information. Of course there is the possibility that some of the information already is outdated, e.g., some professors might have changed universities in the meantime or the chairman might have changed. However, this should only be true for a few cases, and even then the correct information should be tracked down easily.

But please always keep in mind that most of the description is based on the information the departments have given to us. It should be clear that the better and more detailed the information we received, the better the departments could be described.

Acknowledgements

I would like to thank everyone who helped to assemble this guide.

Many thanks to the Computing Research Association for sending us the latest edition of the "Forsythe List"; Dr. Weingarten also made some helpful initial remarks. Other very helpful hints and remarks came from Prof. Dr. Gerhard Seegmüller, Prof. Dr. Gerhard Goos, Prof. Dr. Klaus Beier and Dr. Charles N. Brownstein. I am also indebted to all the unnamed people in the different departments who helped us to obtain the necessary information.

Last but not least, quite a few people in the GMD office in Washington, D.C. have been involved in the planning and preparation of this guide. My very special thanks go to Mr. Jason Yasner, whose contributions were many; he not only prepared many of the profiles, but also took most of the burden of the technical preparation of the guide, and he also helped in contacting the departments and in gathering the information. Dr. Michael Pieper, who prepared some of the profiles, also gave some very helpful advice. Mrs. Erika Feulner arranged many of the initial contacts and helped in gathering and preparing the information. I am also grateful for the support from Ms. Margot Apelt and Mrs. Christa Parrish.

Washington, D.C., June 1992   Wolfgang Tölle

Introduction

Our initial step in planning the guide was to develop a layout or overall structure which would be uniform for all departments, and which would be specific yet broad enough to handle all the information under similar headings.

The basic information (address, phone number, email address, chairman, administrative assistant) was obtained from the latest edition (March 1991) of the "Forsythe List of Ph.D. Granting Departments of Computer Science and Computer Engineering", which is sponsored by the Computing Research Association. It includes basic information on approximately 130 Ph.D.-granting computer science and computer engineering departments in the U.S.A. and Canada. We included most of this basic information in the profiles of the departments, and used most of the listed phone numbers and names for our initial contacts.

Our first step in obtaining the necessary information was to contact the selected departments by phone and we usually asked them to send general and detailed information about their department, e.g., curriculum, faculty (with research areas), facilities, funding, projects, collaborations, etc. (e.g., brochures, annual reports, etc.). We scanned these brochures for the information we were looking for, and assembled it into our layout.

Since we were only aiming at profiles of the departments (and not at a complete description), we restricted the information to the given structure/layout as well as to only a few pages per department. In order to achieve this, we sometimes had to make a selection. In the case of a whole range of known research projects, for example, we usually selected those which had not expired at that time.

In some cases we had to recontact some of the departments by phone to get more detailed information. But still some information was not available, and we wanted to make absolutely sure that everything was correct. Therefore, we sent these preliminary profiles back to the departments to have them verified, and again we asked for more detailed information. We ensured two things with this procedure: first, the departments themselves were involved and had the possibility to correct any mistakes or misleading information, and second, this enhanced the chance of getting the latest and best information.

According to the responses from the departments, we corrected the profiles, entered missing information, etc., and finally, the profiles were finished. Some of the departments did not answer our last inquiry, and we therefore assumed that the preliminary profiles were correct.

After this, our next and last step was to derive two index lists from the information within the profiles:

* an alphabetical list of all the mentioned faculty, and

* a list of the faculty by (alphabetical) research areas.

Furthermore, for the sake of convenience, we added an address list of the included departments.

How to Use This Guide

This guide contains the following information:

*   a list of abbreviations and terms employed, a preface, and an introduction together with an explanation of the general structure of this guide,

*   profiles of selected computer science departments in the U.S.A. (in alphabetical order),

*   an abbreviation list of universities,

*   a faculty list by alphabet,

*   a faculty list by research areas (in alphabetical order),

*   an address list of the included departments,

*   a list of references.

The structure/layout of the profiles is uniform for every university and is as follows:

*   Basic information about the departments:

    –   name of the university,
    –   address of the department,
    –   phone number (and occasionally fax number)
    –   electronic mail (email) address,
    –   name of the current chairman of the department,
    –   name of the current administrative assistant,
    –   the year of the establishment of the department,
    –   number of undergraduate students in the department,
    –   number of graduate students in the department,
    –   number of faculty in the department.

*   Curriculum:

Although the general requirements for obtaining degrees in the U.S. are the same at any university, they are not as clear-cut as in some other countries; specific requirements for the different programs may differ from state to state and even from university to university within one state. Therefore, this section contains information about the degree programs offered by the department. We did not attempt to assemble a full description in every detail, but usually a brief description of the requirements for each program is given. Emphasis is put on special programs (e.g., joint programs with other departments or schools) and special requirements (e.g., language requirements). Therefore, this section should be especially interesting for students.

*   Courses for Graduates (Selection):

Contains a selected list of courses for graduate students offered by the department. This gives an overview of the spectrum of research and education areas and should be interesting for students and researchers. Courses for undergraduates are not listed.

*   Faculty:

We divided this section into three groups:

–   Professors were listed together with their research areas. Information about their degree(s), and where they received them, is also given (if available).
–   Associate Professors are only listed by names.
–   Assistant Professors are only listed by names.

Lecturers, researchers, etc., who might also belong to the faculty and staff are not listed in this section. In the Appendix, all the Professors (including the Associate and Assistant Professors) are listed alphabetically in the "List of Professors". Furthermore, the Professors (excluding Associate and Assistant Professors) are listed by research area in the "Research Areas with Professors"; every single research interest is given there.

*   Affiliated Institutions:

The structure of departments at universities in the U.S. sometimes is not very clear. Next to the department itself there are laboratories and other institutions which directly belong to the department, but, for example, sometimes offer special degree programs. At the same time, there might be institutions or laboratories which belong to other departments or even other schools or universities, but which are also pursuing (sometimes joint) research in the area of computer science, or are offering joint degree programs. Whenever information about these kind of institutions was available, we placed it under the common heading of "Affiliated Institutions", and gave a brief description of their purpose in most cases.

*   Facilities:

We tried to give an overview of the computer (and sometimes special) equipment used within the department and (if available) within the affiliated institutions. This also gives an overview of possible research and education areas. This should be interesting for students and researchers. The latter might, for example, be interested in special supercomputers.

*   Research Areas, Funding, and Selected Projects:

This is a broad section where we tried to give an outline of the research being pursued within the department (or affiliated institutions). If not already clear by other sections (and if possible), we first give an overview of the main research areas. Afterwards, we selected specific projects and listed them (if possible) with a short description of their purpose as well as information about the principal investigator(s) , the sponsor(s), the amount of funding (usually rounded), and the expiration date of the project (if available). The list of projects at some departments was seemingly endless and we therefore had to make a selection in many cases. We tried to select only projects which are currently running or did not expire before 1991, and which – at the same time – give a broad overview of the spectrum of research pursued within the department. This is the section where we most heavily relied on good and detailed information by the department; many official brochures did not mention any specific projects, and only some mentioned the sponsor(s), the funding, etc. Some of the general funding information (e.g., for "separately budgeted research expenditures") was obtained from the "Engineering College Research & Graduate Study; Edition March 1991" published by the American Society for Engineering Education.

*   Collaborations:

In this last section we tried to give some information about special (national and international) collaboration or cooperation of the department with industry, other universities, etc. However, many departments did not have much information available, and especially information about international cooperation was very hard to obtain.

The Appendix is very useful in several ways and for several groups:

*   List of Universities:

This is a quick reference to the addresses of the departments described in the profiles.

*   Abbreviations of Universities:

Only the short names of the universities are used in the faculty list by alphabet. These abbreviations might occasionally not correspond to the official abbreviations.

*   List of Professors (alphabetical):

We assembled an alphabetical list of every Professor (including Associate and Assistant Professors) together with the (abbreviated) name of the university where he or she is currently employed. This list is very useful to anybody looking for a special professor; he or she then can turn to the profile of the department to gather more information. Approximately 1050 professors have been included in the profiles.

*   Research Areas with Professors:

We also assembled an alphabetical list of every single research area mentioned in the faculty list in the profiles. For every research area we listed the names of all the professors pursuing research in that specific area (since we only mentioned research areas for Professors, and not Associate and Assistant Professors, the latter ones naturally are not part of this list). This is most useful for any researcher looking for persons doing research in similar or the same specific research area. After having found interesting persons, he or she then may use the faculty list by alphabet in order to find out the university where these persons are employed. After that, he or she can turn to the profile of the department to get more detailed information (e.g., about the professor or specific projects) and may eventually contact these persons. Approximately 800 specific research areas have been included in the profiles.

*   References:

For further general information.

List of Abbreviations

AFOSR	Air Force Office of Scientific Research
AITRC	Applied Information Technologies Research Center
ARO	Army Research Office
B.A.	Bachelor of Arts
B.M.E.	Bachelor of Mechanical Engineering
B.S.	Bachelor of Science
CAD	Computer-Aided Design
D. E.	Doctorat d'Etat
DARPA	Defense Advanced Research Projects Agency
DoD	Department of Defense
DoE	Department of Energy
D.Phil.	Doctor of Philosophy
Dr. Eng., Eng. Sc. D., Dr.-Ing.	Doctor of Engineering Science
Dr. rer. nat.	Doctor of Science
EECS	Electrical Engineering and Computer Science
FBI	Federal Bureau of Investigation
GPA	Grade Point Average
GRE	Graduate Record Examination
M. Eng.	Master of Engineering
M.A.	Master of Arts
M.B.A.	Master of Business Administration
M.C.S.	Master of Computer Science
M.Phil.	Master of Philosophy
M.S.	Master of Science
M.S.E.	Master of Science in Engineering
M.S.T.C.S.	Master of Science for Teaching in Computer Science
n.a.	not available
NASA	National Aeronautics and Space Administration
NIH	National Institutes of Health
NSF	National Science Foundation
ONR	Office of Naval Research
Ph.D.	Doctor of Philosophy
USAF	United States Air Force
USPS	United States Postal Service

Brown University

Department of Computer Science
Box 1910
Providence, Rhode Island 02912-1910
Phone: (401) 863-7600
email: jes@brown.cs.edu

Chairman: Prof. Eugene Charniak
Administrative Assistant: Katrina Avery

Established: 1979
Undergraduates: n.a.
Graduate students: n.a.
Faculty: 18

Curriculum:
The Department offers B.S., B.A., a master's and Ph.D. programs.

For a M.S. eight approved courses and either a project or thesis have to be completed; this can be done in a year of full-time work by those with an adequate undergraduate background. Two of the courses may be reading and research courses leading to the project/thesis. Of the remaining six courses, two must be "practice", two "theory" and the other two are elective.

Ph.D. students must pass a comprehensive examination (e.g. written test, programming assignment, research project) by the end of the second year, complete eight course credits (as in M.S.), a major requirement (normally thesis proposal document and oral presentation by the end of the third year), and two minor requirements (each met by two approved one-semester courses; usually one inside and one outside the field of computer science). The dissertation, together with an expository talk and the defense of dissertation are the final requirements.

Courses for Graduates (selection):
Introduction to Computer Graphics, Computer Construction, Software Engineering, Artificial In-

telligence, Theory of Computation, Analysis of Algorithms, Logic and Computation, Computational Complexity. Database Management Systems, VLSI, Systems Architecture, Software Systems Design.

Topics in Operating Systems, Database Management, Computer Architecture Systems, Interactive Computer Graphics, Advanced Compiler Construction, Software Engineering, Natural Language Understanding, Artificial Intelligence, Analysis of Algorithms, Mathematical Analysis of Algorithms, Applied Theory of Computation, Computational Geometry, Combinatorial Optimization: Algorithm and Complexity, Semantics of Parallel Computation, Programming Languages, Programming Language Theory, Constraint Logic Programming.

Faculty (Professors with Research Areas):

Professors:

Eugene Charniak, Chairman, Ph.D., Massachusetts Institute of Technology, 1972 - Artificial intelligence, natural language processing.

Paris C. Kanellakis, Ph.D., Massachusetts Institute of Technology, 1981 - Databases, theory of computation, distributed computing, combinatorial optimization, logic programming.

Franco P. Preparata, Dr. Eng., University of Rome, 1959 - Computational geometry, parallel and VLSI computation, design and analysis of algorithms, computer arithmetics.

Steven P. Reiss, Ph.D., Yale University, 1977 - Theory of programming, graphical programming, programming languages and systems, semantics, compilers, database management systems, computational geometry.

John E. Savage, Ph.D., Massachusetts Institute of Technology, 1965 - Computational complexity, parallel and VLSI computation, design and analysis of algorithms.

Andries van Dam, Ph.D., University of Pennsylvania, 1966 - Computer graphics, multimedia document preparation systems, workstations in research and education.

Jeffrey S. Vitter, Ph.D., Stanford University, 1980 - Mathematical analysis of algorithms, computational complexity, parallel algorithms, machine learning, software systems design and optimization.

Peter Wegner, Ph.D., London University, 1968 - Programming languages, software engineering.

Associate Professors:

Thomas L. Dean
Thomas W. Doeppner
John F. Hughes
Stanley B. Zdonik

Assistant Professors:

Leslie P. Kaelbling
Philip N. Klein
Daniel Lopresti
Roberto Tamassia
Pascal Van Hentenryck
F. Kenneth Zadeck

Affiliated Institutions:
Institute for Research in Information and Scholarship: is working on research on educational applications.

Facilities:
The facilities include a network of over 170 SUN color SPARCstations, DEC VAXstations, DECstations, HP graphics workstations, five Symbolics workstations, a large number of Macintoshes, and many high-resolution graphics systems. All systems are connected by Ethernet and to the university's BRUnet. The university's central facility is an IBM 3090.

Research area, funding and selected projects:
Research areas highlight the following:
- Artificial Intelligence (especially reasoning with incomplete knowledge, but also natural language understanding, robot problem solving, and temporal and spatial reasoning for decision support in planning and scheduling),
- Foundations of Computer Science (including design and analysis of algorithms, computational complexity, parallel processing, combinatorial optimization, and machine learning),
- Systems (including parallel, distributed, and VLSI system architectures, object-oriented programming and databases, graphics research, and multi-paradigm design environments).

Interesting projects include:
The FIELD system: is a visual integrated UNIX programming environment that lets programmers create and visualize programs.

The ENCORE object-oriented database: serves as a testbed for research on transaction management, object servers, query languages, and other database topics.

The Threads system: for lightweight processes is intended to support concurrent programming on a variety of machines, including parallel processors.

Collaborations:
In 1991 Brown University and four other universities (California Institute of Technology, Cornell University, University of North Carolina, University of Utah) were awarded a Science and Technology Center grant for Computer Graphics and Scientific Visualization by the National Science Foundation.

Carnegie Mellon University

Department of Computer Science
Schenley Park
Pittsburgh, PA 15213
Phone: (412) 268-2592
email: nico.habermann@cs.cmu.edu

Chairman: Prof. A. Nico Habermann (Dean)
Administrative Assistant: Sharon Burks

Established: 1965
Undergraduates: n.a.
Graduates: 170 (Ph.D. only)
Faculty: 86

Curriculum:

The department offers five programs: Master of Software Engineering (M.S.E.), Doctoral Program in Computer Science, Doctoral Program in Robotics, Doctoral Program in Pure and Applied Logic, and Doctoral Program in Algorithms, Combinatorics and Optimization. No individual credit or grades are given. Instead, near the end of each semester, the entire faculty meets to evaluate the progress of each student.

For a M.S.E. the student takes courses that emphasize software engineering during the first year. The second year is based on a studio model with a master/apprentice relationship between faculty and student. This is the student's major project. A software engineering seminar follows for in-depth discussion. The full-time student completes the M.S.E. program in two years.

The Doctoral Program in Computer Science begins with an "immigration course". This familiarizes the student with the Carnegie Mellon Computer Science community and helps them choose a faculty advisor. The student must then pass four qualifying examinations in the fields of Theory, Programming Systems, Computer Systems and Artificial Intelligence. There is no structured course requirement; students should take specific courses to improve their understanding in weak areas. The

student must then pass an area qualification with guidance from the advisor and a small committee. The student can then prepare and defend a doctoral thesis.

The Doctoral Program in Robotics stresses three areas: Perception, Cognition and Manipulation. Students devise their own individualized course of study and carry out research in the unique laboratories of the Robotics Institute. Students have the opportunity to publish their results by writing scientific papers.

The Doctoral Program in Pure and Applied Logic is an interdisciplinary venture jointly sponsored by the Department of Mathematics, the Department of Philosophy, and the School of Computer Science. Each of the three departments administers a "track program" which are united by a joint core of courses and seminars. The student must complete the Program Core, Program Electives in a specialized field, Computer Science Doctoral Requirements, and a thesis.

The Doctoral Program in Algorithms, Combinatorics and Optimization is sponsored jointly by the Graduate School of Industrial Administration (Operations Research group), the School of Computer Science (Algorithms group) and the Mathematics Department (Discrete Mathematics group). Students pursue a common curriculum that draws from the three above-mentioned groups. The students perform research with faculty from all three groups and prepare a dissertation.

Courses for Graduates (selection): n.a.

Faculty (Professors with Research Areas):

Professors:

A. Nico Habermann, Chairman (Dean), Ph.D., University of Eindhoven, 1967 - Operating systems, programming languages.

Bruce G. Buchanan, Ph.D., Michigan State University, 1966 - Artificial intelligence.

16

Jaime G. Carbonell, Ph.D., Yale University, 1979 - Artificial intelligence, machine learning, natural language processing, knowledge-based machine translation, knowledge acquisition for expert systems, knowledge representation, analogical reasoning, integrated architectures planning and learning.

Stephen W. Director, Ph.D., University of California at Berkeley, 1968 - CAD for VLSI circuits.

Takeo Kanade, Ph.D., Kyoto University, 1974 - Computer vision, mobile robots, manipulators.

H. T. Kung, Ph.D., Carnegie Mellon University, 1974 - Parallel computers, computer architecture.

James L. McClelland, Ph.D., University of Pennsylvania, 1975 - Parallel distributed processing models of perception, memory, language and thought.

Tom M. Mitchell, Ph.D., Stanford University, 1978 - Artificial intelligence, machine learning, robotics.

James H. Morris, Ph.D., Massachusetts Institute of Technology, 1969 - Distributed computer systems for human communication, functional programming languages, empirical studies of programming.

Allen Newell, Ph.D., Carnegie Mellon University, 1957 - Artificial intelligence, cognition.

Raj Reddy, Ph.D., Stanford University, 1966 - Man-machine communication, artificial intelligence, robotics.

John C. Reynolds, Ph.D., Harvard University, 1961 - Type theory, programming languages.

Dana S. Scott, Ph.D., Princeton University, 1958 - Model theory, automata, set theory, information retrieval, electronic publishing.

Mary Shaw, Ph.D., Carnegie Mellon University, 1972 - Software engineering.

Daniel P. Siewiorek, Ph.D., Stanford University, 1972 - Design automation, reliable computing, multiprocessors.

Herbert A. Simon, Ph.D., University of Chicago, 1943 - Artificial intelligence.

Richard Statman, Ph.D., Stanford University - Mathematical logic, theory of computation, combinatorics and graph theory, theoretical computer science.

Associate Professors:

Randal E. Bryant
Edmund M. Clarke, Jr.
David A. Evans
Mark S. Fox
Merrick L. Furst
Ravindran Kannan
Matthew T. Mason
Richard F. Rashid
Rob A. Rutenbar
M. Satyanarayanan
William L. Scherlis
Zary Segall
Alfred Z. Spector
Richard M. Stern
Andrew P. Witkin

Assistant Professors:

Ronald P. Bianchini, Jr.
Guy E. Blelloch
Stephen D. Brookes
Eric C. Cooper
Michael A. Erdmann
Allan L. Fisher
Thomas R. Gross
Maurice P. Herlihy
Peter Lee
Steven Rudich
Daniel D. Sleator
Masaru Tomita
Doug Tygar
Kurt VanLehn
Jeannette M. Wing

17

Affiliated Institutions:

Robotics Institute (RI): is an interdisciplinary research organization dedicated to advanced research and development in the burgeoning field of robotics. In addition to research in its core areas - perception, cognition, manipulation, manufacturing automation and mobile robots - RI pursues activities related to manufacturing decision systems, hazardous environments, automonous vehicles and planetary rovers.

Center for Machine Translation (CMT): has a primary focus on high-quality machine translation, merging aspects of artificial intelligence, computational and theoretical linguistics, speech recognition and algorithm design.

Information Technology Center (ITC): was established in 1979 as a joint project between Carnegie Mellon University and IBM. ITC currently focuses on prototyping of information and communication systems.

Software Engineering Institute (SEI): is a federally funded research and development center for the development of high-quality software.

Facilities:

Research facilities total more than 400 machines including various model DEC VAXstations, HP 9000, IBM RT-PC, and SUN workstations. Larger multiprocessors include DEC (8800, 785-4, 8200-6), Encore (Multimax-16), and Sequent (Balance 2100-26).

The department has also developed a series of programmable systolic array machine such as the Carnegie Mellon VLSI Warp, Andrew distributed computer system, and other experimental computers and devices.

All facilities are on a campus-wide, Ethernet-based network which accesses ARPAnet.

Research area, funding and selected projects:

The faculty perform research in four broad areas: Artificial Intelligence, Computer Systems, Programming Systems and Theory. The department has hundreds of research projects currently running.

Here is a small sample:

GANDALF (Habermann, Siemens Corporation)

Research in Wait-Free Synchronization (Herlihy, ONR, 7/91)

Understanding the Immediate Interaction Cycle Using the Soar Unified Theories of Cognition (John and Newell, ONR, 7/91)

Sensor Algorithm Research Expert System (Kanade, The Analytic Sciences Corporation, 4/91)

The Acquisition and Utilization of Spatial and Functional Knowledge (McKeown, AFOSR, 5/91)

PREP Editor: Support for Co-Authoring and Commenting (Morris et al., NSF, 11/91)

Semantically Based Programming Environments (Scott and Reynolds, DARPA, 9/91)

A Future Distributed Real-Time Operating System (Tokuda, Sony Corporation, 1/92)

Collaborations:

During the years 1988-89, the department had the following industrial affiliates: Appollo Computer Inc., Apple Computer Inc., Bell Communications Research, BP Research, Digital Equipment Corporation, Eastman Kodak Co., General Electric Co., Hewlett Packard Co., Hughes Aircraft Co., IBM Corporation, Lockheed Corporation, Microsage Computer Systems Inc., Matsushita Electric Industrial Co., Mitsubishi Electric Corporation, Mobay Corporation, Motorola Inc., Nippon Electric Corporation, North American Philips Corporation, Nynex Corporation, Olin Corporation, Olivetti Corporation, Omron Tateisi Electronics Co., Prime Computer Corporation, R.R. Donnelley & Sons Co., Seiko Epson Corporation, Shell Development Co., Siemens AG, Siemens Corporate Research and Support, Sony Corporation, Sun Microsystems Inc., Tektronix Inc., US West Advanced Technologies.

Columbia University

School of Engineering and Applied Science
Computer Science Department
450 Computer Science Building
New York, NY 10027
Phone: (212) 854-2736
email: galil@cs.columbia.edu

Chairman: Prof. Zvi Galil
Administrative Assistant: Rosemary Addarich

Established: n.a.
Undergraduates: n.a.
Graduates: 170 (107 M.S., 60 Ph.D., 3 Professional)
Faculty: 26

Curriculum:

The Department of Computer Science offers an undergraduate program, graduate programs leading to a M.S., the professional degree of Computer Systems Engineer, and the degrees of Doctor of Engineering Science and Doctor of Philosophy.

The Computer Systems Engineer degree is for people who already hold a master's degree in Computer Science and wish to specialize beyond this level. The course of study entails the equivalent of two full-time semesters. There are no specific course requirements, but 15 credits (out of a total of the required 24) have to be Computer Science courses and in addition an independent project is required.

Courses for Graduates (selection):

Probability Theory, Mathematical Statistics, Linear Algebra, Data Stuctures, Fundamental Algorithms, Software Laboratory, Digital Logic, Computer Organization, Computability and Models of Computation, Programming Languages and Translators, Operating Systems, Artificial Intelligence, Scientific Computation, Analysis of Algorithms, Software Engineering, Theory of Computation, Numerical Algorithms and their Complexity.

Faculty (Professors with Research Areas):

Professors:

Zvi Galil, Chairman - Algorithms, techniques for proving lower bounds, cryptography.

Jonathan L. Gross - Probabilistic algorithms for graph isomorphism and topological invariants, topological methods in VLSI network design, cultural factors in computing environments.

Joseph F. Traub - Randomization, applications of information-based complexity, models of computation, parallel computation, pseudo-random numbers.

Stephen H. Unger - Sequential logic circuits, switching networks for parallel processors, CAD of digital systems, technology-society issues, string manipulating languages, computer conferencing, office automation.

Henryk Wozniakowski - Information-based complexity, numerical stability.

Associate Professors:

Peter Allen
Terrance E. Boult
Steven Feiner
Gail E. Kaiser
John Kender
Gerald Q. Maguire Jr.
Kathleen McKeown
Salvatore Stolfo
Yechiam Yemini

Assistant Professors:

Daniel J. Duchamp
Diane Litman
Shree K. Nayar
Calton Pu

Affiliated Institutions:

Center for Telecommunication Research: established 1985 by the National Science Foundation as one of the Engineering and Research Centers in the United States. The goal is to expand telecommunications research in an environment of cooperation between industry and academia.

Distributed Computing and Communications Laboratory: provides an environment for collaborative research in the named areas, and forms a part of the New York State Center of Advanced Technology and of the Center for Telecommunication Research.

Center for Medical Informatics: faculty of the Computer Science Department and the Center for Medical Informatics (at the College of Physicians and Surgeons) are jointly directing research mainly emphazising applied automated decision-making (expert systems) in medicine. The Department of Clinical Information Services at Columbia Hospital is also participating in this effort.

The Academic Computing department of the Center for Computing Activities (CUCCA): provides centralized computing and communication services to the University as well as consulting support to many of the distributed systems throughout Columbia.

The Microcomputer Consulting Center: provides information and services on microcomputer software and hardware.

Facilities:

The department's research facilities include laboratory areas for robotics, computer vision, computer graphics, distributed computing, and parallel architecture research. The computer facilities consist of an IBM 4381, six VAX 11/750s, numerous HP, SUN, IBM, DEC, and Symbolics workstations and servers, HP real-time 3D shaded graphics workstations and many microcomputers. Most of the computing equipment connects to a departmental Ethernet, which is gatewayed to a campus backbone network, as well as to INTERnet (through NYSERnet), BITnet, and USEnet.

Campus equipment (e.g. at CUCCA) includes SUN, DEC, Encore, and IBM mainframes and microcomputers.

Research area, funding and selected projects:

CLASP (Classification of Scenarios and Plans): knowledge representation system representing and reasoning with large collections of plan descriptions.

COMET (Coordinated Multimedia Explanation Testbed): an integrated system that generates multimedia explanations of equipment maintenance and repair procedures.

ESPLANADE (Expert System for Planing Animation Design and Editing): testbed for experimenting with rule-based generation of 3D animated presentations.

IAIMS (Integrated Academic Information Management System): the National Library of Medicine awarded a research grant for five years to the Center for Medical Informatics to develop and implement this system which allows users to access e.g. clinical, scholarly, and administrative/management information, and a clinical database.

IBIS (Intent-Based Illustration System): a rule-based system that generates 3D technical illustrations.

NETMATE: pursues studies of problems arising in the managment of complex networked systems.

PSi: aims at developing ultra high-speed communication protocol architecture and processors.

RESEARCHER: deals with the generation of responses within an information system.

SYNTHESIS: operating system for distributed and multiprocessor systems.

In 1989-1990, the whole School of Engineering and Applied Science has separately-budgeted research expenditures in the amount of $21.2 million

($14.5 million Federal Government, $5.7 million Business and Industry, $1 million State and Local Government) for 191 projects. The Department of Computer Science had expenditures in the amount of $3.5 million for 27 projects.

Collaborations: n.a.

Cornell University

Department of Computer Science
405 Upson Hall
Ithaca, N.Y. 14853
Phone: (607) 255-7416
email: jeh@cs.cornell.edu

Chairman: Prof. John E. Hopcroft
Administrative Assistant: Heidi Angus

Established: 1965
Undergraduates: 229
Graduates: 100
Faculty: 35

Curriculum:

The Department offers B.A., B.S., M.S., M.Eng. and Ph.D. programs. In 1989-1990, 21 students received a M.S., 10 a M.Eng., and 16 a Ph.D. degree.

Courses for Graduates (selection):

Computer Science and Programming, Advanced Programming Languages, Compiler Design for Parallel Architectures, Advanced Operating Systems, RISC Microprocessor Design, Matrix Computation, Numerical Optimization, Modern Software Techniques, Robotics, Machine Vision, Text Processing and Information Retrieval, Introduction to Automated Reasoning, Artificial Intelligence Programming, Analysis of Algorithms, Theory of Computing, Topics in Parallel Architectures, Topics in Numerical Analysis.

Faculty (Professors with Research Areas):

Professors:

John E. Hopcroft, Chairman, Ph.D., Stanford University, 1964 - Modeling and simulation, robotics, algorithms.

Robert L. Constable, Ph.D., University of Wisconsin at Madison, 1968 - Theory of Computation, programming logics, automated reasoning.

Donald P. Greenberg, Ph.D., Cornell University, 1968 - Computer graphics, CAD, image processing.

David Gries, Dr. rer. nat., Munich Institute of Technology, 1966 - Programming methodology, formal methods in programming languages, semantics.

Juris Hartmanis, Ph.D., California Institute of Technology, 1955 - Theory of computation, computational complexity.

Dexter Kozen, Ph.D., Cornell University, 1977 - Theory of computation, computational complexity, program logic and semantics.

Gerald Salton, Ph.D., Harvard University, 1958 - Information organization and retrieval, text processing.

Charles van Loan, Ph.D., University of Michigan, 1973 - Numerical analysis.

Associate Professors:

Kenneth P. Birman
Thomas Coleman
Fred B. Schneider
Tim Teitelbaum
Sam Toueg
Lloyd N. Trefethen

Assistant Professors:

Bard Bloom
Bruce R. Donald
Douglas J. Howe
Daniel P. Huttenlocher
Keith Marzullo
Keshav Pingali
Alberto M. Segre
Devika Subramanian
Stephen Vavasis

Affiliated Institutions:

Design Research Institute: the goal is to accelerate the pace and reduce the cost of product development and delivery. Research areas include information management, intelligent productivity-enhancing tools, learning and knowledge-sharing within organizations, collaboration technology & methodology, and design visualization.

Advanced Computing Research Institute (ACRI): is a part of the Center for Theory and Simulation in Science and Engineering. Its mission is to conduct research in parallelism and to foster and enhance its use in the solution of scientific computing problems.

Facilities:

The facilities include about 40 SUN SPARCstations, 40 DECstations, ten SUN servers, ten SUN-3, five MicroVAX, 22 Symbolics, a DEC VAX-11/750, a 48-node BBN Butterfly GP1000, five MicroVAX II, 20 AT&T 3B2-310, six HP-9000, two NeXT, 22 Macintoshes, and a Silicon Graphics IRIS. The university provides extensive campus-wide networking through several fiber-optic token rings connecting organizational Ethernets. National and international access is provided by connections to BITnet, NYSERnet, and NSFnet.

The ACRIs' facilities include an Intel iPSC/2-Hypercube (32 processors), a 16-processor IBM Victor, a 16-processor Transtech transputer system, and an 8-processor Topologix transputer system.

The National Supercomputing Facility operates two IBM 3090-600E supercomputers with six processors each.

Research area, funding and selected projects:

The following is a partial list of funded and submitted research grants:

Very Large Fault-Tolerant Distributed Systems (Birman, DARPA, $2,163,000, 5/92)

Theoretical Foundations of Problem Solving (Constable, ONR, $500,000, 11/91)

Coordinated Experimental Research on Systems for Constructing and Manipulating Complex Objects (Department, NSF, $3,600,000, 6/91)

New Algorithmic Techniques for Task-Level Robot Planning (Donald, NSF, $130,000, 6/92)

A New Programming Language and Environment (Gries, NSF, $1,000,000, 3/91)

Structural Computational Complexity (Hartmanis, NSF, $375,000, 3/92)

Using Computer Design and Simulation to Improve Manufacturing Productivity (Hopcroft, DARPA, $2,930,000, 6/91)

A Program of Continuing Research on Representing, Manipulating, and Reasoning about Physical Objects (Hopcroft, ONR, $320,000, 4/92)

Automatic Syntax Based Phrase Construction (Salton, OCLC, $20,000, 6/91)

The Cornell Apprentice Project (Segre, ONR, $127,000, 1/91)

Research in Automatic Reformulation (Subramanian, NSF, $320,000, 6/92)

Incremental Computation (Teitelbaum, ONR, $400,000, 9/91)

The Synthesizer Generator (Teitelbaum, NSF, $100,000, 2/91)

Abstractions that Simplify the Design and Verification of Fault-Tolerant Distributed Protocols (Toueg, NSF, $140,000, 6/91)

Collaborations:

The Computer Science Department operates its own Industrial Affiliates Program. Members of the program are: AT&T Bell Laboratories, Bell Communications Research, DEC, General Electric Company, HP, Intel, IBM, Sandia National Laboratories, Shell Development Company, SUN, Tektronix, and Xerox Corporation. Service provided to members includes: annual two-day conference to update affiliates on recent research advances, timely distribution of technical reports, opportunities for limited informal discussions with faculty, opportunity for an extended visit to the department by an individual from the affiliate organization to work on a project, and the possibility of an arrangement of a recruiting seminar at Cornell.

The Design Research Institute is a joint research relationship by Cornell University and Xerox Corporation.

Duke University

Department of Computer Science
202 North Building
Durham, NC 27706
Phone: (919) 684-3048
email: djr@cs.duke.edu

Chairman: Prof. Donald J. Rose
Administrative Assistant: Dietolf Ramm

Established: n.a.
Undergraduates: n.a.
Graduates: n.a.
Faculty: 21

Curriculum:

The department offers the M.S. and Ph.D. degrees. In addition, the department cooperates with the School of Medicine in offering a M.D.-Ph.D. program.

For the M.S. degree the student must complete 30 credits of work approved by the Director of Graduate Studies. Six of these credits can be done with a well-documented computer project or thesis. The student also must pass a final oral exam administered by a committee of three graduate faculty chaired by the supervisor of the project or thesis. Up to six credits of course work can be transferred from another institution.

For the Ph.D. degree the student must complete a minimum of 60 credits (or 45 credits with approved credit transfer). During the third semester, the student must pass a qualifying exam in three areas of computer science. A residency requirement of two consecutive semesters in the same academic year is needed along with the above requirements before the student is eligible to take a preliminary exam in the fifth semester. After this the student can proceed to the preparation and defense of a dissertation before a supervising committee.

All admissions begin in the fall of each year.

Courses for Graduates (selection):

Programming Methodology, Programming Languages, Applied Discrete Structures, Computer Network Architecture, Fault-Tolerant Computer Systems, Introduction of VLSI Systems, to Scientific Computing, to Nonlinear Dynamics, Artificial Intelligence, Numerical Analysis, Numerical Differential Equations, Numerical Linear Algebra, Analysis of Algorithms, Formal Languages and Theory of Computation, Mathematical Methods for Systems Analysis, Operating Systems, Compiler Construction, Database Methodology, Functional Analysis for Scientific Computing, Computer Systems Organization, Advanced Topics in Computer Science, in Artificial Intelligence, CMOS VLSI Design, Computational Linguistics, VLSI Algorithmics, Topics in Numerical Mathematics, Systems Modeling, Operating Systems Theory.

Faculty (Professors with Research Areas):

Professors:

Donald J. Rose, Chairman, Ph.D., Harvard University, 1970 - Numerical linear algebra, numerical solution of differential equations, scientific computing.

Alan W. Biermann, Ph.D., University of California at Berkeley, 1968 - Computational linguistics, automatic programming, learning and inference.

Donald W. Loveland, Ph.D., New York University, 1964 - Logic programming, algorithm design and analysis, knowledge evaluation, automated theorem proving.

Merrell L. Patrick, Ph.D., Carnegie Mellon University, 1964 - Parallel algorithms, architecture for large-scale scientific computing.

John H. Reif, Ph.D., Harvard University, 1977 - Parallel algorithms, randomized algorithms, graph algorithms, algebraic computations, robot motion planning, data compression, optical computation.

C. Frank Starmer, Ph.D., University of North Carolina, 1968 - Cellular communication, biological modeling, biomedical research data management.

Kishor S. Trivedi, Ph.D., University of Illinois at Urbana-Champaign, 1974 - Modeling and analysis of fault-tolerant multiple processor systems.

Associate Professors:

Joanne Bechta Dugan
Carla Schlatter Ellis
John L. Ellis
Henry S. Greenside
Gershon Kedem
Dietolf Ramm
Robert A. Wagner

Assistant Professors:

Pankaj K. Agarwal
Shyamal Chowdhury
Carl L. Gardner
Hillel Gazit
Mark A. Holliday
Ming-Yang Kao
Anselmo A. Lastra
Gopalan Nadathur

Affiliated Institutions:

Microelectronics Center of North Carolina (MCNC): allows the university access to the MCNC chip design and fabrication facilities to support education and research projects. Through MCNC's two-way television and data communications network, students are able to participate in graduate-level teleclasses in the field of microelectronics. MCNC also has a cooperative effort with the University of North Carolina at Chapel Hill.

North Carolina Supercomputer Center (NCSC): was opened in Fall 1989. A high-speed connection between NCSC and the department provides workstation users access to NCSC's Cray Y-MP4 supercomputer.

Facilities:

The department's equipment includes: a double CPU Convex C1, a 64-node BBN Butterfly GP1000, five SUN-4/280 servers, three SUN-3 servers, a SUN-4/110 diskless workstation, 15 SUN SPARCstations, 44 SUN-3 diskless workstations, a Symbolics 3670 Lisp Machine, several IBM PC AT and PC, 25 Macintoshes, and a variety of smaller microcomputers.

Duke University Computation Center includes an IBM 4381, an IBM 3083, 70 IBM PC, and 140 personal computers.

MCNC runs two DEC VAX-8600, two VAX 11/750, and two Convex C-1 systems.

The university has a campus-wide network based on Ethernet and accesses NSFnet and INTERnet.

Research area, funding and selected projects:

Design and Analysis of Combinatorial Algorithms (Agarwal)

Natural Language Processing Systems (Biermann)

Queueing Theoretic Analysis of Message-Passing Parallel Computer Systems (Chowdhury)

Construction of Fault-Tolerant Systems (Dugan)

NUMA: Non-Uniformity of Memory Access (C. Ellis)

VLSI Design (J. Ellis)

Semiconductor Device and Process Simulations (Gardner)

Parallel Algorithms for Graph Problems (Gazit)

Program Behavior Models for Parallel Programs (Holliday)

Cycle Separator for Graphs (Kao)

Computational Aspects of Genetic Linkage Mapping (Lastra)

Medical Computing as Applied to Gerontology and Psychiatry (Ramm)

BLITZEN: a New Massively-Parallel Machine (Reif)

VLSI Simulation (Rose)

Biological "Communication" and Modeling (Starmer)

HARP: modeling of computer systems (Trivedi, NASA)

SAVE: modeling of computer systems (Trivedi, IBM Yorktown Research Center)

Collaborations:
The university is an integral member of Research Triangle Park (RTP). In RTP, research and development in computers, communications, microelectronics, and other high fields are cooperatively conducted by industry, government, and the other two participating universities: University of North Carolina at Chapel Hill and North Carolina State University.

George Mason University

Department of Computer Science
4400 University Drive
Fairfax, VA 22030
Phone: (703) 323-2713
email: drine@gmuvax.gmu.edu

Chairman: Prof. David Rine
Administrative Assistant: Peggy Redmond

Established: n.a.
Undergraduates: n.a.
Graduates: n.a.
Faculty: 18

Curriculum:

As one of four departments at the School of Information Technology and Engineering, the Department offers a M.S. in Computer Science (MSCS) with special emphasis on software engineering, parallel computation, image processing, and artificial intelligence.

Students seeking admission to the MSCS-program are expected to satisfy the requirements of the Graduate School. Additionally students must hold a bachelor's degree preferably with a major in computer science or a closely related technical field. They are also required to have taken preparatory courses for graduate work in computer science. Required coursework includes data structures and algorithms, assembly language programming, and computer architecture. In addition, students should have completed one year of mathematics beyond first-year science/engineering calculus, including a course in discrete mathematics. Another prerequisite is a grade point average of at least 3.0 for the last two years of undergraduate work. Furthermore, graduate record examination (GRE) scores must total at least 1800.

The MSCS-program requires a total of 33 semester hours of work. This includes a nine-hour core and 12 credit hours of advanced electives. Core courses are in Language Processors, Operating Systems, and Data Structures and Analysis of Algorithms. In consultation with an advisor, a student may elect additional courses in computer science or a closely related field so that the student's degree plan emphasizes strength in software engineering, artificial intelligence, parallel computation, systems software, distributed systems/computer networking or image processing/vision.

A doctoral program in information technology is offered by the School of Information Technology.

Courses for Graduates (selection):

Introduction to Software Engineering, Theory of Computation, Language Processors, Database Knowledge and Engineering, Computer Graphics, Computer Communications and Networking, Computer Systems Programming, Operating Systems, Introduction to Artificial Intelligence, Analysis of Algorithms, Principles of Computer Science, The Use of Computer Statistical Packages, Software Construction, Software Requirements and Prototyping, Software Design, Formal Methods and Models in Sotware Engineering, Software Project Management, Object-Oriented Software Development, User Interface design and Development, Foundations of Parallel Computation, Theory of Programming Language Translation, Interactive Graphics Software, Performance Analysis of Computer Networks, Computer Architecture and Microprogramming, Computer Systems Theory, Computer System Performance Evaluation, Natural Language Processing, Designing Expert Systems, Computer Vision, Analysis of Algorithms, Graph Algorithms, Image Processing and Applications, Neural Network Principles, Advanced Topics in Computer Science, Advanced Software Requirements, Advanced Software Design Methods, Real-time Systems Design and Development, Machine Learning.

Faculty (Professors with Research Areas):

Professors:

David Rine, Chairman, Ph.D., University of Iowa, 1970 - Database support for software engineering, programming logic and language specifications.

Alan Mark Davis, Ph.D., University of Illinois at Urbana-Champaign, 1975 - Requirements analysis and specification, software project management, design techniques, configuration management.

Ryszard S. Michalski, Ph.D., University of Silesia in Poland, 1969 - Artificial intelligence, pattern recognition, cognitive science and multiple-valued logic, symbolic methods of inductive inference, conceptual clustering, expert systems with learning capabilities, constructive induction, clustering, variable-precision logic.

Arun K. Sood, Ph.D., Carnegie Mellon University, 1972 - Parallel and distributed processing, computer networks, database machines, performance modeling, computer vision, signal processing, simulation and modeling, optimization.

Harry Wechsler, Ph.D., University of California at Irvine, 1975 - Computer and robot vision, automatic target recognition, digital image processing, neural networks, artificial intelligence, machine learning, expert systems.

Associate Professors:

Kenneth A. De Jong
Henry J. Hamburger
Eugene M. Norris
Pearl Y. Wang

Assistant Professors:

James B. Acquah
Richard H. Carver
Jorge L. Diaz Herrera
Oluseyi O. Farotimi
Ophir Frieder

Bradley Kjell
David C. Littman
Piotr Pachowicz
Donna J. Quammen
Michael C. Tanner
Gheorge Tecuci

Affiliated Institutions:
Artificial Intelligence Center, Image Processing and Computer Vision Center, Parallel Computation Center, Center for Software Systems Engineering

Facilities:
Students and faculty have access to a variety of central campus resources, including a VAX 8820 and a VAX 8530. The Computer Science Department laboratories house a number of networked SUN, HP, Macintosh, and Micro Vax II workstations. Machines are connected via Ethernet and are available through 300-2400 baud dialup and all major networks. Advanced students may work on parallel computers including an Intel Hypercube and Transputer.

Research area, funding and selected projects:
The primary areas of faculty research are: parallel computation, software engineering, artificial intelligence, and computer vision/image processing.

Use of Genetic Algorithms on NP-hard problems (De Jong)

Use of Genetic Algorithms to learn task programs in domains such as robotics, diagnosis, navigation, and game playing (De Jong)

Design and Implementation of Self-improving Diagnostic Expert Systems (De Jong, DARPA, ONR, NRL)

Collaborations: n.a.

Georgia Institute of Technology

College of Computing
AECAL Bldg., Room 156
Atlanta, GA 30332-0280
Phone: (404) 894-3186
email: pete@cc.gatech.edu

Chairman: Prof. Peter Freeman (Dean)
Administrative Assistant: Debra Kelley

Established: 1963
Undergraduates: 500
Graduates: 200
Faculty: 37

Curriculum:

The Institute offers both M.S. and Ph.D. degrees.

To obtain a M.S. degree, the student must complete either 50 credit hours of approved course work or 33 credit hours and a thesis. The student must have earned a bachelor's degree from an accredited institution, preferably in Computer Science. The M.S. degree program begins in the fall quarter of each academic year.

The Ph.D. program has two phases which normally require 4-5 years. The first two years are devoted to course work and preparing themselves for their specific research area. This phase culminates in a test of in-depth knowledge. Phase two begins with consultation with an advisory committee where the student formulates a research proposal, carries out the research and prepares a dissertation. The Ph.D. student has several options for a program of study. Besides a Ph.D. in Computer Science, an interdisciplinary program for a Ph.D. in Cognitive Science, and an interdisciplinary program for a Ph.D. in Algorithms, Combinatorics and Discrete Optimization are offered.

Courses for Graduates (selection):

Foundations of Information Science, Philosophy of Mind, Theory of Communication, Systems Theory, Information Systems Design, Theory of Automata, Theory of Compiling and Translation, Analysis of Algorithms, Complexity of Computation, Advanced Theory of Computability, Organization and Management of Information Industry, Knowledge Structures for Machine Intelligence, Computer-aided Modeling, Artificial Intelligence, Pattern Recognition, Information Control Methods, Computer Networks, Computer Language Design, Compiler Construction, Computer Operating Systems, Computer Systems Evaluation, Database Design, Graph Theory, Queueing Theory and Application, Advanced Small-scale Computer Systems, Advanced Computer Organization, Human-Computer Interface, Computer Integrated Manufacturing Systems.

Special Topics: Autonomous Robotics, Knowledge-Based Problem Solving, High-Performance Parallel Computing, Advanced Database Systems, Parallelism in Database Systems, Advanced Techniques in Computer Graphics, Hypermedia, Program Visualization, Network Management, Programming Language Semantics, Boolean Circuit Complexity.

Faculty (Professors with Research Areas):

Professors:

Peter A. Freeman, Chairman (Dean), Ph.D., Carnegie Mellon University - Software engineering.

Lucio Chiaraviglio, Ph.D., Emory University - Computer-supported instruction.

Philip H. Enslow, Jr., Ph.D., Stanford University - Computer networks, telecommunication systems, data communications, distributed processing, operating systems, computer systems.

James D. Foley, Ph.D., University of Michigan - Graphics, human-computer interaction, visualization.

Alton P. Jensen, Associate Dean, B.M.E., Georgia Institute of Technology - Computer-aided learning, small-scale systems in instructional environments.

Janet L. Kolodner, Ph.D., Yale University - Artificial intelligence, cognitive science, learning and problem solving, case-based reasoning.

Richard J. LeBlanc, Jr., Ph.D., University of Wisconsin at Madison - Programming languages and environments, compilers, distributed processing, software engineering.

Sham Navathe, Ph.D., University of Michigan - Database modeling and design, distributed databases and knowledge-based systems, database engineering applications.

Pranas Zunde, Ph.D., Georgia Institute of Technology - Information science, information systems, system theory, pattern recognition.

Associate Professors:

Ian F. Akyildiz
William F. Appelbe
Ronald C. Arkin
Albert N. Badre
James E. Burns
Richard M. Fujimoto
Frances E. Kaiser
Daryl T. Lawton
Gary L. Peterson
Karsten Schwan

Assistant Professors:

Mustaque Ahamad
Mostafa H. Ammar
Partha Dasgupta
Kurt P. Eiselt
John J. Goda, Jr.
Ashok K. Goel
Brian K. Guenter
Larry F. Hodges
Hyoung-Joo Kim
E. Robert McCurley
Gil Neiger

Edward R. Omiecinski
Ashwin Ram
Umakishore Ramachandran
John J. Shilling
John T. Stasko
H. Venkateswaran

Affiliated Institutions:

Software Engineering Research Center (SERC): plans, conducts and supports software engineering research on an Institute-wide basis as well as to make software engineering technology available for use in a broad spectrum of industrial, business and government activities.

Georgia Tech Research Institute (GTRI): provides research opportunities to graduate students in computer systems and a broad selection of application areas.

Visualization, Graphics and Usability Laboratory: has an active research program in the closely-allied areas of computer graphics and computer-human interaction.

Parallel Computation for Technical Applications Laboratory (PaCTech): is dedicated to the science of parallel computation. Research concerns are: architecture, operating systems, programming systems and algorithms research targeting certain application domains.

Facilities:
The research computer systems include an Epoch file server with optical jukebox, a 10-node Sequent S-27, a 32-node BBN Butterfly GP 100, 25 SUN-3 and 42 SUN SPARC workstations with file servers, 10 VAXstation 2000 workstations, 12 NeXT workstations, and numerous smaller systems. An iPSC/2 Intel hypercube is available jointly with the School of Electrical Engineering. Most of these connect to the campus-wide network which also supports access to INTERnet. Other specialized systems include: Silicon Graphics Iris 4D superworkstation (graphics research); 13 Symbolics LISP and two Mac/Ivory and three SUN/Ivory systems (artificial intelligence); $4 million worth

of switching, transmission and test equipment, including three Northern Telecom SL-10 packet switches (education and research in computer networking and communications systems).

Office of Information Technology: includes several clusters containing Apple, DEC, IBM, and SUN workstations; a Sequent S-81 parallel computing system, an IBM mainframe running VM and MVS, several Control Data mainframes including a 990 vector computer, and two Silicon Graphics Iris 4D-superworkstations.

Research area, funding and selected projects:
Artificial Intelligence:
MEDIATOR: mediation of resource disputes (Kolodner),
PERSUADER: mediation of labor contracts (Kolodner),
SHRINK, MEDIC: medical diagnosis (Kolodner),
JUDIS: conversation control (Kolodner),
JULIA: meal planning (Kolodner)

Computer Architecture and VLSI:
VTM: Virtual Time Machine (Fujimoto)

Computer Graphics:
Stereoscopic 3-D Computer Graphics (Hodges)

Computer-Human Interaction:
Design of Transitionality into the User-Computer Interface (Badre)

Computer Networks:
Queueing Networks with Blocking (Akyildiz)

Database Systems:
Heterogeneous Database Management (Navathe)

Distributed and Parallel Systems:
Clouds/DARE (LeBlanc, NSF, $3.35 million, Fall 1995),
PRISM: Parallel Programming Environments for Multicomputer and Multiprocessor backends (Schwan),
Chaos: High-Performance and Real-Time Multiprocessor Operating System Kernels (Schwan)

Information Science:
Adaptive Optimization of Inductive Methods in Knowledge-Based Vision Systems (Zunde),
Evaluation of Transform Methods in Computer Vision Systems (Zunde),
Models of Associative Structure of the Mind (Zunde)

Programming Languages and Environments:
PAT: Parallelization Assistant (Appelbe)

Software Engineering:
Software Reusability (McCracken)

Theoretical Computer Science:
Artificial Neural Networks (McCurley)

Collaborations:
SERC is funded by NSF to establish an Industry/University Cooperative Research Center for Information Management Research (CIMR). In conjunction with the University of Arizona, the CIMR contributes to the knowledge of the creation, storage, retrieval, display, transmission, management and use of information and the integration of all of these processes through the total systems approach. SERC is also working with the Purdue University Software Engineering Research Center on the development of the Mothra environment, an integrated set of tools and interfaces that support the planning, definition, preparation, execution, analysis and evaluation of tests of software systems.

Indiana University

Department of Computer Science
101 Lindley Hall
Bloomington, IN 47405
Phone: (812) 855-6486
email: fpp@iuvax.cs.indiana.edu

Chairman: Prof. Franklin Prosser
Administrative Assistant: Dedaimia Whitney

Established: 1971
Undergraduates: 130
Graduates: 180 (117 M.S., 63 Ph.D.)
Faculty: 23

Curriculum: n.a.

Courses for Graduates (selection):
Introduction to Computer Programming, Advanced Computer Programming, Logic Functions and Machine Theory, Advanced Operating Systems, Advanced Artificial Intelligence, Software Engineering Management, Advanced Concepts in Programming Languages, Logic and Program Verification, Programming Language Type Systems, Very Large Scale Integration, Data Communication and Networks, Computer Systems Architecture, Compilers III, Theory of Operating Systems, Database Design Theory, Analysis of Algorithms, Natural Language Understanding, Computer Models of Learning, Representations Issues for Artificial Intelligence, Algorithms for Sampled-Data Systems, Specials Topics in Computing, Computer Science Reading and Research.

Faculty (Professors with Research Areas):

Professors:

Franklin Prosser, Chairman, Ph.D., Pennsylvania State University, 1961 - Digital hardware, computer science education.

K. Jon Barwise, Ph.D., Stanford University, 1967 - Logic, information-theoretic approaches to semantics, heterogeneous inference.

J. Michael Dunn, Ph.D., University of Pittsburgh, 1966 - Algebraic logic, proof theory, non-standard logics, relations between logic and computer science.

Daniel P. Friedman, Ph.D., University of Texas at Austin, 1973 - Programming languages.

Stanley Hagstrom, Ph.D., Iowa State University, 1957 - Computer hardware, computer graphics, operating systems, software engineering, analysis of algorithms for *ab initio* quantum chemistry.

Douglas R. Hofstadter, Ph.D., University of Oregon, 1975 - Artificial intelligence, philosophy of mind, cognitive science.

Daniel Leivant, Ph.D., University of Amsterdam, 1975 - Theory of computing, theory of programming languages, mathematical logic.

Paul W. Purdom, Ph.D., California Institute of Technology, 1966 - Analysis of algorithms, rewriting systems, compilers, game playing.

Edward L. Robertson, Ph.D., University of Wisconsin, 1970 - Database systems, theory of computation, computational complexity, software engineering.

George Springer, Ph.D., Harvard University, 1949 - Programming languages, numerical analysis, complex analysis.

David E. Winkel, Ph.D., Iowa State University, 1957 - Digital design, applicative architectures.

David S. Wise, Ph.D., University of Wisconsin, 1971 - Applicative programming, multiprocessing architectures and algorithms.

Associate Professors:

Dennis Gannon
Andrew J. Hanson
Christopher T. Haynes
Steven D. Johnson
Robert F. Port

Assistant Professors:

R. Kent Dybvig
Michael Gasser
David Leake
Jonathan W. Mills
Lawrence S. Moss
Gregory J.E. Rawlins
Gregory E. Shannon
Peter Shirley
Dirk Van Gucht

Affiliated Institutions:

Center for Innovative Computer Applications (CICA): works in close cooperation with the department on projects such as visualization efforts relating to theoretical chemistry, astronomy, artificial intelligence, applied mathematics, geology, psychology and cognitive science.

Center for Research on Concepts and Cognition: is an interdisciplinary research group which focuses research on emergent models of high-level perception and analogical thought.

Indiana University Logic Group: is a multidisciplinary group in logic spanning departments of Computer Science, Linguistics, Mathematics and Philosophy.

Indiana Center for Database Systems: promotes the state of Indiana as a center for database software product development and supports Indiana industries and organizations in the development of application of database technology.

Computational Logic Laboratory: was established in 1991 to encourage research projects which bring logic to bear on computation, and vice-versa.

Facilities:

The department's facilities include a DEC VAX 8800, a DEC VAX 780, DEC MicroVAX II, a DECstation 3100, a BBN Butterfly, an Alliant FX/8, a Stardent Titan, a Symbolic, and assorted Apollo, NeXT, SUN, IBM PC clone, and Macintosh workstations. The campus-wide network is based on Ethernet and connects to INTERnet.

Research area, funding and selected projects:

Interactive Modular Programming (Dybvig, Motorola, $15,000, 7/91)

Introspective Computation (Friedman and Jefferson, NSF, $126,000, 6/92)

The Incubator Laboratory: A Multi-Purpose Undergraduate Lab for Experimental Human-Computer Interface Design (Gannon et al., NSF, $181,000 [$90,500 NSF, $90,500 matching funds], 8/91)

Algebra for Digital Design Derivation (Johnson and Winkel, NSF, $203,000, 11/92)

Lukasiewicz Logic Arrays (Mills, NSF, $60,000, 11/92)

Summer Undergraduate Research Experiences in Computer Science: Stimulating Discovery and a Positive Attitude toward Research (Mills and Shannon, COAS, $15,000, 3 summers: 1991, 1992, 1993)

Faculty Research Award (Shannon, RUGS, $3,000, 6/91)

Equipment Grant for Faculty Development (Shannon, Hewlett Packard, $50,000, 1/92)

Parallel Graph Algorithms (Shannon, NSF, $43,000, 1/92)

Coordinated Experimental Research Program: A Conduit from Theory to Practice (Winkel, NSF, $2.7 million, 12/91)

Supplemental to Coordinated Experimental Research Program: A Conduit from Theory to Practice (Winkel et al., NSF, $50,000, 12/91)

A Hierarchy of Memory for Parallel Functional Programming (Wise, NSF, $65,000, 7/91)

Collaborations:
The university also had corporate donations for research in the year 1990 by the following institutions: AT&T Foundation, Alcoa Foundation, Amoco Corporation, Andersen Consulting Company, Arthur Andersen & Company, Bloomington Bicycle Club, Caterpillar Tractor Foundation, Coca Cola Bottling Company, Cray Research Inc., Data Processing Services Inc., Digital Equipment Corporation, E.I. DuPont De Nemours & Co., Eli Lilly & Company, Exxon Corporation, Hewlett Packard Company, IBM Corporation, MPAC, NCR Foundation, Northern Telecom Inc., Printed Wiring Inc., Proctor & Gamble Company, Summit Group Inc., Upjohn Company, Waste Management Inc., Westinghouse Foundation.

Massachusetts Institute of Technology

Department of Electrical Engineering and Computer Science
545 Tech Square
Cambridge, MA 02139
Phone: (617) 253-6001
email: corbato@lcs.mit.edu

Chairman: Prof. Fernando J. Corbato (Associate Department Head)
Administrative Assistant: Neena Lyall

Established: Renamed EECS in 1975
Undergraduates: n.a.
Graduates: 185 (Computer Science only)
Faculty: 45 (Computer Science only)

Curriculum:

Academic programs for graduate students in the field of Computer Science lead to the M.S., Electrical Engineer, Doctor of Philosophy, or Doctor of Science degrees.

Most graduate courses assume a strong background in the fundamentals of Computer Science and the related mathematics. Some courses and research areas may require background in other fields such as Linguistics or classical Mathematics. Dissertations based on original research by the student are required for each of the degrees in Computer Science.

For a Master's degree the student must pass a Preliminary Written Examination (PWE). Within this breadth requirement each student has to qualify in five core fields of Computer Science: Languages, Architecture, Artificial Intelligence, Computability, and Algorithms. In each core field the student has to maintain a grade of A or B. The M.S. degree program normally requires two years to be completed. With an additional year of study a student who does superior research can receive the degrees of Electrical Engineer and Master of Science concurrently.

As part of the Doctoral program, the student must complete two further examinations: the Oral Qualifying Examination (OQE), and the Area Examination. The OQE tests the student's knowledge, problem-solving skills and intellectual preparedness for doctoral research. It is normally taken in the fourth or fifth graduate term. The student must have qualified in three of the five core fields of the PWE (no more than one of these can be Computability and Algorithms). The Area Examination is an in-depth examination on an area related to the student's Doctoral research topic, and is typically taken in the sixth or seventh term. The student must have qualified in each of the five core fields of the PWE before taking the Area Examination.

The department also offers the possibility to pursue a Master of Science degree program while working at the facilities of participating industrial organizations (Master in Industry Program). Students who are accepted into this program fulfill their academic requirements through half-time daytime study spread over two academic years after one year of full-time work at the industrial organization.

Courses for Graduates (selection):

Programming and Systems: Data-Communication Networks, Introduction to VLSI Systems, Programming Languages, Computer System Architecture, Principles of Computer Science, Concurrent Systems for Artificial Intelligence, Concurrent VLSI Architecture, Data Flow Architecture and Languages, Computer Systems.

Algorithms and Theory: Introduction to Optimization, Computation and Communication in Distributed Systems, Program Semantics and Verification, Theory of Computation, Advanced Complexity Theory, Theory of Parallel and VLSI Computation, Advanced Parallel and VLSI Computation, Theory of Algorithms, Distributed Algorithms, Advanced Algorithms, Distributed Network Protocols and Graph Algorithms, Cryptography and Cryptoanalysis, Advanced Topics in Cryptography, Geometrical Algorithms.

Artificial Intelligence: Automatic Speech Recognition, Artificial Intelligence, Concurrent Systems for Artificial Intelligence, Natural Language and the Computer Representation of Knowledge, Legged Locomotion in Robotics and Animals, Machine Vision, Robot Manipulation, The Society of Mind, Knowledge-Based Application Systems.

Furthermore, pertinent classes are also offered by the Departments of Architecture, Brain & Cognitive Sciences, Linguistics and Philosophy, Mathematics, and the Sloan School of Managment, e.g.
Architecture: Computers and Graphics Workshop I and II, Image Representation for Vision, Advanced Computer Graphics, Learning Environments, Conversational Computer Systems.
Brain and Cognitive Sciences: Research in Natural Computation, Computational Approaches to Motor Control, Theory of Neuronal Mechanics, Visual Information Processing: from Computation Theory to Neuronal Mechanics.
Linguistics and Philosophy: Problems of Mental Representation, Topics in Logic.
Management: Information Technology I and II, Advanced Computer Systems, Information Systems and Law.

Faculty (Professors with Research Areas):

Professors:

Fernando J. Corbato, Chairman (Associate Department Head) - Operating systems, computer architecture, networks, and user interfaces.

Harold Abelson - Artificial intelligence, scientific computation, educational computing.

Jonathan Allen - Natural language processing, speech recognition, speech generation, speech understanding, computer architecture, design of custom integrated cicuits, CAD tools.

Arvind - Programming languages, distributed processing, parallel processing, parallel architectures, dataflow systems, functional and logic languages.

Randall Davis - Artificial intelligence, model-based reasoning, causal reasoning about designed artifacts.

Michael L. Dertouzos - Multiprocessor systems, computer productivity.

Peter Elias - Information theory, information efficiency of representations, algorithms for storing, retrieving and manipulating information.

John V. Guttag - Programming methodology, formal specifications, theorem proving, programming multiprocessors.

Frederick C. Hennie III - Theory of computation, theory of algorithms, automata theory, applications of discrete mathematics, relational database applications.

Berthold K. P. Horn - Machine vision, advanced automation, artificial intelligence, photogrammetry, visual perception.

Barbara H. Liskov - Distributed computing, programming methodology, programming languages.

Tomás Lozanzo-Pérez - Robotics, algorithms for spatial reasoning, computational geometry, artificial intelligence.

Nancy A. Lynch - Distributed computing, distributed data management, complexity theory.

Albert R. Meyer - Semantics of programming languages, logic of programs, concurrent programs, lambda calculus, category theory, computational complexity.

Silvio Micali - Randomness and computational complexity, cryptography, secure protocols, distributed computation.

Marvin L. Minsky - Artificial intelligence, robotics, machine vision, musical concepts, understanding the principles of intelligence, applications to psychology, education and industry.

Joel Moses - Organization of large scale systems, application of knowledge-based systems, algebraic manipulation systems.

Marc H. Raibert - Robotics, legged locomotion, computer graphics, biological motor systems.

Ronald L. Rivest - Machine learning, cryptography, analysis of algorithms (on leave).

Jerome H. Saltzer - Computer systems, computer networks.

Stephen A. Ward - Computer architecture, operating systems.

Patrick H. Winston - Artificial intelligence, learning theory, machine vision, productivity technology, analogy-based reasoning.

Associate Professors:

Robert C. Berwick
Rodney A. Brooks
William J. Dally
David K. Gifford
Shafrira Goldwasser
William E.L. Grimson
Carl E. Hewitt
Charles E. Leiserson
Peter Szolovits
William E. Weihl

Assistant Professors:

Anant Agarwal
David A. McAllester
Gregory M. Papadopoulos
Lynn A. Stein
David L. Tennenhouse

Affiliated Institutions:

Artificial Intelligence Laboratory (AIL): its goal is to make machines more intelligent in order to make them more useful and to learn about the nature of intelligence. Work at the laboratory encompasses robotics, computer vision, expert systems, learning, common sense reasoning, making computers understand natural language, and computer architecture.

Center for Cognitive Science (CCS): provides an intellectual and administrative focus for individual and collaborative research in cognitive science at M.I.T. The members of the Center's Policy Committee represent the departments of Linguistics and Philosophy, Electrical Engineering and Computer Science, Artificial Intelligence Laboratory, the Research Laboratory of Electronics, and the Whitaker School of Health Science, Technology, and Managment. The Center coordinates a number of research projects, coordinates graduate and undergraduate study in cognitive science, and administers a program of postdoctoral fellowships and visiting scholar appointments.

Laboratory for Computer Science (LCS): is an interdepartmental laboratory whose principal goal is to conduct research in computer science and engineering. Founded in 1963 as Project MAC, the Laboratory developed CTSS and Multics. These two major developments stimulated research in the application of online computing in such diverse areas as engineering, biology, medicine, library science, and management. Today the laboratory's pursuits have expanded to encompass research in the areas of expert sytems, networks, cryptography, distributed and multiprocessor systems, new computer architecture, theory, VLSI design, and educational computing.

Laboratory for Information and Decision Systems (LIDS): is an interdisciplinary, interdepartmental research laboratory with the fundamental goal to advance the field of systems, communication, and control, recognizing the interdependence of theses fields and the key role that computers and computation play in this research. This work, both theoretical and applied, has broad implications for such diverse areas as data communication networks, flexible manufacturing systems, aerospace systems control, statistical signal processing techniques, and decision making in distributed environments.

Center for Intelligent Control Systems (CICS): is an interuniversity, interdisciplinary center for research in the foundations of intelligent machines and intelligent control systems sponsored by the University Research Initiative program of the U.S. Army Research Office. CICS is directed by a consortium of Brown University, Harvard University, and with headquarters at M.I.T.'s Laboratory for Information and Decision Systems. Research activities are loosely grouped into five areas: Signal Processing, Image Analysis and Vision, Automatic Control, Mathematical Foundations of Machine Intelligence, Distributed Information and Control Systems, and Algorithms and Architectures.

The Media Laboratory: offers an environment to pursue diverse interests in the field of media technology. It includes an experimental theater for video, computer graphics, holography, and computer music. There are laboratories for research areas in signal processing, and advanced television. The laboratory includes twelve research groups: Advanced Television, Computer Graphics and Animation, Electronic Publishing, Epistemology and Learning, Film/Video, Human Interface, Movies of the Future, Music and Cognition, Spatial Imaging, Speech Research, Visible Language, and Vision Science.

The Operations Research Center: provides educational and research opportunities for students and faculty interested in the interdisciplinary field of Operations Research. The center admits its own students and administers its own Master's and Doctoral programs.

The Microsystems Technology Laboratory: provides facilities that support a broad spectrum of research in microsystems technology including: Solid State Devices, Integrated Circuits, Materials for Electronic Applications, Process Technologies, Microsensors, and Computer-Aided Fabrication of Integrated Circuits.

Research Laboratory of Electronics (RLE): already founded in 1946, the RLE is M.I.T.s oldest interdisciplinary research laboratory. Research within the RLE has a very heterogeneous character, but has two major thrusts: Electronics & Op-

tics, and Language, Speech & Hearing. Within these main thrusts a selected list of specific topics includes: Electronic Materials and Fabrication, Submicron Studies, High-Speed Electronics and Optical Devices, Optical Probing and Interfacing, Circuit Design and Performance Evaluation, VLSI Design Tools, Digital Systems Design, Specialized Architectural Studies, Auditory Physiology, Sensory Communication, Speech Communication, and Linguistics.

Facilities: n.a.

Research area, funding and selected projects: The Department of Electrical Engineering and Computer Science classifies the main research interests into six main areas: Area I (Systems, Communications & Control), Area II (Computer Science), Area III (Electronics, Computers and Systems), Area IV (Energy and Electromagnetic Systems), Area V (Materials and Devices), and Area VII (Biomedical Engineering). Throughout the whole description we concentrated on Area II (Computer Science), although there might be many interconnections to other areas. Within Computer Science the main research areas are: Theory of Computation, Artificial Intelligence, Software Systems, and Computer Architecture & Hardware.

Overall, the research areas at M.I.T. are very diverse and so is the list of projects. Every above mentioned "affiliated institution" has a whole range of research projects in a wide range of different research areas. Here is a very small sample, arranged by affiliated institution:

Artificial Intelligence Laboratory:
Design of a Message-Driven Processor: is a high performance processing node for a message-passing, MIMD concurrent computer.

The J-Machine: fine-grain concurrent computer that provides low-overhead primitive mechanics for communication, synchronization, and translation.

Autonomous Mobile Robots: investigates all aspects of building intelligent, fully autonomous mobile robots for indoor, outdoor, underwater, and space applications.

Parallel Networks for Machine Vision, Direct Motion Vision by Fixation, Optimal Filtering in Machine Vision, Motion and Structure Recovery from Sequences Using Shading Information, Dynamic Motion Vision: all five projects aim at new developments in the area of machine vision and motion.

Center for Cognitive Science:
Psychology of Graphic Displays: an exploration of how graphic displays are recognized by humans.

Mental Representation of Space: experimental research on the human ability to recognize, visualize, attend to, and mentally manipulate three-dimensional objects and displays.

Language Learnability and Language Development: development of a theory on the computations children perform to induce grammar of the language of their community.

Knowledge of Language: Thematic Structure, Binding, and Control: aims both to systematize current work on the nature of binding and control in languages and to examine the consequences of this systematization for the structure of the lexicon.

Laboratory for Computer Science:
ALEWIFE: A Large-Scale Multiprocessor: design of a scalable multiprocessor for high performance scientific and symbolic computing.

APRIL: VLSI RISC Processor for a Large-Scale Multiprocessor: design and implementation of a VLSI RISC processor with special hardware support for rapid context switching, data typing, futures, and synchronization.

High Resolution Systems Architecture: an architectural framework for High Resolution Systems including HDTV workstations and video applications.

Advanced Network Architecture (ANA) and Gigabit Network Research: proposes key concepts for future networks and studies critical issues underlying the next generation of data networks, in particular architectural issues such as congestion control, multiple qualities of service, autonomy, etc. The Gigabit Network research is part of the ANA project and involves experimental work related to Broadband Network Architectures (B-ISDN).

Computer Speech Recognition: the long-term goal is to provide graceful human/machine interactions using spoken language. In the near term, focus is on the problem of developing high performance phonetic recognition systems that can accept continous speech from multiple speakers.

Cryptography: high security encyphering schemes which can also supply "digitized signatures" are being investigated based on the difficulty of factoring natural numbers.

Computer-Supported Cooperative Work: investigates research on office systems that support multiperson informational activities, focusing on the use of the computer as the main communication channel.

Laboratory for Information and Decision Systems:
Architectures for Distributed Intelligence Systems: Petri Net and High Level Net theory is used to develop algorithms for the generation of architectures for distributed intelligence systems.

The Nematode as a Model Complex System: long-term, multidisciplinary research program based on a "simple" biological model, the nematode species. Studies are under way to construct multiple interconnected computer representations of the organism, and to determine underlying principles of organization.

Computational Aspects of Control Theory: a theoretical study of the computational requirements of the major classes of problems in stochastic control.

Information Structures in Decision Making Systems: Petri Net concepts are used to describe the information structure and the protocols in a decision making organization.

Expert Computer Information Retrieval Assistant: expert computerized search assistants are being evaluated experimentally for their potential for enhancing bibliographic information retrieval.

The Media Laboratory:
Eye as Output: introduction of eye movements and fixations as part of human/computer dialogue.

Multimodal Natural Dialogue: research into combination of speech, gesture, and eye input/output at the human/computer interface.

Back Seat Driver: computer program that rides with someone in the car, keeping track of the current position, giving spoken directions to the destination of ones choosing.

ISDN Interface: explores issues in interfacing ISDN basic rate service to computer workstations.

Movies of the Future: addresses the digital representation and processing of moving image sequences.

Real-Time Vision Systems: the goals are to develop real-time machines vision techniques, using massively parallel and pipeline computers, for object recognition, non-machine communication systems, and tracking people and vehicles in unconstrained environments.

Interactive Cinematics: development of a workstation environment for retrieval, editing and seamless playback of video segments.

The total campus research budget in 1990 was $306.4 million (the campus academic budget in 1990 was another $338 million).

Collaborations:
M.I.T runs an Industrial Liaison Program (established in 1948) which aims at a partnership between the university and industry. A member of the professional staff works closely with designated individuals at the member company. The goal is to build a mutually beneficial relationship between the member company's staff and members of the M.I.T. community. Members receive "The MIT Report", a monthly newsletter which highlights research advances, identifies promising new areas of investigation, reports on the latest patent licensing opportunities, and lists the latest research reports and papers. The program produces a yearly series of over 30 seminars and symposia that are offered free to members. As of March 1991, there were 245 corporate members, of which 121 were foreign, including 57 Japanese, 56 European (e.g. Italy-14, France-10, Germany-6) and eight members from other regions. About 3% of the campus research budget (and 20% of all industrial funding) came from foreign-based companies.

M.I.T. runs its own office in Tokyo, Japan to address the difficulties that distance and cultural differences pose for management of M.I.T.'s relationships in Japan. A comparable office might be installed in Europe.

International students constituted about 33% of M.I.T.'s graduate student population compared to 26% a decade ago, but the distribution across the fields is quite uneven. For example, international students comprise 55% in mathematics and 25% in electrical engineering and computer science.

41

New York University

Department of Computer Science
Courant Institute of Mathematical Sciences
251 Mercer Street
New York, NY 10012
Phone: (212) 998-3103
email: schonberg@cs.nyu.edu

Chairman: Prof. Edmond Schonberg (Acting)
Administrative Assistant: Victoria Macaulay

Established: 1969
Undergraduates: n.a.
Graduates: n.a.
Faculty: 29

Curriculum:
The department offers M.S. and Ph.D. programs.

For a M.S. the student must pass two written comprehensive exams and proceed to one of the following programs: complete 36 credits of approved coursework (28 credits must be taken at NYU), complete 32 credits of approved coursework (24 credits must be taken at NYU) and submit a thesis, or complete 32 credits of coursework in three successive semesters (including a summer semester). The last option is the accelerated M.S. program available only to well-qualified students. A GPA of 3.0 (B grade) must be maintained throughout the program.

For a Ph.D. the student must complete 72 credits of course and research work (42 credits must be taken in the Graduate School of Arts and Sciences), take three written exams which must be passed with a grade of A, write a Ph.D. proposal which must include a survey paper on the intended area of research, complete an acceptable survey research paper and pass an oral preliminary exam, demonstrate language proficiency in either Chinese, French, German, Japanese or Russian, and write and defend a dissertation.

Courses for Graduates (selection):

Fundamental Algorithms, Programming Languages, Scientific Computing, Advanced Topics in Programming Languages, Compilers and Computer Languages, Computer Systems Design, VLSI Design, Logic Design Laboratory, High Performance Computer Architecture, Design of Operating Systems, Data Communications, Network Design, Computer Graphics, Computer Vision, Elements of Discrete Mathematics, Theory of Computation, Mathematical Logic, Numerical Methods, Database Systems, Advanced Data Structures and Graph Algorithms, Symbolic Mathematical Computation, Artificial Intelligence, Robotics, Textual Information Processing, Distributed Computing, Parallel Algorithms and VLSI Systems, Compiler Optimization Techniques, Linear Programming, Performance Analysis of Computer Systems, Topics in Numerical Analysis, Monte Carlo Methods and Simulation of Physical Systems.

Faculty (Professors with Research Areas):

Professors:

Edmond Schonberg, Acting Chairman, Ph.D., University of Chicago, 1969 - Programming languages, compiler design, analysis of algorithms, program transformations.

Richard Cole, Ph.D., Cornell University, 1982 - Algorithm design and analysis, parallel algorithms, amortized analysis, computational geometry.

Martin Davis, Ph.D., Princeton University, 1950 - Mathematical logic, theory of computation, logic programming.

Robert Dewar, Ph.D., University of Chicago, 1968 - Programming languages, compilers, operating systems, microprocessor architectures.

Max Goldstein, M.S., New York University, 1962 - Mathematics.

Allan Gottlieb, Ph.D., Brandeis University, 1973 - Parallel computing, computer architecture, operating systems, parallel algorithms.

Ralph Grishman, Ph.D., Columbia University, 1973 - Natural language processing, artificial intelligence.

Malcolm Harrison, Ph.D., Leeds University, 1962 - Programming language design and implementation, operating systems, artificial intelligence, theorem proving, computer architecture.

Zvi Kedem, Chairman, D.Sc., Technion University, 1974 - Parallel and concurrent processing, algorithmically-driven programming constructs, database and knowledge-based systems. (on leave 1990-91)

Michael Overton, Ph.D., Stanford University, 1979 - Numerical analysis, optimization, numerical software, linear and nonlinear programming.

Richard Pollack, Ph.D., New York University, 1962.

Jacob Schwartz, Ph.D., Yale University, 1951 - Robotics and computer vision, computer design, language design, compiler optimization, nonnumerical computation, operating systems.

Joel Spencer, Ph.D., Harvard University, 1970 - Combinatorics, probabilistic methods, theory of algorithms.

Elaine Weyuker, Ph.D., Rutgers University, 1977 - Software testing, software engineering, software metrics, theory of computation.

Olof Widlund, Ph.D., Uppsala University, 1966 - Numerical analysis, numerical software, partial differential equations, mathematical analysis.

Paul Wright, Ph.D., University of Birmingham, 1971 - Robotics, automated manufacturing.

Chee Yap, Ph.D., Yale University, 1979 - Algorithms, complexity, compuational geometry, computer algebra, robotics.

Associate Professors:

Marsha Berger
Ernest Davis
Robert Hummel
Bhubaneswar Mishra
Robert Paige
Dennis Shasha
Alan Siegel

Assistant Professors:

Ravi Boppana
Benjamin Goldberg
Zexiang Li
Stephane Mallat
Kenneth Perlin
Tomasz Strzalkowski

Affiliated Institutions:
The Ultracomputer Laboratory: is devoted to parallel processing computing.

The Robotics and Manufacturing Research Laboratory: is equipped with various industrial and experimental robots. A major focus of the laboratory is the theoretical study of motion planning and related geometric algorithms in robotics.

Facilities:
Departmental facilities include 75 SUN workstations, several DEC VAX machines, an IBM 4381 and 4361, Convex and Astronautics minisupercomputers and several advanced graphics systems (Silicon Graphics, Evans & Sutherland, Stellar).
The Ultracomputer Laboratory operates several 8-processor Ultracomputer protoypes, an IBM 4381 and a network of IBM PC-RT's.
The Robotics and Manufacturing Research Laboratory has a wide range of robotics, vision and graphics equipment, including a Utah/MIT dexterous hand, a VPL dataglove, an Exoskeleton, a wrist

43

Polhemus, a four-finger force-controlled manipulator, a PUMA robot arm, an IBM RS/2 robot arm, two IBM SCARA robot arms, a Vicom image processing system, and an AT&T Pixel Machine. All computers are on a network which allows access to NYSERnet, ESnet and INTERnet.

Research area, funding and selected projects:
The general areas of research are: Algorithms, Artificial Intelligence and Natural Language Processing, Computer Systems, Numerical Analysis, Programming Languages and Programming Methodology, Robotics and Manufacturing.

Here is a sample of current projects:

SETL: language design and implementation (Dewar and Schonberg)

PROTEUS: natural language processing (Grishman)

RAPTS: program development methodology (Paige)

Linguistic String Project (Sager)

Ultracomputer Project (Schwartz et al.)

Collaborations:
The PROTEUS project is being conducted in conjunction with a group at UNISYS. The university is also a member of the John von Neumann Computer Consortium at Princeton.

Department of Electrical Engineering and Computer Science
2145 Sheridan Road
Evanston, IL 60208-3118
Phone: (708) 491-3641
email: ahaddad@eecs.nwu.edu

Chairman: Prof. Abraham Haddad (EECS)
Administrative Assistant: George Mach

Established: n.a.
Undergraduates: 78 (Computer Science only)
Graduates: 137 (Computer Science only)
Faculty: 46 (EECS)

Curriculum:

The Department offers two distinct curricula, namely Electrical Engineering, and Computer Science, each of which offers a broad range of programs leading to the B.S., M.S., and Ph.D. degrees. However, the graduate research program is grouped in a way that cuts across the disciplines.

The Department also offers a Graduate Cooperative Engineering Education program in which highly qualified master's and doctor's candidates combine paid work experience in research, business, clinical or manufacturing positions with alternate periods of full-time academic study.

For the M.S. degree at least 12 units of graduate study are required, and a minimum of nine courses must be taken and approved. In addition, each student must either write a thesis, which counts for two or three units toward the 12 unit requirement (Plan A), or he must complete a project and write a project report, which counts for one or two units (Plan B). A grade average of B is required in all work presented, and each student is required to pass a final examination. All work for the M.S. degree must be in the Northwestern Graduate School and must be completed within a a period of five years.

At least 33 units are required for the Ph.D. degree, and a minimum of 18 courses must be taken and approved. Students with the M.S. degree from the EECS Department at Northwestern University are automatically granted 12 units of graduate credit towards the 33-unit total. Students with a master's degree from another recognized institution may be granted up to 12 units. Students with tuition support are expected to complete the 33-unit requirement in nine quarters of full-time registration. Each student must pass the Initial Ph.D. Qualifying Examination, and the Oral Qualifying Examination (OQE) before being allowed to enter the program. Every candidate is required to present a dissertation and must pass the oral Final Examination within a period of five years from the date of the OQE.

Courses for Graduates (selection):

The research in the Department is grouped into six broad areas and every group offers specific courses. Here is a selection relevant to Computer Science:

Algorithms and Computation: Formal Languages, Compiler Construction, Numerical Analysis I, II and III, Design and Analysis of Algorithms, Applied Graph Theory, Combinatorics and Applications, Complexity of Algorithms, Advanced Algorithmic Processes, VLSI Algorithms, Discrete and Iterative Methods in Numerical Linear Algebra, Optimization I and II, Discrete Optimization, Combinatorial Optimization.

Artificial Intelligence: Artificial Intelligence Programming, Expert Systems, Automated Theorem Proving, Neural Networks and Pattern Recognition, Logic Programming and Computer Architecture, Logic and Databases, Advanced Topics in Computer Vision, Special Topics in Computer Science, Introduction to Artificial Intelligence, to Theorem Proving, to Computational Linguistics, to Robotics.

Communications, Systems, and Signal Processing: Communication Circuits, Digital Communications, Digital Image Processing, Mathematical Foundations of Communication Theory, Optical

Communications, Information Theory, Linear Integrated Circuits, System Theory, Advanced System Theory, Introduction to Queueing Theory, Computer Networks, Local Area Networks, Queueing Models for Computer Communications.

Computer and Information Engineering Systems: Design of Real-Time Digital Systems, Operating Systems I and II, Microprocessor System Design, Computer Architecture, Computer Subsystems, VLSI Architecture, Biomedical Computing, Computer Systems Measurement and Evaluation, Relational Database Theory, Logic and Computer Architecture, Computer Graphics, Formal Methods of Syntactic Analysis, Introduction to Database Systems, to Computer Graphics.

Electronic Devices and Materials: Design of Custom VLSI, Semiconductor Theory, Semiconductor Devices, Gallium Arsenide Devices, Introduction to Superconductivity and Applications, Microelectronic Fabrication.

Optical Systems and Technology: Introduction to Applied Optics, Optoelectronics, Optical Communications.

Faculty (Professors with Research Areas):
Since the research and education for Computer Science and Electrical Engineering at the EECS Department is so closely coupled, and since the official brochures did not distinguish them, we list all the professors who listed research interests directly and obviously relevant to Computer Science:

Professors:

Abraham H. Haddad, Chairman (EECS), Ph.D., Princeton University - Stochastic systems, modeling, applications to communications and control.

James S. Aagaard, Ph.D., Northwestern University - Real-time information retrieval, operating systems, data management systems, data communications.

Erwin H. Bareiss, Ph.D., University of Zurich - Applied linear algebra, applied analysis, computational complexity, numerical analysis, transport theory.

Alvin Bayliss, Ph.D., New York University - Numerical analysis, large-scale scientific computing.

Robert Chang, Ph.D., Princeton University - Optoelectronic device applications.

Lawrence J. Henschen, Ph.D., University of Illinois at Urbana-Champaign - Artificial intelligence, theorem proving, deductive databases.

Carl R. Kannwurf, Ph.D., Northwestern University - Optical phenomena, superconductors.

Gilbert K. Krulee, Ph.D., Massachusetts Institute of Technology - Artificial intelligence, mathematical linguistics, computer processing of natural language.

Chung-Chieh Lee, Ph.D., Princeton University - Computer networks, digital communications, computational complexity.

Der-Tsai Lee, Ph.D., University of Illinois at Urbana-Champaign - Design and analysis of algorithms, data structures, VLSI systems, computational geometry, computational complexity, parallel algorithms.

Michael E. Marhic, Ph.D., University of California at Los Angeles - Optical networks, optical processing, holography.

Gordon J. Murphy, Ph.D., University of Minnesota - Microprocessors, design of computing systems, communications.

Martin A. Plonus, Ph.D., University of Michigan - Optical communication, optical fibers.

Zenonas V. Rekasius, Ph.D., Purdue University - Dynamic systems, analysis of large-scale systems.

Roger C. Schank, Ph.D., University of Texas - Artificial intelligence, cognitive science, natural language processing, learning theory, models of human reasoning and human memory, computers and education.

Allen Taflove, Ph.D., Northwestern University - Computational optics, optical phenomena, supercomputing.

James A. Van Ness, Ph.D., Northwestern University - Numerical analysis, control systems, large-scale dynamic systems.

Bruce Wessels, Ph.D., Massachusetts Institute of Technology - Optical materials, semiconductor devices.

Horace P. Yuen, D.Sc., Massachusetts Institute of Technology - Optical communication.

Associate Professors:

Arthur R. Butz
Kenneth Forbus
Srikanta Kumar
Jorge Nocedal
Christopher K. Riesbeck
Peter Scheuermann
Chi-haur Wu

Assistant Professors:

Ibrahim M. Abdel-Motaleb
Lawrence A. Birnbaum
Gregg C. Collins
Paul Copper
Lisa Hellerstein
Scott Jordan
Aggelos K. Katsaggelos
Wei-Chung Lin
Ghassan Z. Qadah
Janet C. Rutledge
Alan V. Sahakian
Majid Sarrafzadeh
Barry J. Sullivan
David Weir

Affiliated Institutions:
The EECS Department has instruction and research laboratories for electronic devices, digital curcuits, solid-state electronics, thin-film device development, biomedical electronics, microwave techniques, real-time control systems, holography and coherent light optics, biological control systems, digital and analog computation, and digital systems design. The Department also uses facilities at the Materials Research Center, and at the Manufacturing Engineering Center

The major institutions for Computer Science are the Computer Science and Engineering Laboratory (CSEL), the Vogelback Computing Center, and the Center for Information and Telecommunication Technology.

Furthermore, there are the Basic Industry Research Laboratory, the Basic Industry Research Institute, and the Institute for the Learning Sciences.

Facilities:
The CSEL has a number of interconnected mini/ microcomputers, including a four-processor Encore Multimax-320, a Britton-Lee IDM 500 Database Machine, an Intel Hypercube iPSC-MX/D4, a Silicon Graphics IRIS-2400, a HP9000, a number of Sun SPARCstations, and SUN-3 and Apollo workstations.
The Vogelback Computing Center has a DEC VAX-11/785 and an IBM 4381 multiprocessor system. Network acces is provided through NSFnet, USEnet, and UUCP.

Research area, funding and selected projects:
As already mentioned above, the EECS department's research is grouped into six broad areas. The fields of study in Computer Science include Operating Systems, Software Engineering, Database Management, Computational Complexity, Automata Theory, Algorithmic Processes, Numerical Analysis, Large-Scale Computation, and Artificial Intelligence. Further fields of study are included in both Electrical Engineering and Computer Science programs.

The following is a selected list of projects, arranged by the identified six research groups:

Algorithms and Computation: VLSI Layout Algorithms: seeks to design an analysis of efficient algorithms for VLSI layout such as floor planning, routing, and wiring.

Geometric Optimization: emphasis is placed on efficiency of algorithms when solving large-scale problems in computational geometry, or other organizational problems.

Algorithms for Optimization and Inverse Eigenvalue Problems: concerns the development of a new algorithm for large nonlinear systems of equations.

Artificial Intelligence and Automation: Learning in Competitive Planning: development of explanation-based and failure-driven learning techniques to permit the acquisition of abstract planning knowledge in competitive domains, including conservatism and deterrence.

Design of Intelligent Systems for Libraries: involves the design of intelligent support systems for retrieving information from a library.

Automated Inference: involves the application of formal logic to various problem areas such as theorem proving and intelligent databases.

Communications, Systems, and Signal Processing: Communication Network Architecture and Protocols: involves the design and analysis of protocols for high-speed network operation/managment, fiber-optic and integrated networks, and architecture to support privacy in LAN/MAN systems.

Automated Document Recognition and Transmission: focuses on fast document recognition via efficient segment coding techniques.

Computer and Information Engineering Systems: Massively Parallel Deductive Database Systems: is concerned with new storage schemes suitable for mapping intelligent database systems with deductive capabilities onto massively parallel hardware.

Domain Knowledge Directed Parallel Logic Inference: syntactic and semantic knowledge is used to guide distributed logic inference efficiently so that the processors cooperate in deriving the answer.

Electronic Devices and Materials: Compound Semiconductors: compound semiconductors are used for numerous electronic devices, including lasers, infrared detectors, and field effect transistors.

Optical Systems and Technology: All-Optical Coding/Decoding or Processing by Optical Networks: passive optical networks made from single-mode fibers and couplers are being studied as a possible means to process information.

Collaborations
The Northwestern University/Evanston Research Park is a joint venture between the university and the city, and offers opportunities for multi-disciplinary research. The Research Park is anchored by the university owned and operated Basic Industry Research Laboratory, a $26 million applied research laboratory. This laboratory is the companion facility of the Basic Industry Research Institute on Northwestern's campus, which coordinates faculty research and graduate training in areas of concern to basic industry. Research Park tenants include the Institute for the Learning Sciences, which focuses on developing artificial intelligence software, and computer technology for educational uses in the public and private sectors.

Ohio State University

Department of Computer and Information Science
2036 Neil Avenue Mall
Columbus, OH 43210-1277
Phone: (614) 292-5813
email: muller-m@cis.ohio-state.edu

Chairman: Prof. Mervin E. Muller
Administrative Assistant: Marty Marlatt

Established: 1968
Undergraduates: 880
Graduates: 236
Faculty: 49

Curriculum:

The M.S. degree offered through the Department of Computer and Information Science may serve as either a terminal degree or as a step towards the Ph.D. degree. All programs of graduate study require a set of core courses in computer and information science: Computability and Unsolvability, Programming Languages, Operating Systems, Computer Architecture, Data Structures and Analysis of Algorithms, Seminar on Research Topics in Computer and Information Science (can be substituted with Introduction to Doctoral Studies), and Advanced Seminar in Computer and Information Science. Total credit hours in Core: 18 hours.

All additional courses taken require the approval of the student's advisor. The minimum number of credit hours for the M.S. degree is 45 credits for Plan A (with thesis) or 48 hours for Plan B (without thesis). Some M.S. programs may require more than the minimum credit hours. Students in Plan A are required to successfully write and defend a M.S. thesis. Students in Plan B must demonstrate their mastery of computer and information science by passing the M.S. Comprehensive Examination. However, students who have passed the Ph.D. General Examination receive the M.S. degree without having to satisfy either of the above requirements.

The doctoral program emphasizes research under advisory of a faculty member, who should be chosen at the earliest possible opportunity. The General Examination, which determines the student's admission to the Ph.D. program, is usually taken during the ninth quarter of residency and consists of a written and an oral part. The Final Oral Examination deals intensively with the candidate's field of specialization and dissertation. The Qualifying, General and Final Oral Examiniations enable the faculty to ensure that only students of outstanding scholastic ability and proven creative research skills will receive the doctoral degree. There is no foreign language requirement for either the M.S. or the Ph.D. program.

Courses for Graduates (selection):

M.S. program (600 and 700 level courses): Introduction to: Automata and Formal Languages, Storage and Retrieval, Principles of Programming Languages, Operating Systems, Database Systems, Computer Architecture, Interactive Graphics, Automata and Language Theory, 3D Image Generation, Parallel Computing, Distributed Computing; Survey of Artificial Intelligence: Basic Techniques, II: Advanced Topics, Topics in Artificial Intelligence: Expert Systems, Operating Systems and Systems Programming, Naive Physics Theory in Artificial Intelligence, Numerical Analysis, Numerical Linear Algebra, Operating and Advanced Operating Systems Laboratory, Comparative Operating Systems, Operating Systems and Systems Programming, Database and Information Management for Manufacturing, Data Structures, Management Information Systems, Database Systems, Microcomputer Systems, Computer Networks, Algebraic Algorithms, Computability and Unsolvability, Computational Complexity, Knowledge-based Systems, Computational Linguistics, Compiler Design and Implementation, Software Engineering, Computer Architecture, CAD and Testing of VLSI Circuits Analysis of Algorithms, Advanced 3D Image Generation, Geometric Modeling, Intermediate Study in Computer and Information Science, Computational Geometry, Symbolic Computation, Logic and Programming, Topics in Parallel Computation, Parallel and Distributed Computing, Human-Computer Interaction, Programming Environments, Computer Graphics, Advanced LISP Programming.

Ph.D. program (800 & 900 level courses): Introduction to Doctoral Studies, Advanced Computer Architecture, Advanced Studies in CIS, Seminar on Research Topics in CIS; one Interdepartmental and 28 Research Seminars on various topics are offered as 800 level courses in the doctoral program.

Faculty (Professors with Research Areas):

Professors:

Mervin E. Muller, Chairman, Ph.D., University of California at Los Angeles, 1954 - Management systems, statistical computations, distributed data and information systems, simulation designs and analyses, financial systems, quality and production concepts, system performance analysis, software engineering.

Balakrishnan Chandrasekaran, Ph.D., University of Pennsylvania, 1967 - Artificial intelligence, expert systems, knowledge-directed databases, pattern recognition, computer program testing, interactive graphics.

Ming T. Liu, Ph.D., University of Pennsylvania, 1964 - Computer architecture and organization, computer communications and networking, parallel and distributed processing, operating systems, performance evaluation.

Sandra A. Mamrak, Ph.D., University of Illinois at Urbana-Champaign, 1975 - Distributed processing, operating systems, performance evaluation.

Ramon E. Moore, Ph.D., Stanford University, 1963 - Numerical analysis and interval analysis.

Associate Professors:

Eitan M. Gurari
Douglas S. Kerr
Ten-Hwang Lai
Dik Lun Lee

Timothy J. Long
William F. Ogden
Richard E. Parent
Anthony E. Petrarca
P. Sadayappan
Mukesh Singhal
Neelamegam Soundararajan
Kenneth J. Supowit
Bruce W. Weide
Stuart H. Zweben

Assistant Professors:

Mohan Ahuja
Thomas C. Bylander
Kikuo Fujimura
Judith D. Gardiner
Chua-Huang Huang
Doddaballapur N. Jayasimha
Phillip E. Krueger
Wolfgang W. Kuechlin
D. Panda
Terry Patten
Gary Perlman
Jordan B. Pollack
Prasad Vishnubhotla
DeLiang Wang
Roni Yagel

Affiliated Institutions:
Laboratory for Parallel and Distributed Computing (PADRE): uses the power of parallel computing in computer algebra, natural language processing, communication protocols, and computer graphics.

Laboratory for Research in Artificial Intelligence (LAIR): creates and applies theories about intelligence by building useful tools to solve real-world problems in a number of domains such as diagnosis in medicine, engineering, neural networks, and natural language processing and computational linguistics.

Performance Analysis Lab (PAL): conducts research in factors affecting computer hardware and software performance.

Ohio Supercomputer Center

Facilities:

Departmental facilities include a CRAY YMP/48, an IBM 3081, three IBM 4341, 25 SUN-4/75, 22 SUN-3/180, two SUN-4/280, an HP 330 MH, an HP 9000/375, two HP 9000/345, 11 HP 9000/425T, two HP 9000/425S, a 32-node Intel Hypercube, a Convex, a 12-processor Encore Multimax, a 10-node BBN Butterfly, seven HP 330 CH, two HP 350 SRX, 247 SUN-4/20, a SUN-3/160, 11 Xerox Dandelions, six Xerox Dandytigers, a TI Explorer, 305 Apple Macintoshes, four IBM PC, ten IBM RT, five Apple Macintosh II.

All facilities are on a campus-wide, Ethernet-based network (SONnet) which allows access to USEnet, BITnet, CSnet, ARPAnet, NSFnet

Research area, funding and selected projects:

As of June 1991, there are 37 ongoing research and development awards in the department. The total value of these awards is $3 million. Here is a sample:

Design and Diagnosis Problem Solving with Multifunctional Technical Knowledge Bases (Chandrasekaran, DARPA, $872,000, 8/92)

Research on Cylindrical Algebraic Decomposition (Collins, NSF, $210,000, 5/93)

Parallel Algorithms for Algebraic Riccati Equations (Gardiner, University Seed Grant, $18,000)

Numerical Solution of Large-Scale Algebraic Riccati Equations (Gardiner, Research Initiation Award, $60,000)

Strategy for Subcube Management in a Hypercube Computer with Direct Connect Communication (Lai, NSF, $60,000)

Computer Communication Protocols for ISDN's (Liu, Army Communications-Electronics Command, $325,000, 2/91)

High-Level Connectionist Models (Pollack, ONR, $256,000)

Collaborations:

Sponsoring agencies include: AT&T Bell Laboratories, the Army Research Office, AFOSR, Battelle Memorial Institute, DARPA, DoD, DoE, Encore, Hewlett-Packard Company, IBM Scientific Center, Intel, National Library of Medicine, the National Cash Register Company, NSF, ONR, Sun Microsystems, the Thomas Alva Edison Program, and the State of Ohio.

Pennsylvania State University

Department of Computer Science
333 Whitmore Laboratory
University Park, PA 16802
Phone: (814) 865-9505
email: mji@psuvax1.cs.psu.edu

Chairman: Prof. Mary Jane Irwin
Administrative Assistant: Helen DeFurio

Established: 1969
Undergraduates: 425
Graduates: 150
Faculty: 29

Curriculum:
The department offers B.S., M.S., and Ph.D. programs.

For a M.S. all of the following background courses or approved equivalents are necessary: Data Structures and Algorithms, Programming Language Concepts, Operating Systems, Computer Architecture, Theory of Automata, Formal Languages, and Computability, Numerical Analysis, Matrix Algebra.
Required Advanced Course Work:
- Algorithm Design and Analysis,
- Two of the following four courses:
Operating Systems Design, Science of Computer Programming, Compiler Construction, Database Management Systems,
- Three other advisor-approved advanced-level courses,
- and the Master's Thesis or Paper.
Total Number of required credits: 30, and a grade-point average of at least 3.0.

For a Ph.D. all of the background courses for the M.S. program are necessary plus additional courses leading to an area of specialization. Coursework normally totals approximately 60 credits beyond the B.S. degree. Admission to doctoral candidacy is based on the results of a written examination to

be taken within approximately one year after the admission to the program. The student has to choose any three of the following areas: Architecture and VLSI, Data Structures and Algorithms, Numerical Analysis, Principles of Operating Systems, Principles of Programming Languages, Theory of Automation.

Furthermore, there is a special language requirement: the student must pass an examination in French, German, Russian or another approved language.

Courses for Graduates (selection):
Operating System Design, Computer Systems Performance Evaluation, Computer Networks and Distributed Systems, VLSI Computer-Aided Design Tools, Science of Computer Programming, Compiler Construction, Semantics of Programming Languages, Theory of Graphs and Networks, Numerical Optimization Techniques, Parallel Algorithms, Database Management Systems, Information Processing Systems, Numerical Algebra, Numerical Solution of Ordinary and Partial Differential Equations, Approximation Theory, Finite Element Methods, Theory of Formal Languages and Automation, Contemporary Computer Architectures, VLSI Systems Design, Machine Intelligence and Heuristic Programming, Computer Linguistics, Digital Integrated Systems Design, Architecture of Arithmetic Processors, Sequential and Parallel Complexity Theory, Design and Specification of Distributed Systems, Algorithm Design and Analysis, Complexity of Combinatorial Problems, Integer Programming, Probabilistic Algorithms.

Faculty (Professors with Research Areas):

Professors:

Mary Jane Irwin, Chairman, Ph.D., University of Illinois at Urbana-Champaign - Computer architecture, computer arithmetic, VLSI design, CAD tools.

Webb C. Miller, Ph.D., University of Washington - Algorithms and software for molecular genetics.

Associate Professors:

Jesse Barlow
Piotr Berman
Martin Fürer
Jonathan Goldstine
Gerald G. Johnson, Jr.
Krishna Kant
Joseph M. Lambert
Robert M. Owens
Georg Schnitger

Assistant Professors:

Donald R. Beaver
C. Mic Bowman
Thang N. Bui
Sitaram Lanka
Barry M. Pangrie
Panayote Pardalos
Alex Pothen
S. Purushothaman
William H. Winsborough

Affiliated Institutions:
Center for Academic Computing: service-oriented to all segments of the University.

Facilities:
Departmental research equipment includes: nine SUN-4, 12 SUN-3, 18 SPARCstations, Intel iPSC/d4 (16 processors), 50+ IBM RT/6152, seven IBM RT/6150, all networked via Ethernet with gateways to NSFnet, BITnet, USEnet and PREPnet. At the Center for Academic Computing: an IBM ES/3090-600S is the main computer. Access to all the national supercomputer centers is provided via INTERnet.

Research area, funding and selected projects:
The basic research activities consist of:
1. Programming Languages,
2. Computer Systems,
3. Theory of Computation and Analysis of Algorithms,
4. Numerical Analysis and Optimization,
5. Design and Theory of VLSI Systems and Architectures.

Current funding includes NSF grants for CAD Tools and Design Automation research; for developing a VLSI Signal Processing Prototype; a five-year Small Scale Infrastructure grant to fund equipment (with multiple faculty involvement); Numerical Solution of Least Squares and Eigenvalue Problems research; Undergraduate Education and Research in Software Development for MAssively Parallel Computers; and Analysis of Coordination in Asynchronous Communications research.

ARO funding is used for a Study of VLSI Theory, and NIH funding is available for research on Algorithms for Analyzing Biosequence Data.

Collaborations:
Chip designs are fabricated (with NSF-support) by MOSIS, a silicon foundry in California.

Princeton University

Department of Computer Science
35 Olden Street, Computer Science Bldg.
Princeton, NJ 08544-2087
Phone: (609) 258-5030
email: rs@princeton.edu

Chairman: Prof. Robert Sedgewick
Administrative Assistant: Charlotte Amsted-Jameson

Established: 1985 (as Computer Science)
Undergraduates: 90
Graduates: 50
Faculty: 22

Curriculum:
The department offers M.S.E. and Ph.D. programs.

Students fulfill the M.S.E. degree by successfully completing eight courses, of which at least four must be at the graduate level. One of the courses may be replaced by a Master's Project. The M.S.E. requirements can be completed in one year with full-time residency.

Although there are no formal course requirements for a Ph.D., the student and a faculty advisor must develop an integrated program of study. Before the student takes a general examination, a programming requirement and a research seminar must be completed. The programming requirement can be satisfied by completing a project that involves substantial programming under the supervision of a faculty advisor, or completing a course that involves substantial programming with a B+ or higher grade. The research seminar is prepared under supervision of a faculty member and should be attended by at least three Computer Science faculty members. The research seminar can be in the same area as the student's dissertation. After these two requirements have been met, the student can take the written and oral components of the general examination. The written part stresses the areas of theory, systems, and hardware. The oral part stresses the student's area of specialization. A final oral examination is given as a defense of the student's dissertation.

Courses for Graduates (selection):
Mathematical Foundations of Computer Science, Distributed Systems, Computer System Organization and Modeling, VLSI Circuits, Computer Hardware, Computer Graphics, Programming Languages, Foundations of Artificial Intelligence, Combinatorial Optimization Algorithms, Mathematical Analysis of Algorithms, Probabilistic Algorithms, Data Structures and Graph Algorithms, Algorithmic Discrete Mathematics, Advanced Topics in the Theory of Algorithms, in Software Systems, in Computer Science.

Faculty (Professors with Research Areas):

Professors:

Robert Sedgewick, Chairman, Ph.D., Stanford University, 1975 - Analysis of algorithms, algorithm visualization.

Bernard Chazelle, Ph.D., Yale University, 1980 - Computational geometry, data structures.

David Dobkin, Ph.D., Harvard University, 1973 - Graphics, analysis of algorithms, geometry.

Hector Garcia-Molina, Ph.D., Stanford University, 1979 - Database systems, distributed computing.

David Hanson, Ph.D., University of Arizona, 1976 - Programming languages, user interfaces.

Patrick Hanrahan, Ph.D., University of Wisconsin at Madison, 1985 - Computer graphics, image synthesis and rendering.

Richard Lipton, Ph.D., Carnegie Mellon University, 1973 - Architecture, complexity, VLSI.

László Lovász, Dr.rer.nat., Eötvös Loránd, 1971 - Combinatorial optimization, graph theory.

Kenneth Steiglitz, Eng.Sc.D., New York University, 1963 - Combinatorial optimization, VLSI, architecture.

Robert Tarjan, Ph.D., Stanford University, 1972 - Data structures, graph algorithms, complexity.

Andrew Yao, Ph.D., University of Illinois - Computational complexity, analysis of algorithms.

Associate Professors:

Andrea Lapaugh
Avi Wigderson (Visiting)

Assistant Professors:

Rafael Alonso
Andrew Appel
Jim-Yi Cai
Joel Friedman
Kai Li
Eric Sven Ristad
Anne Rogers
Elisha Sacks

Affiliated Institutions: n.a.

Facilities: n.a.

Research area, funding and selected projects: n.a.

Collaborations:
The department has extensive collaborations with many universities and corporations through its Colloquia. In the years 1989-90, the Departmental Colloquia included (selection): University of Rochester, Stanford University, Digital Equipment Coporation, International Computer Science Institute at Berkeley, Cornell University, Massachusetts Institute of Technology, IBM T.J. Watson Research Center, AT&T Bell Laboratories, Technical University of Denmark, Xerox PARC, University of Frankfurt, Yale University, Brown University, Bulgarian Academy of Sciences.

Professor Hanson has had collaborations on language development with the University of Arizona and AT&T Bell Laboratories.
Professor Lipton conducts joint research with the Department of Biology to discover fundamental patterns in DNA sequences.

Rice University

Department of Computer Science
P.O. Box 1892
Houston, TX 77251
Phone: (713) 527-4834
email: ivy@rice.edu

Chairman: Prof. Ken Kennedy
Administrative Assistant: Iva Jean Jorgensen

Established: 1984
Undergraduates: n.a.
Graduates: 54 (11 M.C.S., 4 M.S., 39 Ph.D.)
Faculty: 14

Curriculum:

The Department offers three graduate programs:
the professional master's (M.C.S.), the research
master's (M.S.) and the doctoral (Ph.D.)

The professional program, a terminal degree program for students intending to pursue a technical
career in the computer industry, awards the Master
of Computer Science degree. To earn the degree,
the student must successfully complete 30 semester credits of approved coursework. Up to six
credits may be transferrable another institution.
The normal completion time for the M.C.S. is three
semesters.

The research master's program requires a thesis in
addition to the coursework and culminates in the
M.S. degree. Admission is reserved for special
occasions.

To earn a Ph.D., in addition to coursework, the
student must pass a comprehensive examination
covering the core areas of computer science, pass
a qualifying examination in an area of specialization, conduct original research, submit an acceptable thesis proposal, successfully defend the thesis
proposal, submit an acceptable thesis reporting
results, and pass a final oral defense. Upon successful completion of the comprehensive exam, the
qualifying exam and the proposal defense, the
student will be awarded the M.S. degree. After
sucessful thesis defense and completion of all
departmental and university requirements, the student will be awarded the Ph.D. degree.

Courses for Graduates (selection):

Programming Languages, Operating Systems and
Concurrent Programming, Compilation for Parallel Target Machines, Distributed Systems, Advanced Computer Architecture, Computer Networks: Architecture and Protocols, Algorithmic
Algebraic Geometry, Advanced Algorithms, VLSI
Algorithms, Advanced Topics in Theory of Computing.

Faculty (Professors with Research Areas):

Professors:

Ken Kennedy, Chairman, Ph.D., New York University, 1971 - Parallel computing in science and
engineering, scientific programming environments,
optimization of compiled code, computer architecture, performance analysis and graph algorithms.

Robert S. Cartwright, Ph.D., Stanford University,
1977 - Abstract programming and specification
languages, program semantics, and program validation.

Ron Goldman, Ph.D., Johns Hopkins University,
1973 - Mathematical representation, manipulation, and analysis of shape using computers, algorithms for polynomial and piecewise polynomial
curves and surfaces, parametrically and implicitly
represented geometry.

Associate Professors:

Keith D. Cooper
Willy E. Zwaenepoel

Assistant Professors:

Alan Cox
Hristo Djidjev

Mark Krentel
Alejandro Schäffer
Joe Warren

Affiliated Institutions:
Close ties are maintained with the Department of Mathematical Sciences and Electrical and Computer Engineering. Faculty in the three departments are collaborating in several interdisciplinary research efforts in parallel computing. New research efforts in distributed computing, algorithms, and computational geometry have been started.

Facilities:
Campus-wide network of over 100 SUN-3 and SUN-4 workstations, plus several large, time-shared SUNs, six IBM RT/PC-II workstations, a VAX 11/750 system running 4.3 Berkeley Unix, and a collection of miscellaneous personal computers (and Macintoshes), laser printers, and other devices. For experimentation with parallel computation, a 20-processor Sequent Symmetry shared-memory multiprocessor, an Intel Hypercube, a 16-processor loosely coupled multiprocessor, and an 8192 processor CM-2 from Thinking Machines. All equipment has access to the major national networks. Rice is an active member of CSNet, is the lead institution in SEQUInet, and has connections with NSFnet and BITnet.

Research area, funding and selected projects:
PRISM: aims at developing a comprehensive programming language and program validation system to support scientific programming (Cartwright et al.)

A prototype programming environment for FORTRAN (Kennedy et al.)

In 1989-1990, the department had separately-budgeted research expenditures in the amount of $2.6 million for 22 projects.

Collaborations: n.a.

Rutgers University

Department of Computer Science
Hill Center - Busch Campus
New Brunswick, NJ 08903
Phone: (201) 932-3546
email: kaplan@cs.rutgers.edu

Chairman: Prof. Kenneth Kaplan
Administrative Assistant: Priscilla Rasmussen

Established: 1966
Undergraduates: n.a.
Graduates: 250
Faculty: 35

Curriculum:

A M.S. and a Ph.D. are offered to students with an accredited undergraduate program in computer science. Some credits from other schools are transferable toward the M.S. and Ph.D. programs.

For a M.S. degree the student must complete 24 credits of coursework and present a thesis/essay for six credits which has been approved by a thesis committee. The student must also give a seminar in the department presenting the thesis research. The student must maintain an academic standing of 3.0 (B grade) and pass a comprehensive written exam at the beginning of each semester.

For a Ph.D. the student must complete a minimum of 48 credits of successful coursework (M.S. degree credits count toward this). He must complete a significant project in systems software or in an application area. The project should involve problem formulation, program development, and testing. A faculty member must be obtained for the project. After the project is approved, the student must pass two linked exams, oral and written. After the above requirements are fulfilled, the student can proceed to the preparation and defense of a doctoral thesis.

Courses for Graduates (selection):

Language Software, Numerical Methods, Operating Systems Design, Modeling and Simulation of Continuous Systems, Computer Methods in Statistics, Software Engineering, Formal Languages and Automats, Data Structures and Algorithms, Introduction to System Programming, Computer Structures, Introduction to the Foundations of Computer Science, Numerical Analysis, Design and Analysis of Data Structures and Algorithms, Programming Languages and Compilers, Queueing Systems and Performance Models, Operating System Theory, Introduction to Artificial Intelligence, Computational Methods for Linear Programming Problems, Network and Combinatorial Optimization Algorithms, Computer Graphics, Nonlinear Programming Algorithms, Advanced Numerical Analysis, Computer Methods for Partial Differential Equations, Parallel Numerical Computing, Intermediate Artificial Intelligence, Artificial Intelligence Software: Techniques and Languages, Natural Language Processing, Pattern Recognition, Machine Learning, Complexity of Computation, Theory of Computation, Combinatorial Methods in Complexity Theory, Database Systems, Problems in Simulation, Problems in Computer Graphics.

Expert Systems, Introduction to VLSI Systems, Parallel Computation: Algorithms and Complexity, Topics in Computers in Biomedicine, in Software Engineering, in the Foundations of Knowledge Based Systems, in Operating Systems, in Programming Languages, in the Foundations of Computer Science, in Problem Solving Methods.

Faculty (Professors with Research Areas):

Professors:

Kenneth Kaplan, Chairman, Ph.D., Polytechnic Institute of Brooklyn - Design of algorithms.

Saul Amarel, Dr. Eng., Columbia University - Artificial intelligence, problems of representation and modeling in problem solving, interpretation problems, theory of algorithms.

Vaclav Chvatal, Ph.D., University of Waterloo - Analysis of algorithms, combinatorics, graph theory, operations research, linear programming.

Michael L. Fredman, Ph.D., Stanford University - Algorithms, data structures, complexity theory, combinatorics.

Michael D. Grigoriadis, Ph.D., University of Wisconsin - Mathematical programming, large-scale structured problems, graph and network optimization, design of computer networks.

Peter L. Hammer, Ph.D., University of Bucharest - Boolean methods in operations research and related areas.

Jeffry Kahn, Ph.D., Ohio State University - Combinatorics, foundations of geometry.

Leonid Khachiyan, Visiting Professor, Ph.D., D.Sc., USSR Academy of Sciences - Mathematical programming, computational complexity, discrete optimization, convex analysis and geometry.

Casimir Kulikowski, Ph.D., University of Hawaii - Artificial intelligence and pattern recognition, computer aided modeling and simulation, consultation systems, databases, graphics and computer aided design.

L. Thorne McCarty, J.D., Harvard Law School - Artificial intelligence and legal reasoning.

Naftaly Minsky, Ph.D., Hebrew University of Jerusalem - Software engineering, programming languages, artificial intelligence.

Marvin C. Pauli, B.S., Clarkson University - Design and analysis of algorithms.

Irving N. Rabinowitz, Ph.D., Princeton University - Programming languages, software engineering, formal definitions of programming languages, compiler construction.

Charles Schmidt, Ph.D., University of Iowa - Human and machine planning and plan recognition, human-computer interaction.

Eduardo D. Sontag, Ph.D., Florida State University - Control theory, applied algebra, robotics.

William Steiger, Ph.D., Australian National University - Computational geometry, parallel computation, analysis of algorithms, optimization theory, statistical computing.

Endre Szemeredi, Ph.D., Stanford University - Number theory, external graph theory, theoretical computer science.

Robert Vichnevetsky, Ph.D., University of Brussels - Numerical analysis, computer methods for partial differential equations, optimization theory, modeling and simulation of systems, environmental systems.

Associate Professors:

Saul Levy
Gerard Richter
Michael Saks
Chitoor V. Srinivasan
Ann Yasuhara

Assistant Professors:

B.R. Badrinath
Andrew Gelsey
Haym Hirsh
Michiel Norordewier
Stan Raatz

Affiliated Institutions:

Laboratory for Computer Science Research (LCSR): provides the environment for scientific interactions and collaborations between computer scientists and members of other disciplines at the university as well as collaborations with scientists in other institutions in the country. It also provides the administrative basis for all computer science grant-supported projects in New Brunswick, and supports all efforts to obtain new outside grants for research in computer science.

Center for Computer Aids for Industrial Productivity (CAIP): was established in 1985 as an administrative vehicle for chanelling substantial research support to institutions engaged in scientific research in areas critical to the economy of the State of New Jersey. Its primary goals are: to build upon existing strengths at the university in computer-oriented disciplines, strengthen and expand research activities in these areas; and, to encourage increased interaction and research collaboration between the university and industries involved in these areas. A concentration on research in parallel computation is currently running.

Rutgers University Center for Operations Research (RUTCOR): was established in 1982 to coordinate the operations research activities and to act as a focal point for the development of operations research in the State of New Jersey. RUTCOR sponsors interdisciplinary research projects, facilitates research contracts in operations research, sponsors an active colloquium series, puts out four international scientific journals and a technical report series, and hosts distinguished long and short-term visiting scholars from around the world.

The department is also a major participant in the John von Neumann Supercomputer Center and thus has small allocations of supercomputer time.

Facilities:
Primary facilities consist of a network of SUN workstations, Xerox Interlisp-D workstations, two VAX 8650, and an IBM-compatible mainframe (NAS AS-9000). The network is based on Ethernet and is connected to national networks including NSFnet, ARPAnet, CSnet, USEnet, and BITnet.

Research area, funding and selected projects:
Applications of Kolmogorov Complexity: Pseudorandum Generators, Circuit Complexity, and One-Way Functions (Allender, NSF)

Fast Numerical Algorithms for the Approximation of Single Integrals and Integral Equations (Gerasoulis, NSF)

Complexity Tailored Information Systems (Imielinski, NSF)

Research Resource on Artificial Intelligence in Medicine (Kulikowski, NIH)

Empirical Analysis and Refinement of Expert Systems Knowledge Bases (Kulikowski, DARPA)

Concurrent Computer Corporation Award in Support of Expert Systems for Computer Configuration (Kulikowski, Concurrent Computer Corporation)

Architectures for Optical Computers (Levy, AFOSR)

The CAM Project (Levy, DARPA and Syracuse University)

Law Governed Systems (Minsky, NSF)

Topics in Computational Geometry: Curved Objects, restricted-orientation objects, grasping and arrangements (Souvaine, NSF)

A Domain Independent Model of Knowledge-Based Design (Steinberg, DARPA and NSF)

Collaborations:
LCSR also maintains links with industry. As a result, the department is developing software for DEC, conducts IBM research exchange days, is doing research with RCA on cooperative man-machine systems, and is pursuing machine learning projects of interest to industry.

Stanford University

Department of Computer Science
Stanford, CA 94305
Phone: (415) 723-5396
email: ullman@cs.stanford.edu

Chairman: Prof. Jeff Ullman
Administrative Assistant: R. Joyce Chandler

Established: 1965
Undergraduates: n.a
Graduates: n.a.
Faculty: 45

Curriculum:

The Department offers programs for M.S. and
Ph.D. degrees in Computer Science.

The M.S. program can be completed in one to two
years. The degree is intended as a terminal professional degree and does not lead to the Ph.D. degree.

Students admitted to the Ph.D. program are immediately encouraged to become involved with a
research group. Although the program has no firm
course requirements, students must satisfy the
breadth requirement, covering introductory level
graduate material in major areas of Computer Science, and pass a qualifying examination in their
specialty area. The most important degree requirement is the dissertation, which must be approved
by a reading committee of at least three faculty
members and defended in the University Oral
Exam.

Additionally, the Department offers an interdisciplinary Medical Information Sciences Program
which offers instruction and research opportunities
leading to both M.S. and Ph.D. degrees in Medical
Information Sciences, with a particular emphasis
on medical decision sciences, including artificial
intelligence in biomedicine.

Courses for Graduates (selection): n.a.

Faculty (Professors with Research Areas):

Professors:

Jeffrey D. Ullman, Chairman, Ph.D., Princeton
University, 1966 - Databases and parallel computation, use of logic as a database query language.

George B. Dantzig, Ph.D., University of California
at Berkeley, 1946 - Modeling and optimization of
large-scale energy systems, combinatorial mathematics, mathematical programming.

Thomas O. Binford, Ph.D., University of Wisconsin, 1965 - Sensing, machine perception, and geometric modeling for computer vision, manufacturing, mobile robots, and medicine.

Edward A. Feigenbaum, Ph.D., Carnegie-Mellon
University, 1960 - Automated reasoning, knowledge representation.

Robert W. Floyd, B.A./B.S., University of Chicago, 1955/1958 - Design and analysis of algorithms, device-based computability theory.

Michael J. Flynn, Ph.D., Purdue University, 1961
- Computer architecture and organization, simulation and modeling of physical and conceptual processors, parallel machines including sparse
memory, subnanosecond arithmetic processors,
memory hierarchy design, modeling program behavior, performance limits of parallel processors.

Gene H. Golub, Ph.D., University of Illinois, 1959
- Numerical analysis, mathematical programming,
statistical computing.

Leonidas J. Guibas, Ph.D., Stanford University,
1976 - Computational geometry and computer
graphics, representation and manipulation of geometric objects.

John L. Hennessy, Ph.D., State University of New
York at Stony Brook, 1977 - Computer architecture, compiler technology, VLSI technology.

Donald E. Knuth, Ph.D., California Institute of Technology, 1963 - Analysis of algorithms, programming languages, mathematical typography, combinatorial mathematics.

Zohar Manna, Ph.D., Carnegie Mellon University, 1968 - Mathematical theory of computation, logic of programs, automated deduction, logic programming, concurrent programming, artificial intelligence.

John McCarthy, Ph.D., Princeton University, 1951 - Artificial intelligence, nonmonotonic reasoning, computing with symbolic expressions.

Edward J. McCluskey, Sc.D., Massachusetts Institute of Technology, 1956 - Computer design: reliable computers and manufacturing test, expert systems for designing testable circuits, built-in self-test designs.

William F. Miller, Ph.D., Purdue University, 1956 - Computer systems design, software systems, strategic planning and management, economic technological development.

Nils J. Nilsson, Ph.D., Stanford University, 1958 - Distributed artificial intelligence systems and robots, robot architecture, automated reasoning.

Joseph Oliger, Ph.D., University of Uppsala, 1973 - Numerical analysis, numerical methods for partial differential equations.

Vaughan Pratt, Ph.D. Stanford University, 1972 - Process specification languages, logics of programs, relation algebras, applications of universal algebra and category theory.

Gio Wiederhold, Ph.D., University of California at San Francisco, 1976 - Conceptual database models; design of centralized, distributed, and antonomous databases; object models for multiuser database query and update processing interfaces; knowledge-based techniques in database management, query and update; management of large knowledge-bases.

Terry Winograd, Ph.D., Massachusetts Institute of Technology, 1970 - Computer supported cooperative work, artificial intelligence.

Associate Professors:

David A. Cheriton
Michael R. Genesereth
Jean-Claude Latombe
Douglas B. Lenat

Assistant Professors:

David L. Dill
Andrew V. Goldberg
Anoop Gupta,
Monica S. Lam
Mark Leroy
John C. Mitchell
Rajeev Motwani
Serge A. Plotkin
Yoav Shoham

Affiliated Institutions:
Computer Systems Laboratory: operates under the auspices of the Departments of Computer Science and Electrical Engineering. Research areas are Hardware Design and Architecture, Programming Languages and Methodologies, Distributed Systems, Networks and Operating Systems, Database Research, Compilers, and Graphics.

Knowledge Systems Laboratory: concentrates on knowledge-based expert systems, especially those that use symbolic reasoning and heuristic problem-solving processes. Advances in AI research areas include the understanding of knowledge representation, methods for problem-solving, learning and discovery processes, and knowledge engineering, or methods for building expert systems. The laboratory approach involves designing, building, and experimenting with programs that serve to test underlying theories.

The Robotics Laboratory: descended from the Stanford Hand-Eye Project launched in the mid-sixties by Stanford's Artificial Intelligence Laboratory. Research includes manipulation, navigation, vision, tactile sensing, and reasoning. The goal is to make robots both autonomous and dexterous, to increase the self-sufficiency of existing robots, and to enable them to accomplish very delicate tasks. The Laboratory cooperates with other groups in Computer Science and other Departments of Stanford University, e.g. Aeronautics and Astronautics, Mechanical Engineering, and Civil Engineering. It also participates in the Stanford Institute for Manufacturing and Automation, the Center for Integrated Systems and the Center for Integrated Facility Engineering.

Center for Algorithmic Theory: principle emphasis is on theoretical aspects of computation, eg. design and analysis of algorithms, computational geometry, parallel programming, optimization, number theory, theory of programming languages, logics of programs, type theory, and concurrency theory.

Center for Integrated Facility Engineering (CIFE): an industry affiliate program directed towards the problems of the architecture, engineering and construction industry. The major goal is to develop computer-based tools that will permit improved integration and automation of the design, construction and facility management process. CIFE researchers primarily include faculty and graduate students from the Departments of Computer Science and Civil Engineering, and Visiting Fellows from organizations that are members of the center.

Center for Integrated Systems (CIS): a partnership of government, industry and the university, which has more than 80 affiliated faculty representing the Departments of Aeronautics and Astronautics, Applied Physics, Computer Science, Chemical Engineering, Electrical Engineering, Political Science, the Graduate School of Business, and the School of the Humanities and Sciences. Semiconductor technology makes possible improved performance and cost advantages for computer and communication systems by applying design and manufacturing methods and tools. In turn, these systems are applied to research in semicondutor technology and creation of automation systems that improve efficiency and productivity in design and manufacturing. This integration is the basis of CIS programs.

The Center for Large Scale Scientific Computation (CLaSSiC): an interdisciplinary project for the development of computational facilities for large scale scientific problems including faculty, research associates, postdoctoral scholars and doctoral students from Computer Science, Mathematics, and Chemical, Civil and Mechanical Engineering. Current research focuses on the description of complicated geometries and the user interface, adaptive numerical methods for several different classes of problems, theoretical estimates of utilizable parallelism in problems governed by partial differential equations, and language constructs and data structures for the efficient implementation of parallel algorithms.

Center for Scientific Computing and Computational Mathematics (SCCM): a program created to address the need in industry, government and universities for scientists to combine modern computing technology with applicable mathematics. SCCM includes faculty in Chemical Engineering, Computer Science, Electrical Engineering, Mathematics, and Mechanical Engineering. The focus is on the interplay of parallel computation and scientific computation, numerical algorithm development, analysis (including numerical linear algebra), software systems, and applications, especially computational fluid mechanics.

Stanford Institute for Manufacturing and Automation (SIMA): reporting to the Dean of the School of Engineering, SIMA focuses on issues in manufacturing and automation. The design process, the forming and processing of innovative materials, automation, robotics, and manufacturing systems management are areas of particular interest. SIMA is comprised out of four centers of focused expertise and excellence: the Center for Teaching and

Research in Integrated Manufacturing Systems (CTRIMS), the Center for Automation and Manufacturing Systems (CAMS), the Center for Design Research (CDR), and the Center for Materials Formability and Processing Science (CMFPS). Affiliated faculty represent the departments of Aeronautics and Astronautics, Computer Science, Electrical Engineering, Industrial Engineering and Engineering Management, Materials Science Engineering, and Mechanical Engineering.

Center for the Study of Language and Information (CSLI): at CSLI, computer scientists, linguists, logicians, philosophers, psychologists, and artificial intelligence researchers collaborate to build theories about the nature of information and how it is conveyed, processed, stored, and transformed by agents through the use of natural and computer languages. CSLI's goal is to develop and apply theories of information to an analysis of language as intelligent action. Researchers are examining theories of meaning from philosophy, theories of rational action and decision making from philosophy and artificial intelligence, theories of inference and reasoning from logic and psychology, theories of grammatical structure from linguists, detailed programs (large, but less complex units of discourse than natural language) from computer science, and the application of connectionist models to information processing.

Facilities:
The Computer Science Department operates several large computer systems for research, education, and administration. These machines, together with many smaller research computers, are connected to SUNnet, the university-wide Ethernet system and to the nationwide NSF/ARPAnet research network.
The larger systems include a VAX 5400, a SUN-4/390 SPARC Server, and a CYDRA 5. Other equipment includes a DEC VAX 3600, two SUN fileservers, and an Alliant FX/8 with 8 processors. Individual research groups operate a variety of equipment devoted to their specific interests. These machines include 30 MicroVax II, ten VAXstation 2000, 20 VAXstation 3100, 30 SUN-3, 20 Symbolics workstations, 50 Xerox Lisp worksta-

tions, 30 Apple Macintosh II, three NeXT machines, and a VAX 8350.

Research area, funding and selected projects:
Research at the Computer Science Department is divided into the four divisions Foundations of Computer Science, Systems, Scientific Computing, and AI & Robotics. Research areas in these divisions include:

Hardware Design and Architecture, Programming Languages and Methodologies, Distributed Systems, Networks & Operating Systems, Database Research, Compilers, Graphics, Knowledge Representation, Knowledge Acquisition, Use of Knowledge, Uncertain Reasoning.

Selected projects in these divisions are:

HPP - Heuristic Programming Project (Feigenbaum et al.)

AI/CASE - a CASE tool for system design using knowledge-based techniques

Qlisp - an effort to demonstrate the feasibility of parallel Lisp by implementing applications in symbolic algebra, theorem proving and artificial intelligence

PROTEGE - a multilevel program to construct custom-tailored knowledge-acquisition tools that reflect the semantics of particular application areas (Musen)

Integrated robotic systems combining real-time perception, action and language

ONCOCIN - a therapy adviser for oncologists (Shortliffe et al.)

NAIL (Not Another Implementation of Logic) - a knowledge-base system to optimize logic programs (Ullman)

CLaSSiC - an interdisciplinary project for the development of computational facilities for large scale scientific projects (Oliger et al.)

Collaborations:

The Stanford Computer Forum is a cooperative venture of the Computer Science Department, the Computer Systems Laboratory, and over eighty industrial affiliate member companies. The Forum provides a mechanism for developing personal contacts between industrial researchers and their academic counterparts. The Forum is also important to Stanford as a source of significant funding. The corporate membership fee is $15,000 per year. For small businesses with fewer than 500 employees, the fee is $10,000 per year.

Since 1980, the Western Institute in Computer Science has organized and administered advanced training for professional computer scientists every summer with intensive five-day programs. They represent new trends and new research concepts in addition to a series of "core courses", which cover topics involving essential skills and basic concepts. Well over 3,000 students from industry, government, and academic institutions from the United States, Canada, Europe and Asia have participated in this courses.

The Stanford Instructional Television Network (SITN) brings School of Engineering classes to more than 200 corporate sites. SITN students view the live broadcast or videotape, and participate in class discussion through an interactive talk-back system. Stanford furnishes course materials and technical support. Practicing engineers may enroll in a master's degree program in Aeronautics and Astronautics, Civil Engineering, Computer Science, Electrical Engineering, Mechanical Engineering, and other areas.

State University of New York at Buffalo

Department of Computer Science
226 Bell Hall
Buffalo, NY 14260-0001
Phone: (716) 636-3182
email: selman@cs.buffalo.edu

Chairman: Prof. Alan L. Selman
Administrative Assistant: Gloria Koontz

Established: 1967
Undergraduates: 209
Graduates: 112
Faculty: 19

Curriculum:
The department offers M.S. and Ph.D. programs.

For a M.S. a student must complete at least 30 hours of graduate credit (24 within the department), including at most six credits for a thesis or three for a project with a maintained GPA of 3.0 (B grade). The student has the option of writing a thesis, completing a project or passing the core examination at the master's level. There is no foreign language requirement and the student (full-time) should satisfy all requirements by the end of the fourth semester in residence.

There is no course requirement for the Ph.D. degree, but approximately equivalent courses for the M.S. degree should be taken in preparation for the Ph.D. Qualifying examination. The precise program of study will be designed by the student with an assigned faculty advisor. The program must include a minor area of study which consists of up to nine credit hours in any of a variety of fields: e.g., psychology, engineering, mathematics, or a foreign language. The qualifying examinations cover basic material in programming languages, computer architecture, analysis of algorithms, artificial intelligence, and theory of computation. After passing the qualifying examination, the student is assigned a Ph.D. committee consisting of three mem-

bers, the chair of which must be a member of the Department. The student must then submit a Dissertation Proposal, prepare the dissertation, and orally defend it.

Courses for Graduates (selection):
Fundamentals of Programming Systems, Computer Architecture, Analysis of Algorithms, Introduction to Artificial Intelligence, to Theory of Computation, to Operating Systems, to Language Processors, Program Development and Verification.

Faculty (Professors with Research Areas):

Professors:

Alan L. Selman, Chairman, Ph.D., Pennsylvania State University, 1970 - Theory.

Patricia James Eberlein, Ph.D., Michigan State University, 1955 - Numerical linear algebra, parallel computation, analysis of algorithms.

Anthony Ralston, Ph.D., Massachusetts Institute of Technology, 1956 - Software quality measurement, combinatorial and discrete mathematics.

Stuart C. Shapiro, Ph.D., University of Wisconsin, 1971 - Artificial intelligence, computational linguistics, cognitive science, knowledge representation, reasoning, natural language understanding and generation.

Sargur N. Srihari, Ph.D., Ohio State University, 1976 - Pattern recognition, parallel languages, computer architecture.

Associate Professors:

Bharadwaj Jayaraman
Russ Miller
William J. Rapaport
Deborah K.W. Walters

Assistant Professors:

Raj Acharya
Sreejit Chakravarty
Xin (Roger) He
Jonathan J. Hull
Jehuda Kalay
Jeannette G. Neal
Kenneth W. Regan
David B. Sher
Wennie Wei Shu
Shambu Upadhyaya
Patricia VanVerth

Affiliated Institutions:
University Computing Services (UCS)

Laboratory for Document Image Understanding

Facilities:
Departmental facilities include a VAX 11/785, an Encore Multimax, three Intel iPSC Hypercubes, 17 SUN-3 and SUN-4 workstations, five Symbolics Lisp Machines (3620, 3630, two 3640, 3670), six Texas Instruments Explorers, a Tektronix 4406 workstation, and computer vision research equipment such as an Eikonix EC850 4Kx4K CCD digitizing camera, an Adage 3010 image processing system, a Datacube MaxVideo pipeline image processing system, an Imaging Technologies Series 151 pipeline image processing system, and an LSI-11/73 microcomputer as a host processor to an Image Technology IP512 image processing system.
The University Computing Services has a DEC VAX 11/785, an IBM 3081, a Sperry 7000/40, several AT&T 6300 PC's, and several Macintoshes. All campus computers are on an Ethernet-based network which allows access to NYSERnet, BITnet, UUCP, USEnet, MILnet and INTERnet.

Research area, funding and selected projects:
The following is a list of currently running projects:

Test Compaction Algorithms & On-Chip Test Generation Schemes (Chakravarty, NSF, $58,000, 5/91)

Parallel Computation of Eigensystems for Symmetric and Non-Symmetric Matrices (Eberlein, NSF, $121,380, 8/91)

Parallel Algorithms for Special Graphs (He, NSF, $35,580, 5/92)

A Broader Basis for Logic Programming (Jayaraman, NSF, $152,688, 8/92)

Parallel Algorithms for Image Analysis, Computational Geometry (Miller, NSF, $168,623, 2/92)

Complexity, Formal Systems, and Linear-Time Computation (Regan, NSF, $35,000, 6/92)

Complexity of Feasible Computations (Selman, NSF, $130,560, 8/92)

Use of Contextual Information for Automatic Postal Interpretation (Srihari, $1.4 million, 9/91)

Recognition of Handwritten Address Zip Codes (Srihari, $2.1 million, 9/91)

Advanced Research on Real-Time Address Block Location (Srihari, USPS, $3 million, 12/91)

S&F Account for Document Image Understanding (Srihari, $183,612, 9/91)

Collaborations:
Several infrastructure grants ($885,000 in total) have been received by the following institutions: Data General Corporation ($285,000), Digital Equipment Corporation ($500,000), and Sun Microsystems ($100,000).

State University of New York at Stony Brook

Department of Computer Science
1401 Computer Science Building
Stony Brook, NY 11794
Phone: (516) 632-8462
email: pml@suny-sb.csnet

Chairman: Prof. Philip M. Lewis
Administrative Assistant: Pegi Thomas

Established: n.a.
Undergraduates: n.a.
Graduates: 110 (50 M.S., 60 Ph.D.)
Faculty: 24

Curriculum:

The department offers M.S. and Ph.D. programs which focus on the areas of programming, computing systems, theory and applications.

A minimum of 30 credits is needed for a M.S., but the student has the option not to do a thesis. The thesis can be substituted for up to eight credits. There is no residency or language requirement. A GPA of 3.0/4.0 (B/A grade) must be maintained. A student opting to do a thesis must choose a research advisor and a committee who approve the course work and thesis. A student who is enrolled in the Ph.D. program may satisfy the requirements of the M.S. degree without doing a thesis by passing the written Ph.D. qualifying examination, completing the 30 credits of course work and maintaining a GPA of 3.0/4.0.

The Ph.D. program requires residency of two consecutive semesters of full-time graduate study. A qualifying examination (written and oral) must be satisfactorily passed to prepare the student for research. A GPA of 3.0/4.0 must be maintained throughout the study program. Upon approval of the student's research advisor, the student will take a preliminary exam. The major requirement of the preliminary exam is a complete, detailed Ph.D. thesis research proposal. The preliminary exam is customarily an oral one, but a written exam may be requested by the examining committee. The committee consists of no fewer than four members, two of which must be faculty from the department. The student is then advanced to candidacy and can begin a dissertation which must be defended orally before a committee. The student must satisfy all requirements within seven years after completing 24 credits of graduate course work.

Courses for Graduates (selection):

Computer Architecture, VLSI Design, Computing with Logic, LISP and Functional Programming, Advanced VLSI Design, Techniques in Software Design, Advanced Topics in Compiler Design, Laboratory in Computer Science, Operating Systems, Principles in Programming Languages, Introduction to Image Analysis, Computer Graphics, Simulation and Modeling, Theory of Database Systems, Computer Network Communication Protocols, Advanced Operating Systems, Asynchronous Systems, Artificial Intelligence, Natural Language Processing, Expert Systems, Theoretical Foundations of Computer Science, Compatability and Undecidability, Theory of Computational Complexity, Mechanical Inferences, Analysis and Synthesis of Computer Communication Networks, Discrete Mathematics, Analysis of Algorithms, Formal Foundations for VLSI Design, Program Semantics and Verification, Topics in Modern Computer Science.

Faculty (Professors with Research Areas):

Professors:

Philip M. Lewis, Chairman, Ph.D., Massachusetts Institute of Technology, 1956 - Computational complexity, automata theory, compiler design, concurrent systems.

Arthur J. Bernstein, Ph.D., Columbia University, 1962 - Distributed algorithms, design and correctness of operating systems, concurrent programming.

Herbert Gelernter, Ph.D., University of Rochester, 1956 - Artificial intelligence, knowledge-based heuristic problem-solving systems, scientific applications.

Jack Heller, Ph.D., Polytechnic Institute of Brooklyn, 1950 - Database systems, office automation, visualization.

Arie Kaufman, Ph.D., Ben-Gurion University, 1977 - Computer graphics, visualization, computer architecture, computer vision.

Ker-I Ko, Ph.D., Ohio State University, 1979 - Computational complexity, theory of computation, computational learning theory.

Theo Pavlidis, Ph.D., University of California at Berkeley, 1964 - Image analysis, machine vision, computer graphics, interactive systems.

David R. Smith, Ph.D., University of Wisconsin, 1961 - VLSI design, digital systems design, computer architecture.

David S. Warren, Ph.D., University of Michigan, 1979 - Logic programming, database systems, interactive systems, artificial intelligence, natural language and logic.

Larry D. Wittie, Ph.D., University of Wisconsin, 1973 - Distributed operating systems, massively parallel algorithms, computer networks and interconnection topologies, computer architecture, neural networks.

Associate Professors:

Hussein G. Badr
Peter B. Henderson
Jieh Hsiang
Michael Kifer
I.V. Ramakrishnan
Scott A. Smolka
Eugene Stark
Anita Wasilewska

Assistant Professors:

Leo Bachmair
Amit Bandopadhay
Alessandro Giacalone
Prateek Mishra
Shaunak Pawagi
Steven Skiena

Affiliated Institutions:
The department operates reseach laboratories for network computing, image processing, 3-D graphics, robotics vision and heuristic systems. For VLSI research the department has access to facilities for designing, fabricating, and testing 3-micron CMOS chips and those derived from other technologies.

Facilities:
The department's facilities include: 96 SUN-3 workstations, a SUN-4/260, a 20-MIPS SGI 4D120, a 24-MIPS shared memory Sequent S27 multiprocessor, a 12-processor Sequent B20, a DEC 3100, a DEC VAX-11/780, several VAX-11/750, three MicroVAX-II, three Symbolic LISP Machines, SGI 3-D color graphics visualization systems, and many Macintosh, Intel and IBM personal computers.
The campus computing center houses DEC 8600/8350/6320 and IBM 3090/3083 machines.
The campus-wide network is based on Ethernet which connects to ARPAnet, CSnet, NYSERnet and the MOSIS VLSI foundry.

Research area, funding and selected projects:
In 1989-1990, the Department of Computer Science had separately-budgeted research expenditures in the amount of $1.3 million for 17 projects.

Collaborations: n.a.

Syracuse University

School of Computer and Information Science
Suite 4-116
Center for Science and Technology
Syracuse, NY 13244-4100
Phone: (315) 443-2368
email: frieder@top.cis.syr.edu

Chairman: Prof. Gideon Frieder (Dean)
Administrative Assistant: Deborah S. Brown

Established: 1972
Undergraduates: n.a.
Graduates: n.a.
Faculty: 35

Curriculum:
The Department offers a M.S. in both computer science and systems and information science, and a Ph.D. in computer and information science.

Computer Science M.S. - Eleven graduate courses, at least six in the computer science program. A thesis can be substituted for two courses.
Systems and Information Science M.S. - same as above, except choosing not to do a thesis requires a detailed summary and analysis of a technical paper.

For a Ph.D. a qualifying examination leads to establishment of a research committee chaired by the dissertation advisor. Program of five to ten courses to be determined by committee which leads to dissertation preparation and defense before an examining committee.

Courses for Graduates (selection):
Concrete Mathematics for Computer Science, Semantics Programming and Verification, Combinatorics and Graphs Theory, Analysis of Algorithms, Fundamentals of Analysis, Probability and Statistics, Linear Algebra, Group Theory, Methods of Numerical Analysis.

Faculty (Professors with Research Areas):

Professors:

Gideon Frieder, Chairman (Dean), Ph.D., Technion, Israel, 1967 - Distributed architecture, medically-motivated computing, medical graphics.

Klaus J. Berkling, Ph.D., Universität Bonn, 1961 - High-level "new generation" architecture, languages, functional and logic programming.

Per Brinch Hansen, Ph.D., Technical University of Denmark, 1978 - Concurrent programming, programming languages, operating systems, parallel architectures.

Allen Brown, Jr., Ph.D., Massachusetts Institute of Technology, 1975 - Formal bases for document representation and processing, non-monotonic reasoning, foundations of logic programming.

Geoffrey Fox, Ph.D., Cambridge University, 1967 - Supercomputer architectures (hypercube), concurrent algorithms, high energy physics phenomenology, computational science.

Carlos R.P. Hartmann, Ph.D., University of Illinois, 1970 - Theory of decoding, practical decoding algorithms, parallel computation, fault detection in digital systems.

Harold F. Mattson, Jr., Ph.D., Massachusetts Institute of Technology, 1955 - Error-correcting codes, covering radius.

Kishan G. Mehrotra, Ph.D., University of Wisconsin, 1971 - Statistical inference, software reliability, coding theory, neural networks, analysis of algorithms.

F. Lockwood Morris, Ph.D., Stanford University, 1972 - Programming as mathematical exposition, implementation-oriented semantics.

J. Alan Robinson, Ph.D., Princeton University, 1956 - Computational logic, high-level programming languages.

Luther D. Rudolph, Ph.D., Syracuse University, 1968 - Information theory, cryptography and data security, data compression.

Luis Sanchis, Ph.D., Penn State University, 1963 - Non-deterministic computation, selector properties, reflexive structures.

Anne Shelly, Assistant Dean, Ph.D., Syracuse University, 1984 - Logic programming.

Edward F. Storm, Ph.D., Harvard University, 1966 - Design of imperative, nonfunctional programming facilities.

Associate Professors:

Howard A. Blair
James S. Royer

Assistant Professors:

Chilukuri K. Mohan
Peter William O'Hearn
Sanjay Ranka

Affiliated Institutions:
Northeast Parallel Architectures Center (NPAC): established in 1987 as an interdisciplinary research center intended to further research in the design, evaluation, programming and application of parallel computing systems.

Center for Advanced Technology in Computer Applications and Software Engineering (CASE Center): focuses on computer-enhanced reasoning, computer-tools research, and cross-disciplinary studies.

Facilities:
Departmental and campus-wide network including two SUN-3/ servers, an IBM 3090, a VAX/ VMS cluster, and a CAD lab based on VAX/VMS and graphics terminals. At NPAC there are two Encore Multimax systems: a Multimax 520 with 16 extended processors, and a Multimax 320 wtih 20 advanced processors; one CM Model 2 Connection Machine (host computers: VAX8800 and SUN 4260) with 32,768 processors; and one Alliant FX/ 80 with eight vector/parallel computational elements, six interactive processors.

Research area, funding and selected projects:
The CASE center has several currently running projects including: the interconnection of engineering workstations to vector computers, a study of the weather's impact on generation forecasting and system state, a comprehensive analysis of helicopters with bearingless rotors, and development of an expert system to assist in design verification.

Collaborations:
Interdisciplinary projects with the departments of i.e. Chemistry, Engineering, Fine Arts, etc. are available for students interested in not only theories, but also applications of the theories they are developing.

The following private and governmental organizations have sponsored research at the department: NSF, DARPA, IBM, Rome Air Development Center, AFOSR, Bell Communications Research, General Electric, Mutual of New York, Kellogg Foundation, and Intellisys Corporation.

University of Arizona

Department of Computer Science
Tucson, AZ 85721-0001
Phone: (602) 621-4239
email: andrews@arizona.edu

Chairman: Prof. Gregory R. Andrews
Administrative Assistant: Janet Kerr

Established: 1971
Undergraduates: 60
Graduates:90
Faculty: 14

Curriculum:

The university offers both a M.S. and a Ph.D. degree in Computer Science.

The M.S. program consists of 30 credits of required course work which must be maintained at a 3.0 (B grade) average. A comprehensive examination is given in the last semester of the student's program. A thesis option is offered only to the most qualified and prepared students. The thesis counts for six credits and must be defended before a thesis commmittee.

The Ph.D. program is offered directly to students with strong undergraduate records and training in Computer Science. The student must form a doctoral committee consisting of three faculty from Computer Science and two from the minor department. The program consists of 66 credits divided into 36 credits for major course work, 12 units of minor course work, and 18 credits of dissertation work. A qualifying examination must be taken within the first two years of graduate study for students admitted without a master's degree, and within one year for students admitted with a master's degree. A comprehensive examination is given at the end of the student's last semester of regular courses, and a final oral examination is given as defense of the student's dissertation before the doctoral committee and public.

Courses for Graduates (selection):

Mathematical Logic, Principles of Programming Languages, Advanced Systems Modeling and Simulation, Principles of Computer Networking, Software Design, Introduction to Interactive Computer Graphics, Advanced Computer Graphics and User Interface, Computer-Aided Information Systems Analysis and Design, Theory of Graphs and Networks, Design and Analysis of Algorithms, Parallel Computing, String and List Processing, Advanced Operating Systems, Principles of Compilation, Database Systems, Artificial Intelligence, Digital Systems Design, Continuous-System Simulation, Theory of Computation, Digital Logic Design, Numerical Analysis, Computer Architecture, Computational Methods of Algebra, Game Theory and Mathematical Programming, Computational Linguistics, Microprocessors, Minicomputers and Real-Time Distributed Processing, Sequential Circuits and Automata, Advanced Topics in Programming Languages, in Software Systems, in Algorithm Analysis, in Operating Systems.

Faculty (Professors with Research Areas):

Professors:

Gregory R. Andrews, Chairman, Ph.D., University of Washington, 1974 - Design and implementation of concurrent programming languages, parallel and distributed computing, operating systems.

Ralph E. Griswold, Ph.D., Stanford University, 1962 - Programming language design and implementation, string and list processing, program portability.

Udi Manber, Ph.D., University of Washington, 1982 - Design of algorithms, distributed computing, computer networks.

Associate Professors:

Peter J. Downey
Stephen R. Mahaney
Eugene W. Myers, Jr.
Larry L. Peterson

Richard D. Schlichting
Richard T. Snodgrass

Assistant Professors:

Mary L. Bailey
Saumya Debray
Scott Hudson
Sampath Kannan

Affiliated Institutions:
Laboratory for Programming Languages and Software Systems: supports research in software development, programming languages, operating systems, and computer graphics.

Computer and Biological Systems Laboratory: is an interdisciplinary research institute which applies current research in computer science to the substantial data management and analysis problems affecting molecular biologists. Sample research includes decoding the human genome and design pattern detection algorithms for DNA sequences.

Center for Computing and Information Technology (CCIT): provides computer services to the university and supplies instructional computer facilities used by the department in lower-division undergraduate courses. The CCIT machines support a wide range of programming languages, editors, mathematical and statistical programs and specialized applications. All campus mainframes are accessible from CCIT.

Facilities:
The department's facilities include a DEC VAX-8650, a multiprocessor Sequent S81, numerous SUN workstations, Iris and HP high-resolution color graphics workstations, NeXt and DEC workstations, and various microcomputers. The network is based on Ethernet and has access to INTERnet.
CCIT: includes a Convex C240, an IBM 3090, and a cluster consisting of a VAX-8700 and two VAX-8650s.

Research area, funding and selected projects:
Parallel and Distributed Programming (Andrews, NSF)

Parallel Simulation of VLSI Circuits (Bailey, NSF)

Optimization of Logic Programs (Debray, NSF)

Performance Analysis of Concurrent Processes (Downey)

The Icon Programming Language (Griswold, NSF)

User Interface Management Systems (Hudson, NSF)

Constructing Evolutionary Trees (Kannan, NSF)

Structure in Complexity Theory (Mahaney, NSF)

Discrete Pattern Matching (Manber et al., NSF)

Algorithms for Molecular Biology (Myers, NSF/NIH)

The x-Kernel (Peterson, NSF/DARPA)

Distributed Directory Services (Peterson, NSF)

Communication Support for Fault-Tolerant Programs (Peterson et al., NSF/DARPA)

Accessing Remote Scientific Machines (Schlichting)

Fault-Tolerant Programming (Schlichting, NSF/ONR)

Temporal Databases (Snodgrass, NSF/IBM)

Fine Grained Data Management in Software Development Environments (Snodgrass)

The Laboratory for Programming Languages and Software Systems had a $3.6 million Coordinated Experimental Research grant in Programming Sys-

73

tems from NSF in 1984, which was renewed in 1989 providing an additional $1.9 million in funding.

Collaborations:

The department, specifically Professor Schlichting, has a joint research project with colleagues at the Tokyo Institute of Technology in Japan called "Fault tolerant programming based on attribute grammars."

University of California at Berkeley

Department of Electrical Engineering and Computer Science
Division of Computer Science
571 Evans Hall
Berkeley, CA 94720
Phone: (415) 642-0930
email: pattrsn@ginger.berkeley.edu

Chairman: Prof. David A. Patterson
Administrative Assistant: Crystal Williams

Established: 1973
Undergraduates: 400
Graduates: 200
Faculty: 33

Curriculum:
The Computer Science Division offers a B.A. degree through the College of Letters and Science; this program requires two years of computer science coursework as part of the four-year degree program.

The B.S. degree, offered through the College of Engineering, requires four years of computer science and related coursework in engineering.

Graduate programs may lead to one of four degrees: M.S., M.Eng., Ph.D. or D.Eng.

Most of the students are enrolled in M.S. and Ph.D. programs.

Courses for Graduates:
VLSI Systems Design, Computer Architecture, Implementation and Testing of LSI Chips, Advanced Computer Architecture, Parallel Processors, Fault Tolerant Systems, User-Interfaces to Computer Systems, Security in Computer Systems, Advanced Topics in Operating Systems, Design of Programming Languages, Advanced Programming Languages Implementation, Introduction to System Performance Analysis, Computer System Analysis, Analytic Models of Computer Systems, Software Engineering and Large System Design, Combinatorial Algorithms and Data Structures, Randomness and Computation, Probabilistic Analysis of Algorithms, Foundations of Parallel Computation, Computational Geometry, Computational Algebra, Number Theory and Cryptography, Concrete Complexity, Machine-Based Complexity Theory, System Support for Scientific Computation, Computer Vision, Machine Learning, Algebraic Algorithms, Computer-Aided Geometric Design and Modeling, Implementation of Database Systems, Robot Action and Perception, Artificial Intelligence, Concurrent Programming, Distributed Systems and Computer Networks.

Faculty (Professors with Research Areas):

Professors:

David A. Patterson, Chairman, Ph.D., University of California at Los Angeles, 1976 - VLSI computer architecture, high-performance I/O.

Brian A. Barsky, Ph.D., University of Utah, 1982 - Computer graphics, computer-aided geometric design and modeling, visualization in scientific computing.

Lenore C. Blum (Adjunct Professor), Ph.D., Massachusetts Institute of Technology, 1968 - Computer science theory, randomness and complexity.

Manuel Blum, Ph.D., Massachusetts Institute of Technology, 1963 - Computational complexity, computational theory, cryptography.

James Demmel, Ph.D., University of California at Berkeley, 1983 - Scientific computing, numerical analysis, control theory.

Richard J. Fateman, Ph.D., Harvard University, 1971 - Programming environments and systems, programming languages and compilers, scientific computation, symbolic mathematical computation.

75

Jerome A. Feldman, Ph.D., Carnegie-Mellon University, 1964 - Artificial intelligence, biological computation, massively parallel computation.

Domenico Ferrari, Dr. Ing, Politecnico di Milano, 1963 - Computer networks, computer systems, distributed systems, measurement and modeling, operating systems, performance evaluation.

Susan L. Graham, Ph.D., Stanford University, 1971 - Programming language design and implementation, interactive software, development environments.

Michael A. Harrison, Ph.D., University of Michigan, 1963 - Computer security, computer software, document preparation systems, multiple representation.

William M. Kahan, Ph.D., University of Toronto, 1958 - Algorithms, computational theory, computer arithmetic, computer software diagnosis, error analysis, financial computations, matrix computations, numerical analysis, trajectory computations.

Richard M. Karp, Ph.D., Harvard University, 1959 - Combinatorial, parallel and randomized algorithms.

Randy H. Katz, Ph.D., University of California at Berkeley, 1980 - Computer architecture, database management systems, VLSI systems.

Eugene Lawler, Ph.D., Harvard University, 1963 - Combinatorial algorithms, computational biology, coordination theory.

John K. Ousterhout, Ph.D., Carnegie Mellon University, 1980 - Operating systems, distributed systems, user interfaces, window systems.

Beresford N. Parlett, Ph.D., Stanford University, 1962 - Numerical analysis.

Chittoor V. Ramamoorthy, Ph.D., Harvard University, 1964 - Computer architecture, computer networking and distributed systems, software engineering.

Lawrence A. Rowe, Ph.D., University of California at Irvine, 1976 - Application development tools, computer-integrated manufacturing, human-computer interfaces, multimedia applications and databases.

Carlo H. Séquin, Ph.D., University of Basel, 1969 - Computer-aided design of VLSI circuits, computer graphics and geometric modeling, computer architecture and multiprocessors.

Michael R. Stonebraker, Ph.D., University of Michigan, 1971 - Database management systems, expert systems, operating systems.

Robert Wilensky, Ph.D., Yale University, 1978 - Artificial intelligence, knowledge representation.

Lotfi A. Zadeh, Ph.D., Columbia University, 1949 - Artificial intelligence, knowledge-based systems, managment of uncertainty, natural and synthetic languages.

Associate Professors:

Paul N. Hilfinger
Jitendra Malik
Stuart J. Russell
Raimund Seidel
Umesh Vazirani

Assistant Professors:

Thomas Anderson
John F. Canny
David E. Culler
Abhiram Ranade
John Wawrzynek
Katherine Yelick

Affiliated Institutions:

The Division of Computer Science is part of the Department of Electrical Engineering and Computer Science (EECS), which itself is one of seven Departments of the College of Engineering. Because of this construction there are a wide range of interdisciplinary programs and affiliated institutions.

Most of the research conducted within EECS is overseen by the Electronics Research Laboratory, an organizationally independent, administrative unit that manages research grants and contracts for EECS. Next to other specialized, organized research units EECS operates the Engineering Systems Research Center. Furthermore, most of the major research groups operate their own specialized research facilities. Here is a selection:

Quantum Electronics Laboratory: research in the ares of semiconductor lasers, nonlinear optics, electronic probing of semiconductor devices, optical communication systems.

Computer Laboratory for Circuits and Systems: equipped for the analysis and interactive simulation of complicated dynamics in non-linear circuits.

Microfabrication Laboratory: accommodates every step of the fabrication for semiconductor devices and circuits.

Further examples are the Computer-Aided Optimization Laboratory, the Robotics Laboratory, and the Custom VLSI Laboratory.

Though not officially affiliated with the EECS there are some other important institutions, which cooperate frequently:

The International Computer Science Institute: initially supported by the German National Research Center for Computer Science (GMD), the institute sponsors advanced research in computer science by experts from around the world.

The Lawrence Berkeley and the Lawrence Livermore Laboratories: two multidisciplinary research laboratories operated by the University for the Department of Energy.

The Mathematical Sciences Research Institute: collaborates on important projects with the Computer Science Division, especially in the areas of numerical computation and computational theory.

The Berkeley Integrated Sensor Center, the Berkeley Microelectronics Affiliates, the Space Sciences Laboratory, and the Center for Pure and Applied Mathematics are more examples.

Facilities:

The department's computing environment has evolved from mainframes and terminals to an Ethernet-based network of mainframes, workstations, and fileservers; it includes more than 280 Sun workstations, 110 MicroVaxes, 40 DECstations, dozens of Hewlett-Packard and other workstations, Macintoshes and IBM PCs, several models of VAX (from 11/750s to 8800s), and a number of specialized research machines, including an Intel iPSC, a Connection Machine, an NCUBE, and a BBN Butterfly.

The campus computing center maintains an IBM 3090 and a Cray X-MP/14.

Cooperative arrangements provide access to national supercomputer centers through national networks such as ARPAnet, BITnet and MFEnet.

Research area, funding and selected projects:

Computer Science research at Berkeley is divided into nine principal areas: Theory and Algorithms, Computer Architecture, Operating Systems, Programming Languages and Software Development Systems, Database Management Systems, Scientific and Numerical Computing, Computer Graphics and Geometric Modeling, Artificial Intelligence, and Robotics and Computer Vision.

There are dozens of projects in these specific areas and the following is a selection:

Project SEQUOIA: a massive storage system for global research scientists and others.

Project POSTGRES: database managment project to explore ways of storage and accessing large complex data structures such as programs, circuit layouts, and bitmaps.

Project Sprite: developed as part of the SPUR multiprocessor workstation project, which ended 1988, Sprite is intended to provide an experimental distributed operating system for a local-area network or small internet, and its priorities are performance and ease of sharing.

Project DASH: addresses the issues involved in developing an operating system for a high-speed network connecting millions of hosts. A primary focus is integrated multimedia network communication for handling streams of digital audio and video data.

Project XPRS: the goals are to build a high-performance I/O system and to develop operating system and database management software that can take full advantage of the I/O speed.

Project RALPH: the "Rational Agent with Limited Performance Hardware" project is an attempt to create an intelligent agent that can reason about its environment in real time with limited knowledge and limited computational resources.

Project "Model-Based Integrated Assembly System": the goal is to design a robotics assembly system for small mechanical parts that can plan and execute tasks from start to finish, working with a description of the object and the necessary parts and tools.

Principal sources of research support are the Defense Advanced Research Projects Agency, the National Science Foundation, the California MICRO program and the industry. In 1988 the Division was awarded additional major grants by the NSF:

- one Institutional Infrastructure grant for massive information storage, management, and use (project MAMMOTH), which will provide $ 3.8 million over five years. It is involving almost all the computer science faculty to design and implement a massive information storage and management system and to study its applications.

- one grant for exploring redundant arrays of inexpensive disks (project RAID) for $ 1.5 million over three years. The project is supposed to explore high-performance input/output transaction processing, using a large array of medium-capacity disks.

In 1989-1990, the Department of Electrical Engineering and Computer Science had separately-budgeted research expenditures in the amount of $25.2 million for 420 projects. For the whole College of Engineering, the amount was $50.5 million ($26.5 million from the Federal Government, $15.8 million from Business and Industry, $8.2 million from State and Local Government).

Collaborations:
The EECS Department's Industrial Liaison Program (ILP) is intended to encourage productive collaboration and effective technology transfer between the University and industry. Facets of this effort are joint research projects and the annual college-wide ILP conference, attended by representatives of more than 125 member companies.

University of California at Irvine

Department of Information and Computer Science
444 Computer Science Building
Irvine, CA 92717-0001
Phone: (714) 856-7405
email: ljo@ics.uci.edu

Chairman: Prof. Leon Osterweil
Administrative Assistant: Susan Gumbrecht

Established: 1968
Undergraduates: n.a.
Graduates: n.a.
Faculty: 35

Curriculum:
The department offers B.S., M.S. and Ph.D. degrees.

The M.S. degree in Information and Computer Science is awarded only to Ph.D. students who complete necessary requirements. Students are not admitted for graduate study leading only to the M.S.

A student need not have an undergraduate background in computer science for admission into the Ph.D. program. The Ph.D. program has three phases: (I) student must complete nine courses with no grade below a B by the end of the second year, (II) student must take three advanced courses, pass a written comprehensive examination, prepare a survey paper and a research paper of publishable or near-publishable quality, present a research colloquium, receive approval from a faculty committee to take a Candidacy Oral Examination, pass a Candidacy Oral Examination, and (III) teaching activities requirement and dissertation preparation. A student may be awarded a M.S. degree upon completion of all course requirements of phases I and II plus either the phase II paper or the phase II examination. The Ph.D. degree also has a program competence requirement which states the student must be able to read and write programs in assembly, algebraic and nonnumerical languages.

Courses for Graduates (selection):
Data Structures, Formal Semantics of Programming Languages, Computer Systems Architecture, Advanced Topics in Computer Architecture and Operating Systems, Computer Networks, Introduction to Computer Design, High-Performance Architectures and Their Compilers, Design Description and Modeling, Computer Design Synthesis, Analysis of Algorithms, Advanced Analysis of Algorithms, Computational Geometry, Knowledge Representation in Artificial Intelligence, Software Engineering, Computing Resource Management, Automata Theory, Introduction to Artificial Intelligence, Machine Learning.

Faculty (Professors with Research Areas):

Professors:

Leon J. Osterweil, Chairman, Ph.D., University of Maryland - Software process, software environments, software testing and analysis, combinatorics.

Alfred M. Bork, Ph.D., Brown University - Computer-based learning, production systems for computer-based learning, screen design, simulation, computer graphics.

Julian Feldman, Ph.D., Carnegie Institute of Technology - Management of computing resources, problems involved in managing the computer resources of an organization, teaching of programming.

Daniel D. Gajski, Ph.D., University of Pennsylvania - Parallel algorithms and architectures, silicon compilation, expert systems for design, science for design.

Daniel Hirschberg, Ph.D., Princeton University - Analysis of algorithms, concrete complexity, data structures, models of computation.

K.H. (Kane) Kim, Ph.D., University of California at Berkeley - Distributed real-time computer systems, fault-tolerant computer systems, real-time learning systems.

John Leslie King, Ph.D., University of California at Irvine - Economics of computing, policies for computer management and use in organizations, public policy and social impact aspects of computer use.

Rob Kling, Ph.D., Stanford University - Social analysis of computing, computer technology and public policy, sociology of computing.

Kenneth L. Kraemer, Ph.D., University of Southern California - Economics and management of computing, organizational and social impacts of computing, information technology and public policy, management information systems/design support systems.

Lawrence Larmore, Ph.D., University of California at Irvine - Design and analysis of algorithms, optimal coding, parallel compuation.

George S. Lueker, Ph.D., Princeton University - Computational complexity, probabilistic analysis of algorithms, data structures.

Gary S. Lynch, Ph.D., Princeton University - Learning and memory, symaptic change, computational neuroscience.

Thomas A. Standish, Ph.D., Carnegie Institute of Technology - Programming environments, data structures.

Associate Professors:

Lubimir Bic
Peter Freeman
Richard H. Granger
Donald Hoffman
Dennis Kibler
Patrick Langley
Nancy Leveson
Alexandru Nicolau
Richard Taylor
Nicholas P. Vitalari

Assistant Professors:

Nader Bagherzadeh
Douglas M. Blough
Michael Dillencourt
Nikil Dutt
Fadi Kurdahi
Paul O'Rorke
Nohbyung Park
Michael J. Pazzani
Debra J. Richardson
Richard W. Selby
Susan Leigh Star
Tatsuya Suda

Affiliated Institutions:
Computing, Organizations, Policy and Society (CORPS): is a center for research on the social and managerial dimensions of computerization. CORPS research examines the impacts and policy issues that surround computerization, ways in which users develop computing technologies, including workplace negotiations and coalitions, and the economics of computing and different strategies for managing computer resources. CORPS researchers study these topics in various public and private settings including government agencies, hospitals, large and small commercial enterprises and universities.

Educational Technology Center: is dedicated to research and development in educational software, integrated computing/video systems and tools for construction of educational packages. It maintains a close relationship with the informatics group at the University of Geneva.

Facilities:
The department's Computing Facility houses a DEC VAX 11/780, 11/785, 8350 (VMS) and a Sequent Symmetry shared memory multiprocessor (Unix). The department also has research laboratories which include Toshiba T-300 workstations, Macintosh II workstations and many Macintosh Plus. Additional resources include ten SUN-3/

50 workstations, a second Sequent Symmetry Unix timesharing machine, ten Integrated Solutions workstations and over 150 SUN workstations.

Research area, funding and selected projects:
The department has general research areas in Artificial Intelligence, Computer Networks, Parallel Processing, Computer-Aided Design, Educational Technology, Software Engineering, Theory: Algorithms and Data Structures.

Sample research projects are as follows:

Hypertool: Programming Tool for an Intel Hypercube (Bic)

Advanced Strategies for Development Technology-based Learning Units (Bork)

Design Representations and Algorithms for Efficient High Level Synthesis (Dutt)

Computing Resource Management in Organizations (Feldman)

CAD Tools = Silicon Compilers (Gajski)

Parallelization of Application Algorithms (Gajski)

Neural Modeling (Granger)

Data Compression (Hirschberg)

IBL: Instance Based Learning (Kibler)

Evolution of Computing Use in Complex Organizations (King)

ICARUS: an integrated model of perception, planning, action, and learning (Langley)

Safety-Critical Real-Time Systems (Leveson)

Parallel Languages and Parallelizing Compilers (Nicolau)

Abductive Learning and Artificial Intelligence (O'Rorke)

Arcadia: a software development research project (Osterweil and Taylor)

FOCL: First Order Combined Learner (Pazzani)

TEAM: Software Testing and Analysis Techniques (Richardson)

Amadeus Measurement-Driven Analysis and Feedback System (Selby)

Epistemology of Computer Programming (Standish)

Design and Performance of High-Speed Optical Networks (Suda)

Collaborations: n.a.

University of California at Los Angeles

Department of Computer Science
405 Hilgard Ave., 3732 Boelter Hall
Los Angeles, CA 90024-1596
Phone: (213) 825-8878
email: wwc@cs.ucla.edu

Chairman: Prof. Wesley W. Chu
Administrative Assistant: Saba Hunt

Established: n.a.
Undergraduates: n.a.
Graduates: n.a.
Faculty: 42

Curriculum: n.a.

Courses for Graduates (selection): n.a.

Faculty (Professors with Research Areas):

Professors:

Wesley W. Chu, Chairman, Ph.D., Stanford University, 1966 - Distributed processing, distributed databases, computer communication, models for task partition and allocation, fault tolerance in distributed databases, knowledge-based distributed systems.

Masanao Aoki, Ph.D., University of California at Los Angeles, 1960 - Methodology for modeling and control of dynamic data sources, analysis of empirical data in socio-economic areas, stochastic realization theory, simulation and numerical analysis of large dynamic phenomena.

Algirdas Avizienis, Ph.D., University of Illinois at Urbana-Champaign, 1960 - Computer system architecture, dependable computing and fault-tolerance, design diversity in software and hardware, computer arithmetic.

Daniel M. Berry, Ph.D., Brown University, 1974 - Software engineering, programming languages, text processing.

David G. Cantor, Ph.D., University of California at Los Angeles, 1960 - Networks, graphs, sorting and searching.

Alfonso F. Cardenas, Ph.D., University of California at Los Angeles, 1969 - Database management systems, distributed data management, pictorial data management, automatic programming, management information systems.

Jack W. Carlyle, Ph.D., University of California at Berkeley, 1961 - Discrete-state and stochastic systems, data communication and computer methodology, simulation, algorithms and complexity, microcomputer applications.

Joseph J. DiStefano, III, Ph.D., University of California at Los Angeles, 1966 - Scientific computing in the life sciences, modeling theory and methodology in the life sciences, optimal experiment design methodology, expert systems development and applications in physiology and medicine.

Milos D. Ercegovac, Ph.D., University of Illinois at Urbana-Champaign, 1960 - Theory and practice of fast computer arithmetic, special-purpose architectures for arithmetic-intensive computations, supercomputers and parallel architectures, dataflow and functional languages and architectures, specification of VLSI algorithms and structures, logic design.

Gerald Estrin, Ph.D., University of Wisconsin, 1951 - Computer architecture, design of information systems, modeling and analysis of concurrent systems, designer-computer interfaces, computer-assisted collaboration.

Thelma Estrin, Ph.D., University of Wisconsin, 1951 - Expert systems for clinical decision making, application of technology and computer systems to health care, computer methods in neuroscience, engineering education, social implications of computer technology.

Mario Gerla, Ph.D., University of California at Los Angeles, 1973 - Performance evaluation, control of distributed networks and distributed processing systems.

Sheila A. Greibach, Ph.D., Harvard University, 1963 - Complexity theory, algorithms, graph algorithms, models for parallel and distributed computation, automata and formal languages, grammars and generating systems.

Walter J. Karplus, Ph.D., University of California at Los Angeles, 1955 - Modeling and simulation of systems, high-speed scientific computing, realtime computation, neural networks for system simulation, vector and multiprocessors.

Leonard Kleinrock, Ph.D., Massachusetts Institute of Technology, 1963 - Distributed and parallel systems research, performance evaluation and design, application of queueing theory, distributed algorithms, distributed control, distributed communications, data networks.

Allen Klinger, Ph.D., University of California at Berkeley, 1966 - Scientific computing, image indexing, data structures, computer vision, computer graphics, pattern recognition, speech analysis, hypertext and user interfaces.

David F. Martin, Ph.D., University of California at Los Angeles, 1966 - Semantics of programming languages, semantics of computation, theory, implementation and correctness of programming language translators, semantics prototyping systems, program verification, correctness of abstract data type implementation.

Lawrence McNamee, Ph.D., University of Pittsburgh, 1964 - Simulation, computer modeling, VLSI CAD systems for VLSI design, time series analysis, capacity planning of computer systems.

Michel A. Melkanoff, Ph.D., University of California at Los Angeles, 1955 - Programming languages, data structures, database design, question-and-answer systems, CAD, computer-integrated manufacturing, numerical control machining.

Richard R. Muntz, Ph.D., Princeton University, 1969 - Computer system performance and performance evaluation, distributed processing, distributed database algorithms and modeling, query optimization for distributed database systems, task allocation, load leveling, task force scheduling, distributed systems instrumentation and measurement.

Judea Pearl, Ph.D., Polytechnic Institute of Brooklyn, 1965 - Artificial intelligence, automated reasoning, machine learning, neural networks.

Jacques J. Vidal, Ph.D., University of Paris Sorbonne, 1961 - Neurocybernetics and neural models, artificial neural networks, expert systems, parallel architectures, graphics and image processing, human-machine interaction.

Chand R. Viswanathan, Ph.D., University of California at Los Angeles, 1964 - Solid-state electronics, integrated circuit of devices, charge-coupled devices.

Associate Professors:

Michael G. Dyer
Eleizer Gafni
Richard E. Korf
D. Scott Parker
David Rennels

Assistant Professors:

Rajive Bagrodia
David Jefferson
Andrew B. Kahng
Josef Skrzypek
Yuval Tamir

Affiliated Institutions:
Artificial Intelligence Laboratory (AI Lab): conducts research in natural language processing.

Machine Perception Laboratory: conducts research in "real-time general purpose" machine vision based on the human vison system.

Facilities:
AI Lab contains six Hewlett-Packard model 9000 color workstations, four DN4000/3000 series color Apollo workstations, and the CM2 parallel SIMD machine.

Research area, funding and selected projects:
Here is a small sample of contracts:

Research Initiation: Performance Evaluation of Distributed Algorithms (Bagrodia, NSF, 12/90)

Research on Fault Tolerant Databases for Highly Parallel Real Time Distributed Systems (Chu, ONR, 8/91)

LACQ: Language Acquisition (Dyer)

Integrated Voice Data and Video Communications on High Speed Fiber Optics Networks (Gerla, Pacific Bell/MICRO, 12/90)

A Modeling Environment for Performance/Reliability Analysis of Distributed Systems (Muntz and Gerla, NSF, 7/91)

A VLSI Communication Coprocessor: A Building-Block for High-Performance Multicomputer Systems (Tamir, Rockwell/MICRO, 12/90)

Collaborations:
During the academic year 1990, the department had the following industrial affiliates: Bellcore, BNR Northern Telecom, Hitachi, IBM, NCR, Mitsubishi, Northrop, Perceptronics, TRW, Unisys.

The university also has the Cognitive Science Research Program (CSRP), an interdisciplinary, organized research program in the cognitive sciences.

University of California at San Diego

Department of Computer Science and Engineering
Mail Code C-014
La Jolla, CA 92093
Phone: (619) 534-1246
email: burkhard@uscd.edu

Chairman:Prof. Walter A. Burkhard
Administrative Assistant: Patricia Naughton

Established: n.a.
Undergraduates: n.a.
Graduates: 101 (65 Ph.D.)
Faculty: 32

Curriculum:
The Department offers a B.S., B.A., M.S. and
Ph.D. degree. Furthermore the Department of Computer Science and Engineering and the Department
of Electrical and Computer Engineering are jointly
developing a graduate specialization at the master's
and Ph.D. level.

For a M.S. the student has to pass a written comprehensive examination and compile the following
course requirements (out of 48 courses total):
- Software Engineering, Advanced Operating Systems and either Advanced Compiler Design or
Database Systems,
- A Special Project in Computer Science,
- Two of the following 4 sequences:
* Principles on Computer Architecture I and II,
* Advanced Artificial Intelligence I and II,
* Automata; Formal Languages and Computability, Computability and Complexity, Complexity of
Intractability,
* Combinational Algorithms, Mathematical Programming, and Topics in Complexity of Algorithms and Data Structures or Applications of Combinatorial Algorithms.

Courses for Graduates (selection):
Software Engineering, Advanced Operating Systems, Advanced Computer Design, Database Systems, Automation; Formal Languages; and Computability, Computability and Complexity, Complexity of Intractability, Combinatorial Algorithms, Mathematical Programming, Applications of Combinatorial Algorithms, Special Project in Computer Science, Principles in Computer Architecture I and II, Advanced Artificial Intelligence I and II, Algorithm Design and Analysis, Advanced Computer Networks, Computer Vision, Distributed Computation, Connectionists Model and Cognitive Processes, Computer Systems Performance Evaluation, Knowledge Bases, Machine Learning, Design Systems for VLSI Circuits I and II, Natural Language Processing, Parallel Algorithms, Topics in Complexity of Algorithms and Data Structures, in Parallel Complexity Theory, in Distributed Artificial Intelligence, in Parallel Computation.

Faculty (Professors with Research Areas):

Professors:

Walter A. Burkhard, Chairman, Ph.D., University of California at Berkeley -distributed computation, database systems, programming languages and data structures, dynamic voting algorithms, data structures for persistent storage.

William E. Howden, Ph.D., University of California, Irvine - Software engineering, system design, software testing and validation, functional program testing and analysis of real time systems.

T.C. Hu, Ph.D., Brown University - Computer-aided design, VLSI circuit layout, combinatorial algorithms, operations research, floor-planning, placement and routing, compacting PLA and Weinberger's array, linear and integer programming.

Sidney Karin, Adjunct Professor and Director of the San Diego Supercomputer Center, Ph.D., University of Michigan, 1973 - Supercomputers.

Christos H. Papadimitriou, Ph.D., Princeton University - Algorithms and complexity, combinatorial database theory, optimization, parallel computation, artificial intelligence, complexity, parallel algorithms.

Michael E. Saks, Ph.D., Massachusetts Institute of Technology - Computational complexity, algorithms, distributed computing, data structures, combinatorics, complexity of dynamic data structures, distributed computing protocols, circuit complexity.

Walter J. Savitch, Ph.D., University of California at Berkeley - Complexity theory, formal languages, natural language processing.

Associate Professors:

Francine D. Berman
Patrick W. Dymond
Victor Vianu

Assistant Professors:

Scott B. Baden
Richard K. Belew
Laurette A. Bradley
Chung-Kuan Cheng
Garrison W. Cottrell
Charles P. Elkan
Paul R. Kube
Alex Orailoglu
Joseph C. Pasquale
Ramamohan Paturi
George C. Polyzos
Venkat P. Rangan
Augustus K. Uht
S. Heather Woll

Affiliated Institutions:

Multimedia Laboratory, Computer Systems Laboratory, Parallel Computation Laboratory, Artificial Intelligence Laboratory, VLSI Laboratory, the San Diego Supercomputer Center (Adjunct Professor Sidney Karin is the Director), and the Institute for Cognitive Sciences.

Facilities:

Include a VAX 11/780, a Celerity dual processor C1260, a UNISYS 7000/51, a Pyramid 90x, two NCR Tower, four SUN servers, 50 SUN clients (SUN-3 and SUN-4), two DEC MicroVAXs, two VAXstations, 12 AT&T 7300s, 12 AT&T 630 graphics workstations, a AT&T 3B15, a VAX 11/750, a Symbolics 3645 Lisp Machine, a Ametek System-14 (16 Nodes), and several Macintosh IIs. Further SUN and HP 9000 series workstations are used for VLSI design.

Research area, funding and selected projects:

The main research areas include:
Artificial Intelligence, Computational Complexity, Computational Linguistics, Computer Architecture, Data Structures, Distributed Computation and Networks, Parallel Computation, Performance Modeling and Evaluation, Programming Languages, Scientific Computation, Software Engineering, VLSI CAD, and Database Management.

Collaborations: n.a.

University of California at Santa Barbara

Department of Computer Science
College of Engineering
Santa Barbara, CA 93106
Phone: (805) 893-4321
email: grad-advisor@cs.ucsb.edu

Chairman: Prof. John L. Bruno
Administrative Assistant: n.a.

Established: n.a.
Undergraduates: n.a.
Graduates: 100 (60 M.S., 40 Ph.D.)
Faculty: 19

Curriculum:

The Department of Computer Science offers Undergraduate programs leading to B.S and B.A. degrees, and graduate programs leading to M.S. and Ph.D. degrees. Furthermore, the Department of Electrical and Computer Engineering offers additional M.S. and Ph.D. programs.

For graduate degree programs a bachelor's degree is required in some discipline of science, engineering, or mathematics. Applicants must have a GPA of at least 3.0 (B grade) in the last two years of undergraduate study.

The normative time for the M.S degree is two years. The student is required to complete 42 credits of course work approved by the Computer Science Graduate Advisor. After that, the student has either a Thesis Option or a Comprehensive Examination Option. Under the Comprehensive Examination Option, the student is required to pass a comprehensive examination and complete at least ten courses, seven of which must be in the Computer Science Department, and at least six of which are graduate courses. A set of courses constituting one major and one minor area of study must be completed with at least a B average in both areas.

Under the Thesis Option the student must submit an acceptable thesis and complete eight credits of the total credit requirement within the Master's Thesis Research and Preparation Program.

Requirements for the Ph.D. degree typically are completed in three to five years, depending on whether or not a student enters the program with a M.S. in computer science. A M.S. degree with an overall GPA of at least 3.5 is required for entering the Doctoral program, however, highly qualified students may be admitted directly without an M.S. degree.

An examination twice a year administered by the Graduate Examination Committee of the Computer Science faculty screens candidates for continuation in the Ph.D. program. Students must pass this exam within six quarters of residence in the Ph.D. program. After passing the screening examination, the student forms a doctoral research committee. The committee approves the student's proposed major area and tests the student's knowledge of this area. After passing this examination the student prepares a dissertation proposal and passes an oral qualifying examination. The final examination is the defense of the candidate's dissertation.

Courses for Graduates (selection):

Methods of Scientific Computing, Automata-Based Complexity, Formal Languages, Computability, Design and Analysis of Algorithms, Parallel Distributed Processing, Computational Geometry, Computational Aspects of VLSI, Algorithms and Complexity Issues in CAD, Advanced Topics in Translation, Semantics of Programming Languages, Automated Theorem Proving, Advanced Topics in Machine Intelligence, Formal Specification and Verification, Advanced Topics in Operating Systems, Advanced Topics in Distributed Systems, Software Engineering, Advanced Topics in Data Base Management Systems, Performance Evaluation, Distributed Computing and Computer Networks, Computer Security, Simulation, Computer Graphics.

Faculty (Professors with Research Areas):

Professors:

John L. Bruno, Chairman, Ph.D., City College of New York, 1969 - Applications of digital systems to engineering problems, distributed systems, scheduling theory, networks and graphs.

Teofilo F. Gonzalez, Ph.D., University of Minnesota at Mineapolis, 1975 - Computer-aided design, VLSI placement and routing algorithms, scheduling theory, design and analysis of algorithms.

Oscar H. Ibarra, Ph.D., University of California at Berkeley, 1967 - Theory of computation, design and analysis of algorithms, computational complexity, parallel computing, VLSI, learning theory.

Richard A. Kemmer, Ph.D., University of California, Los Angeles, 1979 - Specification and verification of systems, computer system security and reliability, programming and specification language design, software engineering.

Allan G. Konheim, Ph.D., Cornell University, 1960 - Computer communication, computer systems, modeling and analysis, cryptography.

Marvin Marcus, Ph.D., University of California at Berkeley, 1953 - Linear and multilinear algebra, scientific computation, linear numerical analysis.

Jianwen Su, Ph.D., University of Southern California, 1990 - Principles and theory of databases, data modeling and database design, query, transaction, and programming languages for databases, distributed databases, database methodology for software engineering.

Roger C. Wood, Ph.D., University of California at Los Angeles, 1966 - Computer system modeling, design and analysis, computer architecture.

Associate Professors:

Peter R. Cappello
Omer Egecioglu

Assistant Professors:

Divyakant Agrawal
Laura Dillon
Amr El Abbadi
Prakash Ramanan
Ambuj Singh

Yuan-Fang Wang
Earl Zmijewski

Affiliated Institutions:
The Computer Science Instructional Laboratory , the Graduate Student Laboratory, the Machine Vision Laboratory, the Distributed Systems Laboratory, the Reliable Software Laboratory, the Efficient Computation Laboratory, the Concurrent Computation Laboratory, the Center for Computational Sciences and Engineering, the Center for Information Processing Research, the Compound Semiconductor Research Center, the Center for Robotic Systems and Manufacturing, the Optoelectronics Technology Center.

Facilities:
The facilities at the College of Engineering include: a network of several hundred engineering workstations, a Convex, a Alliant FX-1, a FPS 500, an Intel iPSC-D5 hypercube. The bulk of computing is performed using SUN SPARCstations, DECstations, and IBM 6000 series machines. The campus' central computing facility operates an IBM 3090-180, an IBM 4341-2 and 4381-13. The Microcomputer Laboratory, a campus wide facility, maintains and operates hundreds of personal computers including IBM and Apple machines. Access to national networks such as INTERnet and BITnet is provided.

Research area, funding and selected projects:
The department's main research areas include: Computer Systems Modeling and Analysis, Scientific and Engineering Computing, Software Systems, Computer Systems Architecture, Graphics and Image Processing, Integrated Systems, Machine Intelligence, Image Understanding, Computational Models, Algorithms, and Complexity.

Collaborations: n.a.

University of Illinois at Urbana-Champaign

Department of Computer Science
1304 W. Springfield Avenue
Urbana, Illinois 61801
Phone: (217) 333-3373
email: lawrie@cs.uiuc.edu

Chairman: Prof. D. H. Lawrie
Administrative Assistant: Barbara Armstrong

Established: 1948 (as Digital Computer Laboratory), 1964 (CS Department)
Undergraduates: 900
Graduates: 400 (210 M.S., 190 Ph.D.)
Faculty: 43

Curriculum:

Four undergraduate programs, leading to a B.S. in Computer Science, are offered in the Colleges of Engineering and Liberal Arts and Sciences. In the College of Liberal Arts and Sciences, they are joint degree programs in either the Department of Mathematics and CS or the Department of Statistics and CS; an additional program is offered in the College of Liberal Arts and Sciences for students interested in teaching computer science in secondary schools. Four graduate programs are offered leading to the degrees of Ph.D., M.S., M.C.S. (a non-thesis option) and M.S.T.C.S. (for teachers).

The M.S. program requires 7 graduate units (1 unit = 4 semester hours) of coursework plus a master's thesis; the M.C.S. requires 9 units of coursework and no thesis; the M.S.T.C.S. requires 8 units of coursework, teaching experience and no thesis; the M.C.S. is also used in joint degree programs with the Departments of Accountancy, Architecture, and Business Administration; the M.S. can lead toward, and count as part of, a subsequent Ph.D. degree. All degree programs and joint programs require the attendance of specifically assigned courses from the Software, Architecture and Theory lists, and a GPA of 4.0 (B grade) must be maintained throughout the full course of study. To be eligible for the joint program with Accountancy, an overall GPA of 4.3 or more, with at least 4.0 in non-remedial Mathematics and CS courses is required.

The Ph.D. requirements include a total of 16 units of coursework, of which 8 might be supplied by the M.S., passing the Preliminary Examination (Prelim), acquiring 8 units of thesis research credit, and the defense of the dissertation. The department requires Ph.D. candidates to pass two examinations before the Prelim is taken. The first of these is the Comprehensive Examination (Comp), consisting of five three-hour exams in the areas of programming languages and operating systems (software), computer architecture and hardware, theory of computation, numerical analysis, and artificial intelligence. Three areas must be passed. The second exam is the Qualifying Examination (Qual) taken approximately one year after the Comp. The Qual is an in-depth exam covering the intended area of the student's Ph.D. research.

Courses for Graduates (selection):

Advanced Computer Programming, Information Systems, Database Systems, Computer Graphics, Operating Systems Design, Programming Language Principles, Compiler Construction, Software Engineering, Microprocessor Systems, Computer System Organization, Control Structure of Computers, Mechanized Mathematical Interference, Computer Interference and Knowledge Acquisition, Pattern Recognition and Machine Learning, Knowledge-Based Programming, Integrated Circuit Logic Design, Introduction to Computer Arithmetic, Program Verification, Introduction to Computer Memories and I/O, Advanced Computer Circuits, Introduction to Automatic Digital Computing, Programming Language Semantics, Topics in Compiler Construction, in Digital Computer Arithmetic, in Analysis of Algorithms, and in Computer Hardware, Individual Study, Seminar in Computer Science, Individual Project Study, Special Topics in Computer Science.

In addition to those listed above, another 34 CS courses are offered in conjunction with other departments.

Faculty (Professors with Research Areas):

Professors:

Duncan H. Lawrie, Chairman - Computer architecture and systems, operating systems, parallel computing.

Geneva G. Belford - Databases and information systems, distributed systems and networks.

Roy H. Campbell - Communication networks, computer graphics, programming languages, databases and information systems, distributed systems and networks, operating systems, parallel computing, real-time computing systems.

Nachum Dershowitz - Artificial intelligence, programming languages, software engineering, theoretical computing.

Herbert Edelsbrunner - Theoretical computing: analysis of algorithms and data structures, combinatorics, computational geometry.

M. Faiman - Communication networks, CAD of digital systems, computer architecture and systems, distributed systems and networks.

W. J. Kubitz - CAD of digital systems, computer graphics: object-oriented, visual interfaces, programming methods, visualization.

David J. Kuck - Computer architecture and systems, parallel computing.

Chung L. Liu - CAD of digital systems, real-time computing systems, theoretical computing.

J.W.-S. Liu - Communication networks, programming languages, databases and information systems, distributed systems and networks, operating systems, real-time computing systems.

Saburo Muroga - CAD of digital systems.

S. R. Ray - Artificial intelligence, biomedical computing.

Daniel A. Reed - Computer architecture systems, computer graphics, operating systems, parallel computing.

Edward M. Rheingold - Theoretical computing: analysis of algorithms and data structures, combinatorics.

Paul E. Saylor - Numerical and scientific computing, parallel computing.

R. D. Skeel - Numerical and scientific computing: linear algebra, ordinary differential equations, parallel algorithms, mathematical software.

Associate Professors:

Gerald F. DeJong
H. G. Friedman, Jr.
Mehdi T. Harandi
L. V. Kale
S. N. Kamin
S. M. Kaplan
T. Kerkhoven
K.-J. Lin
M. D. Mickunas
David A. Padua
U. S. Reddy
Larry A. Rendell

Assistant Professors:

Gul Agha
Andrew C. Chien
A. M. Frisch
Eric J. Golin
C. C. Hayes
Ralph E. Johnson
L. G. Jones
D. W. Knapp
P. Ng
L. B. Pitt
Jean Ponce
Faisal Saied
Pravin Vaidya
David C. Wilkins
Marianne S. Winslett

Affiliated Institutions

Computing Research Laboratory: coordinates departmental facilities.

NSF National Center for Supercomputing Applications (NCSA), Computer-Based Education Research laboratory.

Facilities

Departmental facilities are organized around a central network with a number of subnets serving various research groups. The central time-sharing machine is a 10-processor Encore Multimax. A second Multimax is used for large, long, and parallel computing tasks. A third Multimax serves as the NFS server for all SUN SPARCstations. Other central facilities are a SUN network server, a SUN software distribution server, and three SUN servers that serve SUN-3 workstations. Additional machines include SUN, IBM RS and RT, Symbolics Lisp, Tektronix, HP workstations, TI Explorer workstions, and Intel Hypercubes.
NCSA operates a CRAY-2, a CRAY X-MP/48, and a Convex C3 supercomputer.
A central network (UIUCnet) with a number of subnets serves the various research groups. Network access is provided to INTERnet, NSFnet, USEnet, and BITnet.

Research area, funding and selected projects

Areas of departmental research include Artificial Intelligence, Biomedical Computing, Communication Networks, CAD of Digital Systems, Computer Architecture and Systems, Computer-assisted Instruction, Computer Graphics, Programming Languages, Databases and Information Systems, Distributed Systems and Networks, Numerical and Scientific Computing, Operating Systems, Parallel Computing, Real-time Computing Systems, Software Engineering, and Theoretical Computing.

The Department of Computer Science is one of the few university groups to design complete systems of hardware as well as software. The department was involved in the design of ILLIACs II, III, and IV and its faculty is now involved in the design of a new supercomputer, CEDAR, in the UIUC Center for Supercomputing Research and Development.

In 1989-1990, the Department of Computer Science had separately-budgeted research expenditures in the amount of $4.9 million for 102 projects, the Department of Electrical and Computer Engineering had $10.2 million for 147 projects (the whole School of Engineering had $83 million).

The National Center for Supercomputer Applications had engineering-related expenditures in the amount of $24 million.

Collaborations: n.a.

University of Maryland

Department of Computer Science
A.V. Williams Building
College Park, MD 20742-3255
Phone: (301) 405-2661
email: tripathi@mimsy.umd.edu

Chairman: Prof. Satish K. Tripathi
Administrative Assistant: Cynthia R. Hale

Established: 1974
Undergraduates: 710
Graduates: 326
Faculty: 44

Curriculum:
The department offers M.S. and Ph.D. programs.

For an M.S. degree a student has the option to write a thesis. All students must complete at least 30 credits of approved coursework with an average of B, 18 of those credits must be at the 600-800 level. The student opting not to write a thesis must pass a written comprehensive exam and write a scholarly paper, which must include an abstract and references to the relevant literature. The student opting to write a thesis must devote six credits to thesis research, complete the thesis, and pass an oral exam on the thesis research.

For a Ph.D. degree, a student must complete written comprehensive exams in three areas, an oral preliminary exam, and demonstrate proficiency in a foreign language. Full-time students must take at least one course at the 600 level or above each semester until they pass the preliminary exam. At least twelve credits must be devoted to dissertation research, and an average of B must be maintained. The student can then prepare and defend a dissertation.

Courses for Graduates (selection):
Computer Systems Theory, Problem Solving Methods in Artificial Intelligence, Database Management Systems, Theory of Programming Languages, Introduction to Computability, Analysis of Algorithms, Numerical Analysis, Performance Evaluation of Computer Systems, Computer Networks, Distributed Algorithms and Verification, Logic for Problem Solving, Computational Linguistics, Connectionist Models of Intelligent Systems, Artificial Intelligence, Computer Processing of Pictorial Information, A Quantitative Approach to Software Management and Engineering, Advanced Theory of Computation, Parallel Algorithms, Mathematical Linguistics, Advanced Linear Numerical Analysis, Numerical Solution of Nonlinear Equations, Modeling and Simulation of Physical Systems, Advanced Topics in Computer Systems, in Information Processing, in Programming Languages, in Theory of Computing, in Numerical Methods.

Faculty (Professors with Research Areas):

Professors:

Satish K. Tripathi, Chairman, Ph.D., University of Toronto, 1979 - Performance evaluation, distributed systems, real-time systems, computer architectures, fault-tolerance, computer networks.

Ashkok K. Agrawala, Ph.D., Harvard University, 1970 - Design and evaluation of systems and networks.

Victor R. Basili, Ph.D., University of Texas at Austin, 1970 - Software engineering, software quality assurance.

Yaohan Chu, Sc.D., Massachusetts Institute of Technology, 1953 - Computer architecture, VLSI design, software engineering.

Larry S. Davis, Ph.D., University of Maryland, 1976 - Computer vision, artificial intelligence.

H.P. Edmondson, Ph.D., University of California at Los Angeles, 1953 - Theory of computing, mathematical linguistics.

John Gannon, Ph.D., University of Toronto, 1975 - Programming languages, distributed systems.

Laveen N. Kanal, Ph.D., University of Pennsylvania, 1960 - Machine intelligence, pattern recognition, computer vision, artificial neural systems.

Raymond E. Miller, Ph.D., University of Illinois at Urbana-Champaign, 1957 - Parallel computation, distributed systems, computer networks, theory of computing.

Jack Minker, Ph.D., University of Pennsylvania, 1959 - Mathematical logic, artificial intelligence, logic programming, nonmonotonic reasoning, databases.

Dianne P. O'Leary, Ph.D., Stanford University, 1976 - Numerical analysis, parallel algorithms.

Nicholas Roussopoulos, Ph.D., University of Toronto, 1976 - Database systems.

Hanan Samet, Ph.D., Stanford University, 1975 - Data structures, image processing.

Ben Shneiderman, Ph.D., State University of New York at Stony Brook, 1973 - Human-computer interaction.

G.W. Stewart, Ph.D., University of Tennessee, 1968 - Numerical linear algebra, parallel computing, perturbation theory, statistical computations.

Marvin V. Zelkowitz, Ph.D., Cornell University, 1971 - Software engineering, programming, program complexity, program development.

Associate Professors:

Richard Austing
Howard Elman
Christos Faloutsas
William I. Gasarch
Clyde P. Kruskal
Dana S. Nau
Donald Perlis

James A. Reggia
A. Udaya Shankar
Carl H. Smith

Assistant Professors:

John (Yiannis) Aloimonos
James H. Anderson
Scott D. Carson
Richard Furuta
Richard Gerber
James A. Hendler
Leo Mark
David M. Mount
Adam Porter
William W. Pugh
James M. Purtilo
H. Dieter Rombach
Kenneth R. Salem
Timos K. Sellis
P. David Stotts
V.S. Subrahmanian

Affiliated Institutions:

Institute for Advanced Computer Studies (UMIACS): broadens the overall base support for computing research throughout the university and focuses on interdisciplinary topics in computing.

Center for Automation Research (CfAR): is dedicated to research on advanced automation in business and industry.

Center for Excellence in Space Data and Information Sciences (CESDIS): was established with funds from NASA and the University's Space Research Association. Its purpose is to sponsor research in areas of computing and information science that will improve the acquisition, analysis and utilization of data from space sensor systems.

Systems Research Center (SRC): was established by NSF and is committed to developing innovative advances in design methods and software systems which address the basic productivity and competitive challenges facing American industry,

Engineering Research Center (ERC): was established to promote industry-university interaction in scientific and technical disciplines.

Facilities:

Departmental facilities include nine DEC VAX computers (an 8600, two 8250, an 11/785, a MicroVAX II, two VAX 3100, and two VAX3200), an Encore 510 Multimax multiprocessor, 13 DEC 3100 RISC computers, approximately 45 SUN-3, 15 SUN-2, four SUN SPARCstations, a 128-node BBN Butterfly multiprocessor, three IBM PC/RT, 40 Xerox 8010 workstations, four TI explorers, and approximately 140 assorted machines like PC's, Macintoshes, Hewlett Packard touchscreen PC's, etc.

All machines are on a campus-wide network which allows access to INTERnet, ARPAnet, CSnet, USEnet and BITnet.

Research area, funding and selected projects:

The department has a vast number and variety of contract- and grant-supported research. Here is a small sample:

Distributed Systems Interconnections and Fault-Tolerance Studies (Agrawala et al., Army Strategic Defense Command, $1.4 million, 3/91)

Robust Routing in Large Dynamic Networks (Agrawala and Sidhu, Rome Air Development Center/DARPA, $862,000, 1/93)

Robust Image Understanding: Techniques and Applications (Aloimonos et al., DARPA-ISTO, $1.9 million, 9/92)

Evaluation of Software Methodologies (Basili, Rombach and Zelkowitz, NASA/SEL, $1.35 million, 9/92)

Studies in Adaptive Mass Storage Systems (Carson, Digital Equipment Corp., $104,000, 1/92)

National Fellowship Program in Parallel Processing (Davis and Rosenfeld, DARPA/NASA, $1.5 million, 12/91)

AI for Foreign Language Training (Hendler and Weinberg [Linguistics], Army Research Institute, $350,000, 1/93)

Neural Network Architectures for 3D Motion and Depth (Kanal, NSF, $260,000, 10/91)

NASA Center of Excellence in Space Data and Information Sciences [CESDIS] (Miller, NASA, $1.7 million, 7/93)

Belief Systems (Minker and Perlis, ARO, $286,000, 6/91)

Efficient Hierarchical Planning (Nau and Hendler, NSF, $404,000, 12/92)

Incremental Evaluation Techniques for Advanced Programming Environments (Pugh, NSF, $66,000, 5/91)

Using Formal Specifications in the Software Component Factory (Purtilo et al., ONR, $322,000, 12/93)

SURANET (Ricart, NSF, $3.2 million, over 3 years)

Advanced Electronic Mail Handling (Ricart, IBM, $800,000, over 3 years)

Process-Based Environment Architectures (Rombach, NSF Presidential Young Investigator Award, $500,000 over five years)

Design Issues for High Performance Engineering Information Systems (Roussopoulos et al., AFOSR, $405,000, 4/92)

Migration of QUILT onto Connection Machine (Samet, Engineer Topographic Laboratory, $184,000, 9/91)

Verification and Logical Construction of Network Protocols (Shankar, NSF, $156,000, 6/92)

Extensions to Hyperties, User Interface for a Portable Touchscreen Computer, Human-Computer Interaction Research (Shneiderman and Plaisant, NCR Corp., $175,000, 12/90)

Human-Computer Interaction Research (Shneiderman, NEC Corp., $90,000, 8/90)

Collaborations:

The Industrial Associates Program (IAP) maintains affiliations with companies committed to research and development in computer science disciplines and technology. IAP is currently sponsored by the Department, the University of Maryland, UMIACS and CfAR. The following companies were members of IAP during 1989-90: Amdahl Corporation, Contel Corporation, Digital Equipment Corporation, General Electric Information Services, GTE Laboratories, Honeywell Inc., Italsiel, MBB, Nippon Electric Company, NCR, Northrop Corporation, Ricoh, Vitro Corporation.

The department also promotes a Colloquium Series which for 1989-90 was jointly sponsored by UMIACS, CfAR and the following corporations: Amdahl Corporation, Contel Corporation, Digital Equipment Corporation, General Electric Information Services, GTE Laboratories, Honeywell Inc., Italsiel, Nippon Electric Company, NCR, Northrop Corporation, Ricoh, Unisys Corporation, Vitro Corporation. In 1990-91, CESDIS will join the group of sponsors.

University of Minnesota

Department of Computer Science
200 Union Street, SE
4-192 EE/CSci Building
Minneapolis, MN 55455-0159
Phone: (612) 625-4002
email: fox@umn-cs.cs.umn.edu

Chairman: Prof. David W. Fox (Resigned)
Administrative Assistant: Kathy Boyer

Established: n.a.
Undergraduates: 433
Graduates: 226
Faculty: 29

Curriculum:
The department offers M.S. and Ph.D. programs.

For a M.S. the student has two options for completion: Plan A with 44 credits total, including eight credits in one or more related fields outside of Computer Science or nine credits in a designated minor field, and a thesis prepared in conjunction with 16 thesis credits; or, Plan B with 16 credits of approved coursework substituted for the thesis. A final examination is required for both plans. The M.S. can be completed in two years with a minimum of four quarters of full-time registration.

For a Ph.D. the student must complete coursework in a major area of Computer Science, coursework in a minor area or a supporting program, a written and preliminary oral examination covering general and specific areas, a dissertation prepared in conjunction with 36 thesis credits, and a final oral examination. The Ph.D. can be completed between three to five years and requires at least nine quarters of full-time registration.

Courses for Graduates (selection):
Modeling and Analysis, Distributed Systems, Languages and Systems, Machine Design, Computation of Special Functions and Formulas, Computational Methods for Initial and Boundary Value Problems, Numerical Analysis, Algorithms, Theory of Computation, Computational Theory and Logic, Computer Vision, Expert Systems, Optimization in Compilers, Special Concepts in Artificial Intelligence, Artificial Intelligence Techniques in Robotics, Control Science, Advanced Topics in Database Systems.

Faculty (Professors with Research Areas):

Professors:

David W. Fox, Chairman (Resigned), Ph.D., University of Maryland, 1958 - Mathematical analysis and its applications, analysis of algorithms.

J. Ben Rosen, Ph.D., Columbia University, 1952 - Mathematical programming algorithms, parallel computing.

Youcef Saad, D.E., France, 1983 - Sparse matrix computations, parallel computing, nonlinear equations, control theory, partial differential equations.

Sartaj K. Sahni, Ph.D., Cornell University, 1973 - Pattern recognition, computer vision, digital signal processing, electronic CAD, graph theory, matrix algebra.

James Slagle, Ph.D., Massachusetts Institute of Technology, 1961 - Expert systems, parallel computing.

Marvin L. Stein, Ph.D., University of California at Los Angeles, 1951 - Parallel computing, algorithms, compilers.

Associate Professors:

Daniel Boley
John Carlis
David Du
K.S. Frankowski
Maria Gini
Vipin Kumar
Arthur Norberg

Eugene Shragowitz
William Thompson

Assistant Professors:

Phillip Barry
Yoon-Hwa Choi
Anthony Chronopoulos
James Held
Ravi Janardan
Haesun Park
Ting-Chuen Pong
Patrick Powell
John Riedl
Shashi Shekhar
Jaideep Srivastava
Anand Tripathi
Wei-Tek Tsai
Shankar Venkatesan
Anastasios Vergis

Affiliated Institutions:

Artificial Intelligence Laboratory (AI Lab): supports major research activities in computational computer vision, robotics, expert systems and a variety of special projects in other aspects of artificial intelligence.

High-Performance Computing Laboratory (HPC Lab): supports the design and analysis of specialized computer algorithms.

Distributed Systems Laboratory (DS Lab): is primarily used to support the NEXUS distributed operating system project.

Computer-Aided Design Laboratory (CAD Lab): supports research in VLSI and systems design.

Academic Computing Services and Systems (ACSS): is primarily used for instructional purposes by the faculty and students.

Minnesota Supercomputer Institute (MSI) and Minnesota Supercomputing Center (MSC): were formed by the university, the Minnesota State Legislature and NSF in 1984 and 1982, respectively, to create a community (academic, govern-mental and industrial) core of powerful computational research programs in basic sciences, engineering and the humanities.

The Charles Babbage Institute for the History of Information Processing: is an archival center, a clearinghouse for information and a center for the contemporary history of information processing.

Apple/Texas Instruments Laboratory for Artificial Intelligence and Graphics: was established by the two companies for instruction in computational graphics, artificial intelligence and robotics, computer music, and advanced database studies.

Microelectronics and Information Science Center (MEIS).

Facilities:

AI Lab: contains a SUN-4 workstation, eight SUN-3 workstations, a SUN-3 file server, and a LABMATE mobile robot.

HPC Lab: houses an Apollo DOMAIN ring network, an NCUBE hypercube and two SUN workstations.

DS Lab: has a SUN-3/280 file server, a SUN-3/160 file server, three SUN-3/60 workstations, seven SUN-3/50 workstations. a VAXstation 2000, an Apollo DOMAIN series 4000, an HP9000 model 310 color workstation and four HP9000 model 310 workstations.

CAD Lab: includes a network of SUN graphic workstations and shares facilities with the HPC Lab.

ACSS: includes an Encore Multimax, a VAX 8650, a Cyber 170-855, and a Cyber 180-830.

MSI and MSC: operate a CRAY-1, a two-pipe Cyber 205 system and a CRAY-2/4-512.

Apple/Texas Instruments Laboratory for Artificial Intelligence and Graphics: contains ten Macintosh II, ten microExplorer Lisp systems, an Explorer II Lisp system and an Explorer LX UNIX/Lisp system.

All facilities are on a campus-wide, Ethernet-based network called UMARnet (University of Minnesota Academic Research Net) which allows access to MRnet, NSFnet, BITnet and INTERnet.

Research area, funding and selected projects:
A Logical Data-Modeling Formalism to Support an ECAD Environment (Berzins and March, Control Data Corp./MEIS/AT&T Bell Laboratories)

Performance Evaluation of a VLSI Array Testing Algorithm (Choi, University of Minnesota Graduate School)

Computer-Aided Design for VLSI (Du and Powell, MEIS)

A Robot Testbed for Artificial Intelligence and Real-Time Programming (Gini, AT&T foundation)

Software for Robot Programming (Gini, IBM)

Structure from Motion and Stereo Vision (Pong, University of Minnesota Graduate School)

Global Optimization for Large-Scale Problems Using Vector Processing (Rosen, NSF/MEIS)

Experimental Research in Computer Algorithms (Sahni et al., NSF-CER)

Layout of Structured Integrated Circuits (Sahni, Control Data Corp.)

Automatic Techniques for Reconfiguring a Multiple Processor (Slagle, NASA)

Expertise in Problem Solving (Thompson and Johnson, SUMEX-AIM)

Structure From Motion (Thompson, AFOSR)

An Object-Oriented Distributed Operating Systems and Programming Environment for Reliable Computing (Tripathi, University of Kansas Research Institute)

An Investigation of Network Flows (Venkatesan, NSF)

The department's FY1990 expenditure was $4.4 million: $3 million (State funds for operations and maintenance); $46,000 (State special appropriations); $624,000 (Federal-sponsored research); $332,000 (Nonfederal-sponsored research); $169,000 (University research support); and, $319,000 (Endowment income, annual gifts, earned income).

Collaborations:
The university maintains many collaborations with industrial and governmental institutions.
In 1985, the department was awarded a five-year coordinated experimental research grant in the total amount of $3.6 million by NSF to support the project "Experimental Research in Computer Algorithms". The NSF has also established the Institute for Mathematics and Its Applications (IMA). The main goal of IMA is to stimulate interaction between junior and senior researchers in various disciplines and create healthy environments for postdoctoral training.

University of North Carolina at Chapel Hill

Department of Computer Science
Sitterson Hall, CB#3175
Chapel Hill, NC 27599-3175
Phone: (919) 962-1777
email: weiss@cs.unc.edu

Chairman: Prof. Stephen F. Weiss
Administrative Assistant: Wanda Smith

Established: 1964
Undergraduates: 0 (see below)
Graduates: 130
Faculty: 24

Curriculum:

While the department does not offer a bachelor's degree in computer science, there are two B.S. programs that have a strong computer science component. The curriculum in Mathematical Sciences offers a computer science option in their B.S. program. The curriculum is oriented toward mathematics and requires approximately five computer science courses. The curriculum in Applied Sciences also offers a computer science option in their B.S. program. The Applied Science curriculum is oriented more toward math and software.

For a M.S. the student must earn 30 credits of coursework. A thesis is optional; if one is written, it counts for six credits. Besides core coursework requirements, the student must pass a comprehensive exam, program and document a program product, and write a significant piece of technical prose. Up to six credits can be transferred from another institution, and usually two years are required for completion of the degree.

For a Ph.D. the student must have fulfilled the M.S. degree requirements, and completed an additional 15 to 18 credits in elective coursework. The student must pass written and oral comprehensive exams, and submit a significant dissertation. The Ph.D. is usually completed in four or five years.

Courses for Graduates (selection):

Algorithms and Analysis, Software Engineering Laboratory, Numerical Computing, Natural Language Processing, Information Retrieval, Models of Languages and Computation, Topics in Computer Science, Introduction to Operating Systems, Files and Databases, Translators, Digital Logic Techniques, Introduction to Programming Languages, Advanced Analysis of Algorithms, Database Management Systems, Discrete Event Simulation, Computer Graphics, Raster Graphics, Exploring Virtual Worlds, Compiler Design, Advanced Compiler Design, Operating Systems, Distributed Systems, Programming Languages, Functional Programming, Logic Programming Semantics and Program Correctness, Monte Carlo Method, Picture Processing and Pattern Recognition, Computer Vision, Visual Solid Shape, Computer Architecture and Implementation, Advanced Computer Architecture, Advanced Computer Implementation, VLSI Systems Design, Advanced Design of VLSI Systems, Mechanized Mathematical Inference, Discrete Optimization: Algorithms and Complexity, Information Theory, Error-Correcting Codes, Topics in Computer Science, Professional Writing in Computer Science, Technical Communication in Computer Science, Computers and Society.

Faculty (Professors with Research Areas):

Professors:

Stephen F. Weiss, Chairman, Ph.D., Cornell University, 1970 - Information storage and retrieval, natural language processing, communications and distributed systems, collaboration support systems.

Frederick P. Brooks, Jr., Ph.D., Harvard University, 1956 - Real-time 3D computer graphics, computer architecture. (on leave 1991-92)

Peter Calingaert, Ph.D., Harvard University, 1955 - Computer-supported cooperative work, communication, control, translator, application software systems.

Henry Fuchs, Ph.D., University of Utah, 1975 - Computer graphics, VLSI design, 3D medical imaging, computer architecture.

John H. Halton, D.Phil., Oxford University, 1960 - Applying combinatorial, probabilistic, and analytic methods to computational, scientific and engineering problems.

Gyula A. Magó, Ph.D., Boston University, 1989 - Parallel computation, computer architecture, programming languages.

Stephen M. Pizer, Ph.D., Harvard University, 1967 - Image processing and display, human and computer vision, graphics, numerical computing, medical imaging. (on leave Spring 1992)

David A. Plaisted, Ph.D., Stanford University, 1976 - Mechanical theorem proving, term rewriting systems, algorithms and logic programming.

Donald F. Stanat, Ph.D., University of Michigan, 1966 - Declarative languages, algorithm design and analysis, data structures, program verification, programming language semantics.

Associate Professors:

Kye S. Hedlund
John McHugh
Jane S. Richardson
F. Donelson Smith
John B. Smith

Assistant Professors:

James M. Coggins
Kevin Jeffay
Jonathan A. Marshall
Jan F. Prins
Akhilesh Tyagi
Hiroyuki Watanabe
Jennifer L. Welch

Affiliated Institutions:
The Graphics and Image Laboratory: supports research and teaching in computer graphics, image processing, computer vision and pattern recognition.

The Microelectronics Design Laboratory (MDL): supports the design and simulation of full- and semi-custom MOS integrated circuits. The laboratory is also used for both teaching and research in CAD and VLSI system design.

The Microelectronic Systems Laboratory (MSL): provides capability for the rapid prototyping of high-performance microelectronic systems.

The SoftLab Software Systems Laboratory: provides the department's experimental research efforts in VLSI and distributed systems design with a software development environment optimized for rapid prototyping of novel architectures.

The TextLab Research Laboratory: supports teaching and research dealing with text and natural language analysis, hypertext and collaboration support systems.

The North Carolina Supercomputer Center.

Facilities:
Departmental facilities include 80 SUN workstations, 65 DEC workstations, 140 Apple Macintoshes, 20 IBM PC's, and ten larger DEC systems.
The Academic Computing Services operates a DEC VAX system, an IBM mainframe and a Convex mini-supercomputer.
The Graphics and Image Laboratory has Pixel-Planes 4 and Pixel-Planes-5 machines (developed at UNC), a Silicon Graphics display computer, a Pixar Image computer, an Evans and Sutherland Picture system, Adage/Ikonas display systems and a varifocal mirror for 3D display.
The North Carolina Supercomputer Center: operates a CRAY YMP supercomputer.
All facilities are on an Ethernet-based network that allows access to all national networks.

Research area, funding and selected projects:
The department is actively engaged in the following research areas: Algorithms and Data Structures, Computer Architectures, Computer Graphics and Image Processing, Computer-Supported Cooperative Work, Databases, Distibuted Systems, Functional and Logic Programming, Human-Machine Interaction, Monte Carlo Methods, Natural Language Processing, Neural Networks, Parallel Computing, Real-Time Systems, Software Engineering Techniques and Environments, Theorem Proving and Term Rewriting, VLSI Systems and Design.

The department's total grants, contracts and gifts expenditures for FY1990-91 was $8.5 million. Here is a sample of current projects:

Advanced Technology for Portable Personal Visualization (Brooks and Fuchs, DARPA)

Interactive Graphics for Molecular Studies (Brooks, NIH)

VISTAnet: a Very High Bandwidth Protoype Network for Interactive 3D Medical Imaging (Chi et al., Corporation for National Research Initiatives)

CISE Institutional Infrastructure Program for Prototyping Complete Digital Systems (Chi and Weiss, NSF)

Image Pattern Recognition (Coggins and Brooks, NASA/URSA)

Supercomputing Power for Interactive Visualization (Fuchs and Poulton, NSF/DARPA)

The Design and Construction of Predictable Real-Time Systems (Jeffay, Digital Equipment Corporation)

Medical Image Presentation (Pizer et al., NIH)

A Hypermedia Environment for Software Development (J. Smith, IBM)

Building and Using a Collaboratory: a Foundation for Supporting and Studying Group Collaborations (J. Smith et al., NSF)

The Impact of Time on Distributed Computing (Welch, NSF)

Collaborations:
The Department of Computer Science has close collaborations with the corporations, goverment agencies, universities and institutions in the Research Triangle Park community. This includes Duke University, North Carolina State University, University of North Carolina at Charlotte, North Carolina AT&T, MCNC Central Laboratories, the North Carolina Supercomputer Center, IBM, Data General, Northern Telecom, Bell Northern Research, and General Electric.

University of Pennsylvania

Department of Computer and Information
Science
Philadelphia, PA 19104-6389
Phone: (215) 898-0051
email: badler@central.cis.upenn.edu

Chairman: Prof. Norman Badler
Administrative Assistant: Karen Carter

Established: 1959
Undergraduates: n.a.
Graduates: n.a.
Faculty: 17

Curriculum:

The Department of Computer and Information
Science (CIS) offers a M.S.E. (in CIS) and a Ph.D.
program. Furthermore, the CIS Department and
the Wharton Graduate Division offer a two-year
joint-degree program leading to both the Master of
Science in Engineering (CIS) and Master of Business Administration degrees.

All M.S.E. students are required to take the following three courses: Programming Languages & Techniques, Introduction to Computer Architecture,
and Analysis of Algorithms. M.S.E. students are
required to do advanced study in at least one area of
Computer Science. Each major requires a special
combination of mathematics and advanced courses.
A thesis is not required, but encouraged. However,
students intending to continue with Ph.D. studies
will be expected to write a thesis.

The M.B.A./M.S.E. program is designed for those
who wish to combine management and information systems education to better manage the requirements and development of information systems in organizations. Work toward both degrees
can be completed in two years by satisfying the
individual requirements of both schools. The
M.B.A. program requires eighteen course units
and an advanced study project. The M.S.E. (CIS)

program requires ten course units and a thesis. The
student would take a total of nineteen course units
and write a master's thesis, which would also
constitute the M.B.A. advanced study project. Six
to seven course units would be in the CIS department, and twelve to fourteen would be in the
Wharton School.

For a Ph.D. a minimum of twenty course units is
required for the Ph.D. degree. The minimum may
include eight course units for which the master's
degree was awarded. Most students should expect
to take more than this minimum number, either in
special topics or independent study and research.
Before undertaking studies for a Ph.D. a written
preliminary examination has to be passed, which
consists of two parts: the core-area exam and the
special-area exam.

Courses for Graduates (selection):

Programming Languages and Techniques, Computer Architecture, Analysis of Algorithms, CAD,
Theory of Computation in Algebra, Basic Logic
for Computer Science, Computational Linguistics,
Operating Systems, Introduction to VLSI Systems,
Database and Information Systems, Image Recon-
struction from Projections, Computer and Inter-
preters, Telecommunications Networks I & II,
Machine Perception, Design and Control of Robotic Manipulators, Connectionists Models of Artificial Intelligence, Introduction to Computer
Graphics, Parallel Algorithms, Computational
Aspects of Robotics.
Advanced Topics in Artificial Intelligence, in Operating Systems, in Databases, in Computer Graphics, in Machine Perception.

Faculty (Professors with Research Areas):

Professors:

Norman I. Badler, Chairman - Computer graphics,
human movement simulation, three-dimensional
modeling and interaction techniques.

Ruzena Bajcsy - Computer vision, robotics, language and vision, biomedical computing.

Peter Buneman - Database systems, knowledge base systems, programming languages, environments, semantics.

John W. Carr III - Programming languages, problem solving, learning theories, VLSI design.

David Farber - High speed computer networks, distributed computer systems, distributed collaboration, software productivity.

Peter Freyd, Ph.D., Princeton University, 1960 - Type theory, category theory, logic, semantics of programming languages.

Jean Gallier - Automated deduction, proof theory, logic programming, theory of computation, programming environments, compilers.

Aravind K. Joshi, Ph.D., University of Pennsylvania, 1960 - Natural language processing, natural language interfaces, artificial intelligence, cognitive science.

Mitch Marcus - Natural language processing, computational theories of grammar, computational analysis of spoken language.

Associate Professors:

Susan Davidson
Insup Lee
Dale Miller
Max Mintz

Assistant Professors:

Val Breazu-Tannen
Carl Gunter
Amarnath Mukherjee
Michael Palis

Affiliated Institutions:
The Artificial Intelligence Center of Excellence: was established in 1989 with funding from the U.S. Army Research Office. The work covers a wide range of topics, e.g. spoken language systems, knowledge representation and reasoning, robotics,

computer vision, computer graphics, natural language processing, and parallel distributed processing. There are four major research laboratories which participate in the AI Center research: GRASP, LINC, Graphics and Theory. Furthermore, the AI Center maintains close ties with Penn's Institute for Research in Cognitive Science, and the Institute for Neuroscience.

The Computer Graphics Research Laboratory: the overall goal of the laboratory is the modeling and animation of human movement. This central topic drives a number of related research interests covering a broad scope from image synthesis to natural language interfaces.

The General Robotics and Active Sensory Perception Laboratory (GRASP): focuses on research in several areas of robotics and machine vision in a multidisciplinary approach (students and faculty are from four departments). Funding comes from governmental and industrial sources.

The Distributed Systems Laboratory: consists mainly of an undergraduate teaching laboratory, the graduate laboratory for VLSI design and computer communications, and the computer networks research laboratory.

The Language, Information and Computation Laboratory (LINC): focuses on computational linguistics and on the development of the technological base for human-computer interaction.

Facilities:
The primary educational computer is a VAX-8650. There is also an educational laboratory with 17 SUN workstations.
The central research computing resource is a two-node VMS VAXcluster with two VAX-11/785. Each of the three laboratories (GRASP, LINC, Graphics) has a dedicated VAX-11/785 as well as other computers such as a whole range of Silicon Graphics IRIS, SUN, Symbolics, HP, and MicroVAX II. Each computer is connected to an Ethernet network which allows access to the Penn Campus Network and ARPAnet.

Research area, funding and selected projects:
Major research areas at present include: artificial intelligence, computer vision, computer graphics, robotics, natural language processing, expert systems, knowledge representation, learning, computer architecture, massively parallel systems, networking, distributed computing, theory of computation, logic, advanced data management systems, and biomedical computing.

Here is a list of selected projects:

Distributed Systems Laboratory:
DAWN: Proposes to build an experimental research network and to develop an architecture and protocols that will be adequate for the next generation of computer communication.
MIRAGE: model for understanding network protocols barriers at a speed of 100Mb/s (Farber)

Language, Information and Computation Laboratory:
Cooperative Response Systems (Joshi et al.)
AI and Medicine (Webber)
Spoken Language Systems (Joshi et al.)
Natural Language and Animation (Badler et al.)
Parallel Processing in Natural Language Processing (Palis)

Graphics Laboratory:
Animation Control Techniques (Badler)
Language-Based Interfaces (Badler et al.)
Three-Dimensional Object Representation (Badler)
Human Occupants in Three-Dimensional Environments (Badler)

GRASP Laboratory:
Active Sensory Perception (Bajcsy et al.)
Perception via Manipulation (Bajcsy et al.)
Sensor Driven Robotics (Bajcsy et al.)
Real-time Distributed Systems (Lee et al.).

Collaborations:
Recent and current support for the Computer Graphics Research Laboratory has been provided by NASA, Army Research Office, NSF, State of Pennsylvania, Deere & Co., FMC Co., Martin-Marietta, Denver Aerospace Co., and Siemens Corporate Research, Munich.

University of Pittsburgh

Department of Computer Science
323 Alumni Hall
Pittsburgh, PA 15260
Phone: (412) 624-8493
email: chang@cs.pittsburgh.edu

Chairman: Prof. Shi-Kuo Chang
Administrative Assistant: Betty Brannick

Established: 1966
Undergraduates: n.a.
Graduates: n.a.
Faculty: 23

Curriculum: n.a.

Courses for Graduates (selection): n.a.

Faculty (Professors with Research Areas):

Professors:

Shi-Kuo Chang, Chairman, Ph.D., University of California at Berkeley, 1969 - Pictorial information systems, information exchange theory.

Bruce Buchanan, Ph.D., Michigan State University, 1966 - Artificial intelligence.

Robert Daley, Ph.D., Carnegie Mellon University, 1971 - Theoretical foundations of computer science, computational complexity, inductive inference (learning algorithms), and philosophical aspects of computer science.

Thomas A. Dwyer, Ph.D., Case Institute of Technology, 1960 - Application of computers and concepts from computer science to education.

Ching-Chung Li, Ph.D., Northwestern University, 1981 - Pattern recognition, computer vision, knowledge-based image processing.

George A. Novacky, Jr., Assistant Chairman, Ph.D., University of Pittsburgh, 1981 - Mathematics.

Mary Louise Soffa, Ph.D., University of Pittsburgh, 1977 - Design and implementation of programming languages, static analysis techniques and their utilization, compilers of parallel systems, parallelizing compilers, incremental compilers.

Associate Professors:

Alfs T. Berztiss
Henry H. Chuang
Rami Melhem
Kurt VanLehn

Assistant Professors:

Donald M. Chiarulli
Rajiv Gupta
William D. Hurley
Bala Kalyanasundaram
Johanna D. Moore
Harry Plantinga
Kirk Pruhs
Taieb Znati

Affiliated Institutions:

The Pittsburgh Computing Center (PSC): is a joint effort by the University of Pittsburgh, Westinghouse, and Carnegie Mellon University. PSC currently operates a CRAY Y-MP/4832 supercomputer which is available to the department of computer science via a fiber optic LAN.

Center for Parallel and Distributed Intelligence Systems (CPDIS): houses computing laboratories for the following research specialties: visual computing, artificial intelligence, adaptive and visual interface design, parallel and distributed computing, software systems, and optical computing. Each laboratory contains a variety of computing resources specific to its research area.

Parallel and Distributed Computing Research Center: includes a 16 node iPSC2/D4 Hypercube multiprocessor. This system is used for the following research projects: fault tolerance in hypercube systems, an integrated parallel finite element system, a framework for parallelizing transformations, and strategies for data partitioning and mapping.

Facilities:

The department operates a DECstation 3100S fileserver, an Intel iPSC/2 Hypercube, two DECstation 3100 workstations, a DEC station 2100 workstation, two SUN SPARCstation IPC workstations, 27 SUN-3 workstations, two NeXT workstations, six Macintosh II workstations, two TI micro-Explorer LISP workstations, eight Visual X19-Turbo terminals, six AT&T micro-computer, and a VAX-11/780. Departmental and campus-wide network (PITTnet) based on Ethernet, as well as connection to the PREPnet and NSFnet regional networks.

The university operates a VMS VAXcluster containing three nodes (one 6420, one 6440, and one 8820), a VAX 8800, and a VAX 9000. Wide area networking and electronic mail are supported by BITnet.

Research area, funding and selected projects:

SF as a Prototyping Language (Berztiss, AITRC)

Information Retrieval and Visualization by Iconic Indexing (Chang, NSF)

A Visual Language Compiler - Phase Two (Chang, AITRC)

Visual Reasoning for Information Retrieval (Chang, AITRC)

Multi-Media Information System (Chang, IBM Watson Research Center)

Center for Parallel, Distributed, and Intelligent Systems: A National Science Foundation Industry-University Cooperative Research (IUCR) Center (Chang, NSF)

Coincident Pulse Techniques for Hybrid Optical Electronic Computer Systems (Chiarulli et al., AFOSR)

Optical Technology in Network Based Multiprocessor (Chiarulli et al., NSF)

Intelligent Systems Laboratory (Clearwater et al., NLM, Alcoa Corp., Digital Equipment Corp., NIH, DoE)

Research in Computational Complexity and Inductive Inference (Daley, NSF)

An Engineering Design Methodology for Interactive Systems (Hurley, NSF)

Topics in Space Bound Computation (Kalyanasundaram, NSF)

Bi-Level Reconfigurations of Fault Tolerant Arrays (Melhem, NSF)

Computational Infrastructure in Science and Engineering (Melhem et al., NSF)

Continuous, Viewer-Centered Object Recognition (Plantinga, Central Research Development Fund)

Fine and Coarse Grain Incremental Compilation of Optimized Code (Soffa, NSF)

User-Oriented and Software-Specific Interface Design and Development (Treu, NCR Corporation)

Adaptive, Visual, and Evaluative Features for HSL Users of N-Chime (Treu, NCR Corporation)

Collaborations: n.a.

University of Rochester

Department of Computer Science
Wilson Blvd.
Rochester, NY 14627-0226
Phone: (716) 275-5478
email: leblanc@cs.rochester.edu

Chairman: Prof. Thomas J. LeBlanc
Administrative Assistant: Jill O. Forster

Established: 1973
Undergraduates: n.a.
Graduates: 50
Faculty: 14

Curriculum:

The department only offers a Ph.D. program. The first year culminates in a Comprehensive examination in the three research areas of the Department (Artificial Intelligence, Systems, and Theory). A programming project with faculty supervision must also be completed. The second year culminates in an indepth exam of one of the three previously-mentioned research areas, and a technical paper demonstrating critical independent thought in some subject within that area. After this the student can proceed to plan, prepare and defend a dissertation. Each student is also required to serve as a teaching assistant for two semesters during the program.

Courses for Graduates (selection):

Uncertain Inference, Logical Foundations of Artificial Intelligence, Mathematical Foundations of Artificial Intelligence, Computer Analysis of Images, Natural Language Processing, Theory of Graphs, Computer Organization, Programming Languages and Compilers, Parallel Programming, Operating Systems, Introduction to Numerical Analysis, Theory of Computation, Design and Analysis of Computer Algorithms, Topics in Programming Systems, in Programming Languages, in Artificial Intelligence, in Cognitive Science, in Theory of Computation.

Faculty (Professors with Research Areas):

Professors:

Thomas J. LeBlanc, Associate Professor, Chairman, Ph.D., University of Wisconsin, 1982 - Parallel and distributed operating systems, parallel programming environments.

James F. Allen, Ph.D., University of Toronto, 1979 - Natural language processing, artificial intelligence, planning, representation of beliefs, goals and action.

Dana H. Ballard, Ph.D., University of California at Irvine, 1974 - Computer vision and robotics, artificial intelligence, computational neuroscience.

Christopher M. Brown, Ph.D., University of Chicago, 1972 - Artificial intelligence, computer vision, graphics, robotics, geometric modeling.

Henry E. Kyburg, Jr., Ph.D., Columbia University, 1954 - Philosophy of science, logical foundations of probability and statistical inference, measurement theory, cognitive science, artificial intelligence.

Lenhart K. Schubert, Ph.D., University of Toronto, 1970 - Knowledge representation and organization, general and specialized inference methods, natural language understanding, automatic planning, aspects of robotics and computer vision.

Associate Professors:

Michael L. Scott
Joel I. Seiferas

Assistant Professors:

Paul F. Dietz
Robert J. Fowler
Mark A. Fulk
Lane A. Hemachandra
Danny D. Krizanc
Randal C. Nelson

Affiliated Institutions:
The Computer Vision and Robotics Laboratory.

Facilities:
The department's facilities include two VAX 11/750, 40 SUN-4 SPARCstations, ten SUN-3 workstations, five SUN file servers, five Symbolics Lisp Machines, four Texas Instruments Explorer Lisp Machines, eight large-screen Macintosh II, an IBM 8CE multiprocessor workstation and four BBN Butterfly Multiprocessors, including a 96-node Butterfly I and a 24-node Butterfly Plus.
The Computer Vision and Robotics Laboratory has a Unimation Puma robot arm, a Utah four-fingered dextrous hand, a custom-designed binocular "head" and numerous DataCube real-time image processing boards.
All computers are linked to a campus-wide Ethernet-based network which allows access to NYSERnet, NSFnet and INTERnet.

Research area, funding and selected projects:
The following are grant-supported projects:

Language, Learning and Discourse (DARPA)

Programming Environment for Parallel Vision Algorithms (DARPA and Department of the Army)

Animate Robotics Vision (NSF)

Basic Research in Representing Plans in Natural Language (NSF)

Multi Model Parallel Computing (NSF)

Parallel Laboratory for Real-Time Vision and Robotics (NSF)

Parameter Networks and Spatial Cognition (NSF)

Presidential Young Investigator: Structural Complexity Theory (NSF)

Problems Arising in Persistent Data Structures (NSF)

Research Initiation Award: Adaptive Image Restoration and Recovery (NSF)

Further Development for a Center of Excellence in Knowledge Representation - Issues in Supporting Natural Language Dialogues (ONR)

Plan-Based Knowledge Representation for Man-Machine Dialogs (ONR)

The Role and Structure of Virtual Memory Management for Large-Scale NUMA Multiprocessors (ONR and University of Maryland)

Tools and Techniques for Parallel Program Analysis (ONR and Young Investigator Program)

Basic Research in Nonmonotonic Reasoning in Support of Message-Driven Intelligence (U.S. Army Communication-Electronics Command)

Image Understanding and Intelligent Parallel Systems (U.S. Air Force)

Collaborations:
The university also received support from the following institutions: AT&T Bell Laboratories, BBN Advanced Computers Inc., BBN Laboratories Inc., Boeing Corporation, Eastman Kodak Company, General Electric Company, IBM Corporation, Nippon Telegraphic and Telephone Corporation, Siemens Inc., SUN Microsystems Inc., Xerox Corporation.

University of Southern California

Department of Computer Science
University Park
Los Angeles, CA 90089-0782
Phone: (213) 740-1460
email: horowitz@pollux.usc.edu

Chairman: Prof. Ellis Horowitz
Administrative Assistant: Sudha Kumar

Established: 1976
Undergraduates: 300
Graduates: 400 (100 Ph.D.)
Faculty: 27

Curriculum:
The department offers M.S. and Ph.D. programs.

For a M.S. the student must complete 27 credits including three core course requirements. No comprehensive exam or thesis is required for the M.S. degree. Full-time students should complete the M.S. in two semesters.

The Ph.D. program is grouped into the following three tracks: 1) theoretical computer science; 2) language, systems, and applications; 3) artificial intelligence, robotics, and neural computation. The student must complete five core courses and additional courses specific to the student's area of specialization. A total of 60 credits with a GPA of 3.5 (B+/A-) must be completed. A student with a M.S. can petition to transfer up to 27 credits. The student then takes the qualifying examination, prepares a dissertation, and defends the dissertation as a public final oral examination.

Courses for Graduates (selection):
Concepts in Programming Languages, Finite Automata Theory, Introduction to Computer Networks, to Systems Design Using Microprocessors, to Artificial Intelligence, Numerical Methods, Design and Construction of Large Software Systems, Computer Graphics, File and Database Management, Numerical Analysis and Computation, Mathematical Programming, Management of Computing, Natural Language Processing, Basic Robotics Laboratory, Software Methods in Robotics, Queueing Theory for Performance Modeling of Computer Systems, Design and Analysis of Computer Communication Networks, Computer Communications, Logic Design and Switching Theory, Computational Solution of Optimization Problems, Real-Time Computer Systems, Operating Systems, Cryptography and Information Security, Computer Systems Architecture, Mathematical Pattern Recognition, Advanced Microcomputer-Based Design, Artificial Intelligence, Brain Theory and Artificial Intelligence, Compiler Design, Analysis of Algorithms, Issues of Programming Language Design, Computer Vision, Man-Machine Interactive Systems, VLSI System Design, Advanced Computer Graphics, Database Systems, Algorithmic Aspects of Graph Theory, Expert Systems, Automata and Formal Language Theory, Parallel Processing, Computer Aided Design of Digital Systems.

Faculty (Professors with Research Areas):

Professors:

Ellis Horowitz, Chairman, Ph.D., University of Wisconsin at Madison, 1970 - Design and analysis of algorithms, software engineering, office information systems.

Leonard Adleman, Ph.D., University of California at Berkeley, 1976 - Complexity theory, public key cryptosystems.

Michael Arbib, Ph.D., Massachusetts Institute of Technology, 1963 - Brain theory in artificial intelligence.

George A. Bekey, Ph.D., University of California at Los Angeles, 1962 - Robotics, artificial intelligence, information processing in biological systems.

Edward K. Blum, Ph.D., Columbia University, 1952 - Numerical analysis, computer programming theory.

Melvin A. Breuer, Ph.D., University of California at Berkeley, 1965 - Fault-tolerant systems, CAD, VLSI systems.

Alvin M. Despain, Ph.D., University of Utah, 1966 - Computer architecture, multiprocessor and multicomputer systems, logic programming, design automation.

Seymour Ginsburg, Ph.D., University of Michigan, 1952 - Automata, formal languages, grammar forms, database theory.

Kai Hwang, Ph.D., University of California at Berkeley, 1972 - Supercomputers, multiprocessors, multicomputers, parallel processing, artificial intelligence-oriented computers.

Christoph von der Malsburg, Ph.D., University of Heidelberg, 1970 - Neural architecture, artificial intelligence, parallel computing.

Ramakant Nevatia, Ph.D., Stanford University, 1975 - Machine vision, robotics, artificial intelligence.

Irving S. Reed, Ph.D., California Institute of Technology, 1949 - Automatic detection and processing of radar data, multiple error-correcting communication codes, logical design of digital computers.

Aristides A. G. Requicha, Ph.D., University of Rochester, 1970 - Programmable automation, geometric modeling.

Associate Professors:

Ming-Deh Huang
Richard Hull
Dennis McLeod
Paul Rosenbloom

Assistant Professors:

Bruce Abramson
Peter B. Danzig
Deborah Estrin
Les Gasser

Shahram Ghandeharizadeh
Kenneth Goldberg
Douglas Ierardi
Dean Jacobs
Kim Korner
Gerard G. Medioni
Shankar A. Rajamoney
Rafael Saavedra-Barrera

Affiliated Institutions:

Information Sciences Institute (ISI): is a research facility involved in a broad spectrum of information processing research and the development of advanced computer and communication technology and systems.

Programmable Automation Laboratory: provides support for research in 3D geometric modeling and automatic planning of manufacturing and inspection tasks.

Robotics Laboratory: has goals to develop intelligent robotic systems connecting perception and action through machine intelligence and mechanical dexterity, and to produce advanced manufacturing automation tools supporting computer integrated manufacturing and concurrent engineering.

Parallel Knowledge Processing Laboratory: conducts research on the analysis of algorithms, and hardware and software for parallel processing of artificial intelligence applications such as natural language processing.

Computer Vision Laboratory: supports research on the development of fundamental methods such as edge detection, scene segmentation and motion analysis, active range sensing, shape analysis, object recognition, and scene matching.

Brain Simulation Laboratory: has research which focuses on computational neurobiology and neural engineering.

Parallel Computing Research Laboratory: provides facilities to design, simulate and debug parallel and distributed multiprocessing systems.

Computer Architecture Laboratory: establishes principles for large improvements in machines to support logic programming, design automation, expert systems, signal processing, and high speed artificial intelligence.

Computer Network and Distributed Systems Laboratory: houses facilities for experimental studies of computer network protocols, and distributed system algorithms and architectures.

Computer Networks and Distributed Systems Performance Laboratory: provides experimental facilities for research in computer networks and distributed systems.

VLSI Design Test Laboratory: has goals dealing with various aspects of testing digital systems, including algorithms for test generation and fault simulation, design-for-test and built-in self-test.

VLSI/CAD Laboratory: produces software tools for use in the design of digital chips and systems, and demonstrate the utility of these tools through the construction of example integrated circuits.

Database Laboratory: provides facilities for both theoretical and experimental database research.

Software Engineering Laboratory: provides an environment for research and teaching of large-scale software design and development.

Computer Animation Laboratory: is a joint endeavor of the Department of Computer Science and the School of Cinema-Television.

Facilities:
Programmable Automation Laboratory has a SUN-3/260, a SPARCstation, two SUN-3/50, and a Tektronix 4337.
Robotics Laboratory includes a SUN-4/260, a SUN-4/110, a SUN SPARCstation 1, five IBM PC (System 2 Model 50, System 2 Model 80, AT/286, AT/386, XT), a Puma 560, two IBM 7545, a US 500, a Hero II Mobile robot, and two dextrous robot hands.

Parallel Knowledge Processing Laboratory includes a SUN-3/280, three SUN-3/50, and an IBM PC/AT.
Computer Vision Laboratory has seven Symbolics Lisp machines, a SUN-3/280 file server, two SUN-3/60 workstations, two IBM PC/AT, and a Denning MRV-3 Mobile Robot System.
Brain Simulation Laboratory has a SUN-3/260 file server, two SUN SPARCstations, a SUN-4/110, two SUN-3/110, a SUN-3/50 Transputers, a SUN 386i, two IBM AT, three IBM RS/6000 MAC, and several Apple Macintoshes.
Parallel Computing Research Laboratory includes two SUN-4/60, a SUN-3/80, a SUN-3/60, two AST 486 PC, a Star 860-Intel i860 development system, and an Apple Macintosh II.
Computer Architecture Laboratory has a SUN-4/65 M2-8 workstation, six SUN-4/65, four SUN-3/50, three SUN-3/160, seven HP 425J workstations, an HP 433S server, two IBM PS/2 PC, an Apollo workstation, a VAX 11/785, a TI Microlaser, and a ZEOS 386sx-16/8 PC.
Computer Network and Distributed Systems Laboratory includes four SUN-3/60, a SUN SPARCstation 1, five DEC MicroVAX III, and six IBM RT.
Computer Networks and Distributed Systems Performance Laboratory has two SUN workstations, four HP workstations, and an HP file server.
VLSI Design Test Laboratory has SUN workstations as its primary equipment.
VLSI/CAD Laboratory uses five SUN-3 workstations, a SUN-2 workstation, and an IBM PC.
Database Laboratory has an Intel iPSC/2 Hypercube, several SUN-3/60 and SPARCstations, and several NeXT machines.
Software Engineering Laboratory includes a SUN-3/80, a SUN-3/60, an IBM PS/2, an IBM RISC System 6000, and a NeXT computer.
Computer Animation Laboratory has an Ardent Titan graphics supercomputer, a Harris HCX-9 super-minicomputer, a Dicomed D48C high resolution film recorder, and Apple, IBM and NeXT computers.
ISI has shared computer equipment which includes two DEC VAX 8650, three DEC VAX 11/780, ten DEC VAX 11/750, three SUN-3/160, three SUN-

4/370, several Symbolics artificial intelligence workstations (3600, 3645, 3650, 3675), several Silicon Graphics IRIS and 4D/70 workstations, several IBM PC/XT/AT/PS2, several Apple Macintosh II, several TI Explorer II workstations, and several Hewlett-Packard 9000 Series Bobcat workstations.

All facilities are on an Ethernet-based network which accesses DARTnet, ISInet, MILnet, CERFnet, NSFnet, INTERnet, and other regional networks.

Research area, funding and selected projects:
The total research dollars for 1990 were $3.8 million (NSF: $2 million, AFOSR: $237,000, Industry: $489,000, ONR: $134,000, AT&T: $686,000, NIH: $70,000, Misc.: $106,000). Here is a sample list of projects:

Computation Complexity and Its Relationship to Number Theory (Adleman, NSF)

The Image Recognition Expert System Applying Neural Networks for Knowledge Representation (Arbib, Nippon Telegraph and Telephone Corporation)

Visumotor Coordinator: Neural Networks and Schemas (Arbib, NIH)

Development of Gait Pathology Expert System (Bekey, NIH)

Network Connections and Security Mechanisms (Estrin, NSF)

Mathematical Foundations of Databases (Ginsburg, AFOSR)

Compiling Logic Programs for Multiprocessor Computers (Jacobs, NSF)

System Factory Approach to Large Scale Software Engineering Environments (Scacchi, ONR)

Signal/Images Processing Algorithm/Architecture Studies (Scacchi, ONR)

Neurobiology and Simulation of Neural Nets for Invariant Object Recognition (von der Malsburg, AFOSR)

Collaborations:
The Department of Computer Science has an unofficial connection with Hewlett-Packard Corporation. Many recent graduates have immediately begun working and performing research at Hewlett-Packard Research Labs.

The department also has an exchange program with the Technical University of Berlin, Germany.

University of Texas at Austin

Department of Computer Sciences
Taylor Hall 2.124
Austin, TX 78712-1188
Phone: (512) 471-7316
Fax: (512) 471-0548
email: aldale@cs.utexas.edu

Chaiman: Prof. A. G. Dale
Administrative Assistant: S.K. Rhoads

Established: 1966
Undergraduates: 996
Graduate students: 238 (157 Ph.D., 81 M.A./M.S.)
Faculty: 40

Curriculum:

Master's and Ph.D. degree programs have been offered by the Department since 1966. The B.A. degree program was offered for the first time in 1974, and the B.S. degree program in 1988.

Courses for Graduates (selection): n.a.

Faculty (Professors with Research Areas):

Professors:

A.G. Dale, Chairman, Ph.D., University of Texas at Austin, 1961 - Database managment systems, database architecture.

W. W. Bledsoe, Ph.D., University of California at Berkeley, 1953 - Automatic theorem proving, artificial intelligence.

Robert S. Boyer, Ph.D., University of Texas at Austin, 1971 - Program verification, automatic theorem proving, artificial intelligence.

J.C. Browne, Ph.D., University of Texas at Austin, 1960 - Parallel computation, parallel architectures, resource managment for parallel systems.

Alan K. Cline, Ph.D., University of Michigan, 1970 - Mathematical software, numerical analysis.

Edsger Wybe Dijkstra, Ph.D., University of Amsterdam, 1959 - Program correctness, algorithms, systems.

Charles Anthony Richard Hoare, Visiting Professor, M.A., University of Oxford, 1959 - Programming theory, applications of formal methods to program and system design.

Simon S. Lam, Ph.D., University of California at Los Angeles, 1974 - Communication protocols, computer networks, performance analysis, specification and verification techniques.

Vladimir Lifschitz, Ph.D., Steklov Mathematical Institute at Leningrad, 1971 - Mathematical logic, artificial intelligence.

Jayadev Misra, Ph.D., Johns Hopkins University, 1972 - Parallel programming.

Abraham Silberschatz, Ph.D., State University of New York at Stony Brook, 1976 - Database Systems, operating systems, distributed systems, logic programming.

Robert F. Simmons, Ph.D., University of Southern California at Los Angeles, 1954 - Language data processing, procedural logic, psycholinguistics, behavior synthesis, simulation via computer.

David M. Young, Ph.D., Harvard University, 1950 - Numerical analysis, partial differential equations.

Associate Professors:

Don S. Batory
E. Allen Emerson
Donald S. Fussell
Mohamed G. Gouda
Henry F. Korth
Benjamin J. Kuipers

Aloysius K. Mok
Gordon S. Novak, Jr.
Vijaya Ramachandran
Louis E. Rosier

Assistant Professors:

William C. Athas
Risto Miikkulainen
Daniel P. Miranker
Raymond J. Mooney
Sean William O'Malley
Greg Plaxton
Bruce W. Porter
Robert A. van de Geijn
Martin D. F. Wong

Affiliated Institutions:
Artificial Intelligence Laboratory: founded in 1984 with major support from the U.S. Army Research Office, from NSF and NASA. The AI lab includes nine faculty, and approximately 35 graduate student researchers, and has received equipment grants for several million dollars.

The Center for High Performance Computing, and the Computation Center.

Facilities:
Departmental Research Equipment: Sequent Balance 21000 (26 processors), Sequent Symmetry 81000 (14 processors), SYMULT 2010 (24 processors), BBN Butterfly (16 processors), 22 SUN-2, 55 SUN-3, a SUN-4, 60 HP-9000/3xx, three Silicon Graphics IRIS, numerous LISP machines (including 18 Symbolics 36x0 and 26 TI Explorer I), ca. 100 Macintoshes: almost all networked by Ethernet including gateways to NSFnet, CSnet, BITnet, and UUCP.

Departmental Teaching Resources: microprocessor laboratory containing ca. 90 Macintosh SE, ten Dell 80286, ten Dell 80386, and 20 IBM PCs, hardware/software lab containing nine Macintosh II, undergraduate workstation lab containing 20 SUN SPARCstation I.

Campus Computers: at the Center for High Performance Computing there are two Cray 1 (a Cray 1 X-MP/24 running COS and a Cray 1 X-MP/14se running UNICOS), at the Computation Center there are dual CDC Cyber-170/750, six VAX-11/780, IBM 3081D, IBM 4341, over 3000 Macintoshes, several hundred IBM PCs. At the Houston Area Research Center there is a NEC SX-2 available via NSFnet.

Research area, funding and selected projects:
Sponsored research support approximated $2.5 million (including equipment grants) for the academic year 1990-1991 in 35 external grants and contracts. The following list is a sample:

Research on Automated Theorem Proving (Bledsoe, NSF, $84,000, 5/91)

STR+VE Distribution Proposal (Bledsoe, NSF, $29,000, 8/91)

Automated Reasoning in Geometry and Mechanics (Boyer and Chou, NSF, $65,000, 5/91)

Application Specific Parallel Programming Environment (Browne, IBM, $350,000, 8/91)

Fault-tolerant, Bounded Time, Parallel Structures Decision Processes (Browne and Mok, ONR, $403,000, 9/91)

Automated Deduction in Programming Language Semantics (Brumfield, Lockheed, $50,000, 7/92)

Qualitive Methods for Robot Exploration (Kuipers, NSF, $252,000, 7/92)

Real-Time Database Systems (Korth and Silberschatz, NEC American, $54,000, 8/91)

Qualitive Modeling and Simulation of Physical Systems (Kuipers, NSF, $160,000, 8/91)

A Theoretical Foundation for Communication Network Protocols (Lam, NSF, $105,000, 8/93)

Towards a Theory of Large-Scale Programming in UNITY (Misra, ONR, $330,000, 9/92)

Specifications and Designs of Large Reactive Systems (Misra, Texas Advanced Research Program, $125,000, 9/91)

Formal Design Methodology for Hard Real-Time Systems (Mok, ONR, $445,000, 12/91)

Real-Time-Based Systems (Mok, Texas Instruments, $25,000, 12/91)

Utility and Incomplete Theories: Addressing Two Important Problems in Explanation-Based Learning (Mooney, NASA, $275,000, 5/92)

Processor-Efficient Parallel Algorithms for Combinatorial Problems (Ramachandran, NSF, $161,000, 5/92)

Research in VLSI Circuit Layout (Wong, NSF, $60,000, 8/91)

Collaborations:
The Department of Computer Sciences established its own component of the College of Natural Sciences' Industrial Associates Program. The purpose is to facilitate the transfer of technology from an academic setting to industry through various channels. Activities include the annual Computer Sciences Industrial Forum (topic for 1991 is technology transfer), and the Frontiers in Computing Symposium (event in 1991 will highlight research in theorem-proving). Companies that participate in the program are also entitled to access the technical information collection, to receive copies of technical reports generated by faculty and graduate students, and to participate in the Visiting Scholars program.

University of Utah

Department of Computer Science
3160 Merrill Engineering Bldg.
Salt Lake City, UT 84112
Phone: (801) 581-7026
email: ksmith@cs.umd.edu

Chairman: Prof. Kent Smith
Administrative Assistant: Gary Reynolds

Established: n.a.
Undergraduates: n.a.
Graduates: n.a.
Faculty: 33

Curriculum:

The department offers M.S., M.Phil., and Ph.D. programs.

For a M.S. the student must complete a minimum of 45 credits with at least 36 credits in resident study. A minimum of 30 credits must be in approved coursework with the balance in thesis research. A comprehensive oral exam is conducted by a supervisory committee as the defense of the student's thesis proposal. A full-time student should complete the M.S. program in two years.

The M.Phil. program is equivalent to the Ph.D. program minus the dissertation and requires 81 credits of coursework.

For a Ph.D. the student must complete at least 74 credits exclusive of independent study and inclusive of M.S. degree requirements. At least 20 credits of dissertation research and 54 hours of approved coursework must be completed. One year of full-time residency at the university is required. The student must pass a comprehensive exam consisting of four Computer Science areas, and one area which is closely aligned to the thesis topic. The qualifying exam is an oral exam which usually focuses on the student's dissertation proposal. A teaching requirement of at least one quarter is also required. The student can then proceed to

the preparation and defense of a dissertation. The student should complete the Ph.D. program in four years.

The student must maintain a B average throughout all programs.

Courses for Graduates (selection):

Programming Language Concepts, Knowledge-Based Programming, Introduction to Theoretical Computer Science, Operating Systems, Compiler Principles and Techniques, Data Communications and Networks, Discrete State Simulations, Programming Linguistics, Logic Design Laboratory, Advanced Robotics, Advanced Computer Vision, Structured Design of Large Scale Integrated Circuits, Modeling of Integrated Circuits, Lisp and AI Programming, Artificial Intelligence, Expert Systems, Advanced Computer Organization, Introduction to Parallel Computer Organization, Microprocessor Laboratory, Digital and Analog Interfaces, Digital Signal Processing, Formal Languages, Program Verification, Computational Complexity, Software Engineering, Database Systems, Computer Graphics, Computer-Aided Geometric Design.

Faculty (Professors with Research Areas):

Professors:

Kent F. Smith, Chairman, Ph.D., University of Utah, 1982 - Structured logic circuits, complexity.

Lee A. Hollaar, Ph.D., University of Illinois at Urbana-Champaign, 1975 - Information retrieval systems, VLSI design, communications networks, distributed systems, legal issues concerning computers.

Robert R. Johnson, Ph.D., California Institute of Technology, 1956 - Computer architecture, system design.

Gary E. Lindstrom, Ph.D., Carnegie Mellon University, 1971 - Programming language design, programming aspects of parallel computers.

Richard F. Riesenfeld, Ph.D., Syracuse University, 1973 - Computer graphics, computer-aided geometric design, animation.

Frank Stenger, Ph.D., University of Alberta, 1965 - Numerical analysis, linear algebra, algorithms.

Associate Professors:

Elaine Cohen
Ran Ginosar (Visiting)
Thomas C. Henderson
Robert Kessler
Kris Sikorski

Assistant Professors:

Beat Bruderlin
Ganesh C. Gopalakrishnan
Jamie Painter
Gary Ridsdale
Joseph Zachary

Affiliated Institutions:
The Software Research Laboratory, the Computer Aided Design and Graphics Laboratory, the Lisp Programming and Artificial Intelligence Laboratory, the Robotics Laboratory, the VLSI Computing Facility, and the Digital Processing Laboratory.

Facilities:
The Software Research Laboratory has a BBN Butterfly GP1000 Parallel Computer, a CSA Transputer Parallel Computer, two HP 9000/835 RISC-based computers, 25 HP 9000/3xx 680x0-based Lisp systems, and a SUN-4 file/compute server.
The Computer Aided Design and Graphics Laboratory has a Silicon Graphics 4D240-GTX, ten Silicon Graphics Personal Iris 4D20 systems, an Apollo DN 10020, an Apollo DN 3500, five SUN-clone Prime/CV Color 3/160 workstations, two HP 9000/3xx 680x0-based systems, an Abekas A60 Digital Video Disk Recorder, a Matrix Instruments OCR Film Recorder, and a Monarch Cortland VMC-45 machining center.

The Lisp Programming and Artificial Intelligence Laboratory has ten HP/9000/3xx 680x0-based Lisp systems, and a HP 9000/835 PA RISC-based system.
The VLSI Computing Facility has five HP/9000/3xx 680x0-based Lisp systems and two SUN SPARCstation-1 systems.
The Robotics Laboratory has a Puma 560 robot arm and controller, a Rhino robot arm, a Technical Arts 100A 3D White scanner, a Vicom Image Processing System, a Textronix 4635 Video Image Printer, a Fairchild CCD camera, a VAX 11/750 server and a HP320 workstation.
The Digital Processing Laboratory has a NeXT System.

Research area, funding and selected projects:
Symbolic Computer Geometry and Interactive Geometric Design (Bruderlin, NSF)

PODS Architecture (Cohen and Drake, State of Utah)

Formal Specification of VLSI Systems for Verification and Automation (Gopalakrishnan, NSF)

Specification Driven Design of Custom Hardware (Gopalakrishnan, NSF)

Dextrous Manipulation (Henderson, NSF)

Robot World Representation (Henderson, NSF/INRIA [France] Cooperative Research)

Precision Architecture (Kessler, Hewlett-Packard)

UNIX Systems Software Development (Kessler, Hewlett-Packard)

Open Languages: Types as Semantic Interfaces (Lindstrom, NSF)

Research Initiation Equipment Grant (Ridsdale, NSF)

Computer Animation of Human Figures (Ridsdale, NSF)

117

NC Machining Center Equipment Grant (Riesenfeld and Cohen, NSF)

Computer Aided Design (Riesenfeld and Cohen, DARPA)

3-D Resonance (Sikorski and Schuster, NSF)

Discrete Relaxation Architecture (Smith, NSF)

PPL Cell Matrix (Smith and Carter, DARPA)

Rapid Prototyping (Smith and Carter, FBI)

Numerical Solution of Inverse Problems (Stenger and Sikorski, ARO)

Collaborations:
In addition to the above list, some professors have consulting contracts and/or collaborate with industrial and governmental institutions. Here is a sample:

Distributed Scientific Computation and Information-Based Complexity (Sikorski, IBM/NSF/USAF)

Computer Graphics, Geometric Design, and Advanced Manufacturing (Bruderlin et al., NSF/DoD)

Consulting Research Efforts (Johnson, Mosaic Systems/Ovonic Imaging Systems/Evans & Sutherland)

University of Washington

Department of Computer Science and Engineering
Seattle, Washington 98195
Phone: (206) 543-1695
email: baer@cs.washington.edu

Chairman: Prof. Jean-Loup Baer
Administrative Assistant: Chris Cunnington

Established: 1967; Department since 1975; moved to College of Engineering and renamed in 1989
Undergraduates: 250
Graduates: 150 (50 M.S., 100 Ph.D.)
Faculty: 29

Curriculum:

The Department grants a Bachelor in Computer Science and a Bachelor in Computer Engineering, and a M.S. and a Ph.D.

There are two options (thesis and non-thesis) leading to the M.S. degree. For both a cumulative GPA of 3.0 and a total of 40 credits are required. There are further specific requirements for each option and a thesis counts for 9 credits.

Ph.D. students have to pass a qualifying and a general examination, have to complete 60 credits of course work (course work toward the M.S. degree is applicable), and prepare and orally defend a dissertation.

Courses for Graduates (selection):

Computers and Society, Compiler Construction, Software Engineering, Concepts of Programming Languages, Design and Analysis of Algorithms I & II, Computational Geometry, Parallel Algorithms, Formal Languages and Automata, Complexity Theory, Theory of Distributed Computing, Discrete System Simulation, Central Processor Architecture, Computer Systems Performance Modeling, Fundamentals of Stochastic Models of Systems, Computer Systems Architecture, High-Performance Computer Architecture, Operating Systems, Distributed and Parallel Systems, Real-Time Systems, Computer Graphics, Computer Aided Geometric Design, Computer Communication and Networks, Introduction to VLSI Systems, Advanced VLSI Laboratory, Artificial Intelligence I & II, Image Understanding, Mathematical Morphology, Parallel Computation in Image Processing, Advanced Topics in Programming Languages, Advanced Topics in Complexity Theory.

Faculty (Professors with Research Areas):

Professors:

Jean-Loup Baer, Chairman, Adjunct Professor of Electrical Engineering, Ph.D., University of California at Los Angeles, 1968 - Parallel processing, system architecture.

Hellmut Golde, Adjunct Professor of Electrical Engineering, Ph.D., Stanford University, 1959 - Computer networks, compilers.

Alistair D. C. Holden, Ph.D., University of Washington, 1964 - Artificial intelligence and applications, speech understanding, neural networks, knowledge-based systems.

Theodore H. Kehl, Ph.D., University of Wisconsin, 1958 - Real-time hardware and software systems, computer design, VLSI.

Richard Ladner, Ph.D., University of California at Berkeley, 1971 - Theory of computation, computational complexity, design and analysis of algorithms, computer communication theory, computers to aid the handicapped.

Edward D. Lasowska, Ph.D., University of Toronto, 1977 - Computer systems: modeling and analysis, design and implementation, distributed and parallel systems.

Walter L. Ruzzo, Ph.D., University of California at Berkeley, 1978 - Computational complexity, parallel computation.

Linda Shapiro, Ph.D., University of Iowa, 1974 - Computer vision, artificial intelligence, robotics, pattern recognition, intelligent information systems.

Alan C. Shaw, Ph.D., Stanford University, 1968 - Operating systems, software specifications, realtime systems.

Lawrence Snyder, Ph.D., Carnegie-Mellon University, 1973 - Parallel computation, VLSI.

Steven L. Tanimoto, Adjunct Professor of Electrical Engineering - Ph.D., Princeton University, 1975 - Image analysis, computer graphics, artificial intelligence.

Martin Tompa, Ph.D., University of Toronto, 1978 - Computational complexity.

Paul Young, Ph.D., Massachusetts Institute of Technology, 1963 - Computational complexity, computability, and connections with mathematical logic.

John Zahorjan, Ph.D., University of Toronto, 1980 - Computer systems, performance modeling and evaluation, performance and scheduling issues in parallel and distributed systems.

Associate Professors:

Richard Anderson
Alan Borning
Tony DeRose
Henry M. Levy
David Notkin
Arun Somani

Assistant Professors:

Paul Beame
Steve Burns
Gaetano Borriello
Craig Chambers
Carl Ebeling
Susan Eggers
Oren Etzioni

Steve Hanks
Dan Weld

Affiliated Institutions:

Computer Science Laboratory: originally established within the department to meet its research and instructional computing needs. Today the laboratory coordinates the aquisition, maintenance, and operation of computing equipment and network services.

Northwest Laboratory for Integrated Systems: industry/University effort to exploit VLSI in high-performance computer architectures and to develop CAD tools for designing such architectures.

Graphics and Artificial Intelligence Laboratory: laboratory of the Department of Computer Science for research related to computer vision and image processing.

Intelligent Systems Laboratory: laboratory of the Department of Electrical Engineering for research related to computer vision and image processing.

Mathematical Sciences Computing Center: instructional Consortium compromising Computer Science, Statistics, Mathematics, and Applied Mathematics.

Facilities:

General purpose research computing is provided by a VAX 8550, two DECsystem 5500s, a number of MicroVAXs, roughly 80 DEC (DECstation 5000 and 3100) and SUN (SUN-4) workstations, plus a number of X-Terminals. Research in parallel computing is supported by a Sequent Symmetry-81 (20 processors), an Intel iPSC II (32 processors), and by ten DEC SRY Firefly workstations. Research in VLSI is supported by SUN workstations and special-purpose CAD equipment. Research in graphics and computer vision utilizes conventional workstations, a Symbolics, and various special-purpose devices.

Roughly 40 DEC and Tektronix workstations and servers, as well as several Macintoshes and IBM RTs, are dedicated to instruction.

The department's local, Ethernet-based network provides access to all major external networks, including NSFnet, CSnet, BITnet and USEnet.

Research area, funding and selected projects:
The Department of Computer Science and Engineering has a total instruction, research expenditures, and equipment budget of over $7.5 million.

Major areas of expertise include:
Computer Architecture and VLSI, Computer Systems and Computer System Performance, Programming Systems, Theory of Computation, Graphics, Image Analysis and Computer Vision, and Artificial Intelligence.

Here is a sample of research projects:

The Parallel Computing Project: provides infrastructure (equipment, maintenance, and staff) for research related to parallel computation (Lazowska et al., NSF Coordinated Experimental Research/Institutional Infrastructure Program, 1992).

Orca: the Orca project is an interdisciplinary research effort studying parallel programming environments (Notkin and Snyder).

Amber: C++ based system for programming networks of multiprocessors (Lazowska et al.).

The funding for the Northwest Laboratory for Integrated Systems is provided primarily by the DARPA, but local industry and the NSF also provide a significant level of support.

Intelligent Machine Vision: the goal is to develop an automated vision system for inspection and robot guidance that bridges the gap from CAD models to machine vision algorithms (Shapiro et al.).

Collaborations:
VLSI chips , developed at the Northwest Laboratory for Integrated Systems are fabricated through the MOSIS facility through DARPA and NSF contracts.

ECSEL (Engineering Coalition of Schools for Excellence in Education and Leadership): five-year multimillion-dollar effort to develop novel interactive courseware to support a new engineering curriculum. The ECSEL project is conducted by one of two (as of 1991) NSF-sponsored coalitions of universities. The other members of the coalition are City College of New York, Howard University, Massachusetts Institute of Technology, University of Maryland, Morgan State University, and Pennsylvania State University (Borning and Tanimoto).

The department has contributed to the local economy by helping attract high-technology companies such as DECWest and Tera Computers, and has a history of association with local and national industry in a wide range of activities, especially through the Industrial Affiliates Program.

121

University of Wisconsin at Madison

Department of Computer Science
1210 West Dayton
Madison, WI 53706
Phone: (608) 262-1204
email: dyer@cs.wisc.edu

Chairman: Prof. Charles R. Dyer
Administrative Assistant: Robert Holloway

Established: 1963
Undergraduates: 150
Graduates: 225
Faculty: 39

Curriculum:
The department offers M.S. and Ph.D. programs.

For a M.S. the student must receive 24 credits in approved coursework. A thesis or project is optional and can count for a maximum of six credits. The thesis need not be an original piece of work (unlike the Ph.D. dissertation). It may serve as a basis and major first step toward subsequent Ph.D. research or be less formal by describing a project carried out under the supervision of a faculty advisor. No credits from other educational institutions can be counted toward the M.S.

For a Ph.D the student must pass qualifying, preliminary, and final oral examinations, and write a dissertation. Each semester the department offers a depth exam and a breadth exam in each of the following areas:
* Artificial Intelligence
* Computer Architecture and VLSI
* Database Systems
* Mathematical Programming
* Modeling and Analysis of Computer Systems
* Numerical Analysis
* Operating Systems
* Programming Languages and Compilers
* Theory of Computing

The student may pass the qualifying exam by either taking the depth exam in one area and the breadth exam in two areas, or take the depth exams in the areas of Mathematical Programming and Numerical Analysis. These exams must be passed by the end of the sixth semester. The student must then pass the oral preliminary exam before a committee of three members. The student can then prepare a dissertation and defend it as the final oral examination before a committee of five members. The student's major professor must be a member of all committees.

Courses for Graduates (selection):
Programming Languages and Compilers, Compiler Construction, Mathematical Techniques for Analysis of Algorithms, Applied Numerical Methods, Numerical Analysis of Differential Equations, Numerical Functional Analysis, Network Flows, Integer Programming, Dynamic Programming and Associated Topics, Nonlinear Programming Theory and Applications, Advanced Nonlinear Programming, Nonlinear Programming Algorithms, Advanced Artificial Intelligence, Topics in Artificial Intelligence, Computational Methods for Large Sparse Systems, Advanced Operating Systems, Computer Systems Performance Evaluation and Modeling, Distributed Systems, Advanced Computer Networks, Advanced Computer Architecture, VLSI Systems Design, Computer-Aided Design for VLSI, Advanced Computer Architecture, Machine Learning, Deduction and Problem Solving by Computer, Topics in Database Management Systems, Perceptual Recognition, Computer Vision, Graph Theory, Computational Linguistics, Problems in Computational Linguistics, Data Models and Languages, Advanced Algorithms and Data Structures, Models and Formalisms for Computation, Arithmetic Algorithms, Algebraic Algorithms, Transcendental Function Algorithms, Theory of Automata and Formal Languages, Abstract and Concrete Complexity Theory, Numerical Methods for Ordinary Differential Equations, Matrix Theory in Numerical Analysis, Approximation Theory:

Faculty (Professors with Research Areas):

Professors:

Charles R. Dyer, Chairman, Ph.D., University of Maryland, 1979 - Computer vision, robotics, artificial intelligence, computer graphics.

Carl de Boor, Ph.D., University of Michigan, 1966 - Approximation theory, numerical analysis.

Edouard J. Desautels, Ph.D., Purdue University, 1969 - Systems programming, personal computer systems and applications.

David J. DeWitt, Ph.D., University of Michigan, 1976 - Database management systems, computer architecture.

Charles N. Fischer, Ph.D., Cornell University, 1974 - Compiler theory and design, interactive program development environments, automatic code generation.

James R. Goodman, Ph.D., University of California at Berkeley, 1980 - Computer architecture, large-scale computing, parallel computing, shared-memory multiprocessors.

Sheldon Klein, Ph.D., University of California at Berkeley, 1963 - Archaeology of cognition, simulation of language transmission and language change, language understanding generation in the context of knowledge structures.

Kenneth Kunen, Ph.D., Stanford University, 1968 - Mathematical logic, logic programming, automated deduction.

Lawrence H. Landweber, Ph.D., Purdue University, 1967 - Computer networks and protocols, electronic mail.

Olvi L. Mangasarian, Ph.D., Harvard University, 1959 - Mathematical programming, pattern recognition.

Robert R. Myer, Ph.D., University of Wisconsin, 1968 - Linear and nonlinear network optimization, parallel algorithms for large-scale optimization.

Seymour V. Parter, Ph.D., New York University, 1958 - Numerical methods for partial differential equations.

Stephen M. Robinson, Ph.D., University of Wisconsin, 1971 - Operations research, management science.

Marvin H. Solomon, Ph.D., Cornell University, 1977 - Distributed operating systems, computer networks, program development systems, programming languages.

Larry E. Travis, Ph.D., University of California at Los Angeles, 1966 - Mechanization of deduction, expert systems, non-procedural knowledge representation, philosophical foundations of artificial intelligence, computing management, social implications of computing.

Leonard M. Uhr, Ph.D., University of Michigan, 1957 - Pattern perception, integrated wholistic systems, models of intelligence, algorithm-structured multicomputer architectures.

Associate Professors:

Eric Bach
Michael J. Carey
Donald R. Fitzwater
Deborah A. Joseph
Miron Livny
Barton P. Miller
Thomas Reps
John C. Strikwerda
Mary K. Vernon

Assistant Professors:

Guido Brunnett (Visiting)
Anne Condon
Renato De Leone (Visiting)
Michael C. Ferris

Stuart A. Friedberg
Mark D. Hill
Susan Horwitz
Yannis E. Ioannidis
James R. Larus
Jeffrey F. Naughton
Raghu Ramakrishnan
Amos Ron
Jude W. Shavlik
Gurindar S. Sohi
Prasoon Tiwari
David A. Wood

Affiliated Institutions:

The Artificial Intelligence Laboratory: has specialized equipment for research in computer vision and robotics.

The VLSI Laboratory: is jointly operated with the Department of Electrical and Computer Engineering.

The Center for Parallel Optimization.

Facilities:

Departmental facilities include two Sequent Symmetry multiprocessors, a 32-processor Intel Hypercube, a DECstation 5400, an 8-stage Aspex Pipe image processor, two DECstation 5000, 140 DECstation 3100, 25 DEC VAXstation 3200, 26 DEC VAX 11/750, a Britton-Lee IDM-500 database machine, 16 SUN-4/110, two SUN-3/50, 43 IBM RT/PC, 27 Hewlett-Packard 9000/360, five Hewlett-Packard 9000/345, 67 Hewlett-Packard 9000/330, three Hewlett-Packard 9000/550, seven Hewlett-Packard 9000/345, two Hewlett-Packard 9000/835, a Hewlett-Packard 9000/350, three Hewlett-Packard 64000, three SUN-3/110, a SUN-3/160, and additional Apple Macintosh and IBM PC computers for instructional purposes.
The Artificial Intelligence Laboratory has a Vicom image processor, a Unimation Puma 560 robot, several DECstation 3100, and a DEC Vax 11/750.
The VLSI Laboratory has three AED color graphics terminals, several DECstations and VAXstations.
All facilities are on a campus-wide network which accesses USEnet, XUnet, CICnet, and NSFnet.

Research area, funding and selected projects:
Research funding for 1989-90 exceeded $5.7 million. Here is a sample of current projects:

Design and Analysis of Arithmetic Algorithms (Bach, NSF/Digital Equipment Corporation, 12/91)

Multivariate Spline Approximation (de Boor, Army Research Office, 9/92)

TOPAZ: a Laboratory for Research in Parallel Computing (DeWitt et al., NSF, 12/91)

Multicube: a Large-Scale, Cache-Coherent Shared-Memory Multiprocessor (Goodman, NSF, 11/92)

Cache Memory Design (Hill, NSF/AT&T Bell Laboratories/Digital Equipment Corporation/Texas Instruments, 11/94)

Language-Based Tools for Programming Environments (Horwitz, NSF/Eastman Kodak/Xerox, 11/94)

Computational Complexity and Geometric Algorithms (Joseph, NSF/AT&T Bell Laboratories/Digital Equipment Corporation/SUN Microsystems, 1/92)

An Experimental X.400/X.500 Network (Landweber, NASA, 6/91)

Common Interface for Network Management Applications (Landweber and Hall, Digital Equipment Corporation, 7/91)

Large-Scale Serial and Parallel Optimization (Mangasarian, NSF, 11/91)

Center for Parallel Optimization (Mangasarian and Meyer, AFOSR, 10/91)

Parallel Optimization of Large-Scale Networks (Meyer, NSF, 2/93)

Transferring the IPS-2 Parallel Program Performance Tools into Supercomputer Environment (Miller, NSF, 2/92)

Combining Explanation-Based and Neural Approaches to Machine Learning (Shavlik, ONR, 5/93)

Studies in High-Performance, Fine-Grain Parallel Architecture (Sohi, NSF, 3/93)

Collaborations:
The department had industrial affiliates who contributed over $770,000 for graduate fellowships, undergraduate fellowships, and research/instructional equipment during the academic year 1989-90. They include: AT&T Bell Laboratories, Arthur Andersen Consulting, Bell Communications Research, Boeing, Cray Research, Digital Equipment Corporation, Dow Chemicals, Eastman Kodak, EPIC Systems, Hewlett-Packard, IBM, Prime Computer, Sequent Computer, Shell Development, Software Publishing, Texas Instruments, Unisys.

Yale University

Department of Computer Science
P.O. Box 2158, Yale Station
New Haven, CT 06520
Phone: (203) 432-1200
email: schultz-martin@cs.yale.edu

Chairman: Prof. Martin Schultz
Administrative Assistant: Bob Dunne

Established: 1969
Undergraduates: n.a
Graduates: n.a (more than 80 full-time doctoral students)
Faculty: 20

Curriculum: n.a

Courses for Graduates (selection): n.a

Faculty (Professors with Research Areas):

Professors:

Martin H. Schultz, Chairman, Ph.D., Harvard University, 1965 - Numerical analysis, scientific computing, application of parallelism to scientific computing.

Stanley Eisenstat, Ph.D., Stanford University, 1972 - Numerical analysis, discrete mathematics, concrete computational complexity.

Michael J. Fischer, Ph.D., Harvard University, 1968 - Theory of parallel and distributed systems, cryptographic protocols, computational complexity.

Drew V. McDermott, Ph.D., Massachusetts Institute of Technology, 1976 - Cognitive mapping, spatial and temporal reasoning, knowledge representation.

Willard Miranker, Professor Adjunct, Ph.D., New York University, 1956 - Parallel computing, associative computing, hybrid digital/analogue computing, numerical analysis.

Vladimir Rokhlin, Ph.D., Rice University 1983 - Numerical scattering theory, elliptic partial differential equations, numerical solution of integral equations, quadrature formulae for singular functions, numerical linear algebra, and large-scale particle simulations.

Associate Professors:

Sandeep Bhatt
Mrina Chen
David Gelernter
Paul Hudak
Ilse Ipsen
Lennart Johnsson

Assistant Professors:

P. Anandan
Richard Beigel
Young-il Choo
Eric Mjolsness
Jeffery R. Westbrook
Kenneth Man-kam Yip
Lenore Zuck

Affiliated Institutions: n.a

Facilities:
A SUN-4/390 file server connected to a local email and bulletin board network, a Multiflow Trace 14/300, 139 SUN SPARCstations and servers, a 64-node Intel Hypercube (IPSC/2) with an Intel 310 front end microprocessor, a Connection Machine (CM-2) with both a VAX 8350 and Symbolics 3645 front end processor, an 18-node Encore MultiMax, a 10-processor Sequent Symmetry, an Apollo DN 10000, an IBM 8CE, a WARP, an IBM RS/6000 Model 320 and an Inmos Transputer.
Educational facilities include 37 color SPARC stations.
All systems are interconnected via Ethernet (TCP/

IP) and have access to external networks including ARPAnet, USEnet, NSFnet, and BITnet

Research area, funding and selected projects:
Research concentrates on four general areas:
- Programming languages and systems (especially focussed on highly parallel computation ranging from VLSI design, systems architecture, and operating systems to parallel computing languages, compilers, and environments. Portability of languages and environments is a major concern),
- Scientific computing, generally focussed on adaption of fast serial algorithms for the solution of linear and non-linear systems of equations for parallel multiprocessor environments, and investigation of policies for the allocation of the resources of a multiprocessor machine (Theoretical Analysis: rates of convergence, optimality, operation counts / Systems Modeling Research: examination of performance implications of the interactions between computationally intensive algorithms, operating systems, and multiprocessor machines / Programming considerations: coding efficiency, numerical accuracy, generality of application, data structures, and machine independence),
- Artificial Intelligence (testbed execution model for robot plans / theory and implementation of an algorithm for projecting probable effects of plans / interactive theorem prover, based on generalized backward chaining / implementation of a frame-based representation language using neural nets / automatic reasonning),
- Theory of computation (logical foundations of algorithms / study of fault tolerant distributed algorithms, synchronization, and communication for parallel computation / computational concepts of time and space complexity and randomness)

Collaborations:
The department of Computer Science runs a "Liaison Program" for Affiliated Institutions.

List of Universities

Brown University
Dept. of Computer Science
Box 1910
Providence, Rhode Island 02912-1910
Phone: (401) 863-7600
email: jes@brown.cs.edu

Carnegie Mellon University
Department of Computer Science
Schenley Park
Pittsburgh, PA 15213
Phone: (412) 268-2592
email: nico.habermann@cs.cmu.edu

Columbia University
School of Engineering and Applied Science
Computer Science Department
450 Computer Science Building
New York, NY 10027
Phone: (212) 854-2736
email: galil@cs.columbia.edu

Cornell University
Department of Computer Science
405 Upson Hall
Ithaca, NY 14853
Phone: (607) 255-7416
email: jeh@cs.cornell.edu

Duke University
Department of Computer Science
202 North Building
Durham, NC 27706
Phone: (919) 684-3048
email: djr@cs.duke.edu

George Mason University
Department of Computer Science
4400 University Drive
Fairfax, VA 22030
Phone: (703) 323-2713
email: drine@gmuvax.gmu.edu

Georgia Institute of Technology
College of Computing
AECAL Bldg., Room 156
Atlanta, GA 30332-0280
Phone: (404) 894-3186
email: pete@cc.gatech.edu

Indiana University
Department of Computer Science
101 Lindley Hall
Bloomington, IN 47405
Phone: (812) 855-6486
email: fpp@iuvax.cs.indiana.edu

Massachusetts Institute of Technology
Department of Electrical Engineering and
Computer Science
545 Tech Square
Cambridge, MA 02139
Phone: (617) 253-6001
email: corbato@lcs.mit.edu

New York University
Department of Computer Science
Courant Institute of Mathematical Sciences
251 Mercer Street
New York, NY 10012
Phone: (212) 998-3103
email: schonberg@cs.nyu.edu

Northwestern University
Department of Electrical Engineering and
Computer Science
2145 Sheridan Road
Evanston, IL 60208-3118
Phone: (708) 491-3641
email: ahaddad@eecs.nwu.edu

Ohio State University
Department of Computer and Information
Science
2036 Neil Avenue Mall
Columbus, OH 43210-1277
Phone: (614) 292-5813
email: muller-m@cis.ohio-state.edu

Pennsylvania State University
Department of Computer Science
333 Whitmore Laboratory
University Park, PA 16802
Phone: (814) 865-9505
email: mjir@psuvax1.cs.psu.edu

Princeton University
Department of Computer Science
35 Olden Street, Computer Science Bldg.
Princeton, NJ 08544-2087
Phone: (609) 258-5030
email: rs@princeton.edu

Rice University
Dept. of Computer Science
P.O. Box 1892
Houston, TX 77251
Phone: (713) 527-4834
email: cork@rice.edu

Rutgers University
Department of Computer Science
Hill Center - Busch Campus
New Brunswick, NJ 08903
Phone: (201) 932-3546
email: kaplan@cs.rutgers.edu

Stanford University
Department of Computer Science
Stanford, CA 94305
Phone: (415) 723-5396
email: ullman@cs.stanford.edu

State University of New York at Buffalo
Department of Computer Science
226 Bell Hall
Buffalo, NY 14260-0001
Phone: (716) 636-3182
email: selman@cs.buffalo.edu

State University of New York at Stony Brook
Department of Computer Science
1401 Computer Science Building
Stony Brook, NY 11794
Phone: (516) 632-8462
email: pml@suny-sb.csnet

Syracuse University
School of Computer and Information Science
Suite 4-116
Center for Science and Technology
Syracuse, NY 13244-4100
Phone: (315) 443-2368
email: frieder@top.cis.syr.edu

University of Arizona
Department of Computer Science
Tucson, AZ 85721-0001
Phone: (602) 621-4239
email: andrews@arizona.edu

University of California at Berkeley
Department of Electrical Engineering and
Computer Science
Division of Computer Science
571 Evans Hall
Berkeley, CA 94720
Phone: (415) 642-0930
email: pattrsn@ginger.berkeley.edu

University of California at Irvine
Department of Information and Computer
Science
444 Computer Science Building
Irvine, CA 92717-0001
Phone: (714) 856-7405
email: ljo@ics.uci.edu

University of California at Los Angeles
Department of Computer Science
405 Hilgard Ave., 3732 Boelter Hall
Los Angeles, CA 90024-1596
Phone: (213) 825-8878
email: wwc@cs.ucla.edu

University of California at San Diego
Department of Computer Science and
Engineering
Mail Code C-014
La Jolla, CA 92093
Phone: (619) 534-1246
email: burkhard@uscd.edu

University of California at Santa Barbara
Department of Computer Science
College of Engineering
Santa Barbara, CA 93106
Phone: (805) 893-4321
email: grad-advisor@cs.ucsb.edu

University of Illinois at Urbana-Champaign
Department of Computer Science
1304 W. Springfield Avenue
Urbana, Illinois 61801
Phone: (217) 333-3373
email: lawrie@cs.uiuc.edu

University of Maryland
Department of Computer Science
A.V. Williams Building
College Park, MD 20742-3255
Phone: (301) 405-2661
email: tripathi@mimsy.umd.edu

Univerisity of Minnesota
Department of Computer Science
200 Union Street, SE
4-192 EE/CSci Building
Minneapolis, MN 55455-0159
Phone: (612) 625-4002
email: fox@umn-cs.cs.umn.edu

University of North Carolina at Chapel Hill
Department of Computer Science
Sitterson Hall, CB#3175
Chapel Hill, NC 27599-3175
Phone: (919) 962-1777
email: weiss@cs.unc.edu

University of Pennsylvania
Department of Computer and Information
Science
Philadelphia, PA 19104-6389
Phone: (215) 898-0051
email: badler@central.cis.upenn.edu

University of Pittsburgh
Department of Computer Science
323 Alumni Hall
Pittsburgh, PA 15260
Phone: (412) 624-8493
email: chang@cs.pittsburgh.edu

University of Rochester
Department of Computer Science
Wilson Blvd.
Rochester, NY 14627-0226
Phone: (716) 275-5478
email: leblanc@cs.rochester.edu

University of Southern California
Department of Computer Science
University Park
Los Angeles, CA 90089-0782
Phone: (213) 740-1460
email: horowitz@pollux.usc.edu

University of Texas at Austin
Department of Computer Sciences
Taylor Hall 2.124
Austin, TX 78712-1188
Phone: (512) 471-7316
Fax: (512) 471-0548
email: aldale@cs.utexas.edu

University of Utah
Department of Computer Science
3160 Merrill Engineering Bldg.
Salt Lake City, UT 84112
Phone: (801) 581-7026
email: ksmith@cs.umd.edu

University of Washington
Department of Computer Science and
Engineering
Seattle, Washington 98195
Phone: (206) 543-1695
email: baer@cs.washington.edu

University of Wisconsin
Department of Computer Science
1210 West Dayton
Madison, WI 53706
Phone: (608) 262-1204
email: dyer@cs.wisc.edu

Yale University
Department of Computer Science
P.O. Box 2158, Yale Station
New Haven, CT 06520
Phone: (203) 432-1200
email: schultz-martin@cs.yale.edu

Abbreviations of Universities

Brown	-	Brown University
CMU	-	Carnegie Mellon University
Columbia	-	Columbia University
Cornell	-	Cornell University
Duke	-	Duke University
George Mason	-	George Mason University
GeorgiaTech	-	Georgia Institute of Technology
Indiana	-	Indiana University
MIT	-	Massachusetts Institute of Technology
Northwestern	-	Northwestern University
NYU	-	New York University
Ohio	-	Ohio State University
Penn State	-	Pennsylvania State University
Princeton	-	Princeton University
Rice	-	Rice University
Rochester	-	University of Rochester
Rutgers	-	Rutgers University
Stanford	-	Stanford University
SUNY Buffalo	-	State University of New York at Buffalo
SUNY Stony Brook	-	State University of New York at Stony Brook
Syracuse	-	Syracuse University
UC/Berkeley	-	University of California at Berkeley
UC/Irvine	-	University of California at Irvine
UC/San Diego	-	University of California at San Diego
UC/Santa Barbara	-	University of California at Santa Barbara
UCLA	-	University of California at Los Angeles
UNC/Chapel Hill	-	University of North Carolina at Chapel Hill
Univ. Arizona	-	University of Arizona
Univ. Ill.	-	University of Illinois at Urbana-Champaign
Univ. Maryland	-	University of Maryland
Univ. Minnesota	-	University of Minnesota
Univ. Penn.	-	University of Pennsylvania
Univ. Pittsb.	-	University of Pittsburgh
Univ. Texas	-	University of Texas at Austin
Univ. Utah	-	University of Utah
Univ. Wash.	-	University of Washington
Univ. Wisconsin	-	University of Wisconsin at Madison
USC	-	University of Southern California
Yale	-	Yale University

Aagaard, James S. - Northwestern
Abbadi, Amr El - UC/Santa Barbara
Abdel-Motaleb, Ibrahim M. - Northwestern
Abelson, Harold - MIT
Abramson, Bruce - USC
Acharya, Raj - SUNY Buffalo
Acquah, James B. - George Mason
Adleman, Leonard - USC
Agarwal, Anant - MIT
Agarwal, Pankaj K. - Duke
Agha, Gul - Univ. Ill.
Agrawal, Divyakant - UC/Santa Barbara
Agrawala, Ashkok K. - Univ. Maryland
Ahamad, Mustaque - GeorgiaTech
Ahuja, Mohan - Ohio
Akyildiz, Ian F. - GeorgiaTech
Allen, James F. - Rochester
Allen, Jonathan - MIT
Allen, Peter - Columbia
Aloimonos, John (Yiannis) - Univ. Maryland
Alonso, Rafael - Princeton
Amarel, Saul - Rutgers
Ammar, Mostafa H. - GeorgiaTech
Anandan, P. - Yale
Anderson, James H. - Univ. Maryland
Anderson, Richard - Univ. Wash.
Anderson, Thomas - UC/Berkeley
Andrews, Gregory R. - Univ. Arizona
Aoki, Masanao - UCLA
Appel, Andrew - Princeton
Appelbe, William F. - GeorgiaTech
Arbib, Michael - USC
Arkin, Ronald C. - GeorgiaTech
Arvind - MIT
Athas, William C. - Univ. Texas
Austing, Richard - Univ. Maryland
Avizienis, Algirdas - UCLA
Bach, Eric - Univ. Wisconsin
Bachmair, Leo - SUNY Stony Brook
Baden, Scott B. - UC/San Diego
Badler, Norman I. - Univ. Penn.
Badr, Hussein G. - SUNY Stony Brook
Badre, Albert N. - GeorgiaTech
Badrinath, B.R. - Rutgers

Baer, Jean-Loup - Univ. Wash.
Bagherzadeh, Nader - UC/Irvine
Bagrodia, Rajive - UCLA
Bailey, Mary L. - Univ. Arizona
Bajcsy, Ruzena - Univ. Penn.
Ballard, Dana H. - Rochester
Bandopadhay, Amit - SUNY Stony Brook
Bareiss, Erwin H. - Northwestern
Barlow, Jesse - Penn State
Barry, Phillip - Univ. Minnesota
Barsky, Brian A. - UC/Berkeley
Barwise, K. Jon - Indiana
Basili, Victor R. - Univ. Maryland
Batory, Don S. - Univ. Texas
Bayliss, Alvin - Northwestern
Beame, Paul - Univ. Wash.
Beaver, Donald R. - Penn State
Beigel, Richard - Yale
Bekey, George A. - USC
Belew, Richard K. - UC/San Diego
Belford, Geneva G. - Univ. Ill.
Berger, Marsha - NYU
Berkling, Klaus J. - Syracuse
Berman, Francine D. - UC/San Diego
Berman, Piotr - Penn State
Bernstein, Arthur J. - SUNY Stony Brook
Berry, Daniel M. - UCLA
Berwick, Robert C. - MIT
Berztiss, Alfs T. - Univ. Pittsb.
Bhatt, Sandeep - Yale
Bianchini, Ronald P., Jr. - CMU
Bic, Lubimir - UC/Irvine
Biermann, Alan W. - Duke
Binford, Thomas O. - Stanford
Birman, Kenneth P. - Cornell
Birnbaum, Lawrence A. - Northwestern
Blair, Howard A. - Syracuse
Bledsoe, W. W. - Univ. Texas
Blelloch, Guy E. - CMU
Bloom, Bard - Cornell
Blough, Douglas M. - UC/Irvine
Blum, Edward K. - USC
Blum, Lenore C. - UC/Berkeley
Blum, Manuel - UC/Berkeley
Boley, Daniel - Univ. Minnesota
Boppana, Ravi - NYU
Bork, Alfred M. - UC/Irvine
Borning, Alan - Univ. Wash.
Borriello, Gaetano - Univ. Wash.

Boult, Terrance E. - Columbia
Bowman, C. Mic - Penn State
Boyer, Robert S. - Univ. Texas
Bradley, Laurette A. - UC/San Diego
Breazu-Tannen, Val - Univ. Penn.
Breuer, Melvin A. - USC
Brookes, Stephen D. - CMU
Brooks, Frederick P., Jr. - UNC/Chapel Hill
Brooks, Rodney A. - MIT
Brown, Allen, Jr. - Syracuse
Brown, Christopher M. - Rochester
Browne, J.C. - Univ. Texas
Bruderlin, Beat - Univ. Utah
Brunnett, Guido - Univ. Wisconsin
Bruno, John L. - UC/Santa Barbara
Bryant, Randal E. - CMU
Buchanan, Bruce - Univ. Pittsb.
Buchanan, Bruce G. - CMU
Bui, Thang N. - Penn State
Buneman, Peter - Univ. Penn.
Burkhard, Walter A. - UC/San Diego
Burns, James E. - GeorgiaTech
Burns, Steve - Univ. Wash.
Butz, Arthur R. - Northwestern
Bylander, Thomas C. - Ohio
Cai, Jim-Yi - Princeton
Calingaert, Peter - UNC/Chapel Hill
Campbell, Roy H. - Univ. Ill.
Canny, John F. - UC/Berkeley
Cantor, David G. - UCLA
Cappello, Peter R. - UC/Santa Barbara
Carbonell, Jaime G. - CMU
Cardenas, Alfonso F. - UCLA
Carey, Michael J. - Univ. Wisconsin
Carlis, John - Univ. Minnesota
Carlyle, Jack W. - UCLA
Carr, John W. III - Univ. Penn.
Carson, Scott D. - Univ. Maryland
Cartwright, Robert S. - Rice
Carver, Richard H. - George Mason
Chakravarty, Sreejit - SUNY Buffalo
Chambers, Craig - Univ. Wash.
Chandrasekaran, Balakrishnan - Ohio
Chang, Robert - Northwestern
Chang, Shi-Kuo - Univ. Pittsb.
Charniak, Eugene - Brown
Chazelle, Bernard - Princeton
Chen, Mrina - Yale
Cheng, Chung-Kuan - UC/San Diego

Cheriton, David A. - Stanford
Chiaraviglio, Lucio - GeorgiaTech
Chiarulli, Donald M. - Univ. Pittsb.
Chien, Andrew C. - Univ. Ill.
Choi, Yoon-Hwa - Univ. Minnesota
Choo, Young-il - Yale
Chowdhury, Shyamal - Duke
Chronopoulos, Anthony - Univ. Minnesota
Chu, Wesley W. - UCLA
Chu, Yaohan - Univ. Maryland
Chuang, Henry H. - Univ. Pittsb.
Chvatal, Vaclav - Rutgers
Clarke, Edmund M., Jr. - CMU
Cline, Alan K. - Univ. Texas
Coggins, James M. - UNC/Chapel Hill
Cohen, Elaine - Univ. Utah
Cole, Richard - NYU
Coleman, Thomas - Cornell
Collins, Gregg C. - Northwestern
Condon, Anne - Univ. Wisconsin
Constable, Robert L. - Cornell
Cooper, Eric C. - CMU
Cooper, Keith D. - Rice
Copper, Paul - Northwestern
Corbato, Fernando J. - MIT
Cottrell, Garrison W. - UC/San Diego
Cox, Alan - Rice
Culler, David E. - UC/Berkeley
Dale, A.G. - Univ. Texas
Daley, Robert - Univ. Pittsb.
Dally, William J. - MIT
Dantzig, George B. - Stanford
Danzig, Peter B. - USC
Dasgupta, Partha - GeorgiaTech
Davidson, Susan - Univ. Penn.
Davis, Alan Mark - George Mason
Davis, Ernest - NYU
Davis, Larry S. - Univ. Maryland
Davis, Martin - NYU
Davis, Randall - MIT
De Jong, Kenneth A. - George Mason
De Leone, Renato - Univ. Wisconsin
de Boor, Carl - Univ. Wisconsin
Dean, Thomas L. - Brown
Debray, Saumya - Univ. Arizona
DeJong, Gerald F. - Univ. Ill.
Demmel, James - UC/Berkeley
DeRose, Tony - Univ. Wash.

Dershowitz, Nachum - Univ. Ill.
Dertouzos, Michael L. - MIT
Desautels, Edouard J. - Univ. Wisconsin
Despain, Alvin M. - USC
Dewar, Robert - NYU
DeWitt, David J. - Univ. Wisconsin
Dietz, Paul F. - Rochester
Dijkstra, Edsger Wybe - Univ. Texas
Dill, David L. - Stanford
Dillencourt, Michael - UC/Irvine
Dillon, Laura - UC/Santa Barbara
Director, Stephen W. - CMU
DiStefano, Joseph J., III - UCLA
Djidjev, Hristo - Rice
Dobkin, David - Princeton
Doeppner, Thomas W. - Brown
Donald, Bruce R. - Cornell
Downey, Peter J. - Univ. Arizona
Du, David - Univ. Minnesota
Duchamp, Daniel J. - Columbia
Dugan, Joanne Bechta - Duke
Dunn, J. Michael - Indiana
Dutt, Nikil - UC/Irvine
Dwyer, Thomas A. - Univ. Pittsb.
Dybvig, R. Kent - Indiana
Dyer, Charles R. - Univ. Wisconsin
Dyer, Michael G. - UCLA
Dymond, Patrick W. - UC/San Diego
Ebeling, Carl - Univ. Wash.
Eberlein, Patricia James - SUNY Buffalo
Edelsbrunner, Herbert, - Univ. Ill.
Edmondson, H.P. - Univ. Maryland
Egecioglu, Omer - UC/Santa Barbara
Eggers, Susan - Univ. Wash.
Eiselt, Kurt P. - GeorgiaTech
Eisenstat, Stanley - Yale
Elias, Peter - MIT
Elkan, Charles P. - UC/San Diego
Ellis, Carla Schlatter - Duke
Ellis, John L. - Duke
Elman, Howard - Univ. Maryland
Emerson, E. Allen - Univ. Texas
Enslow, Philip H., Jr. - GeorgiaTech
Ercegovac, Milos D. - UCLA
Erdmann, Michael A. - CMU
Estrin, Deborah - USC
Estrin, Gerald - UCLA
Estrin, Thelma - UCLA

Etzioni, Oren - Univ. Wash.
Evans, David A. - CMU
Faiman, M. - Univ. Ill.
Faloutsos, Christos - Univ. Maryland
Farber, David - Univ. Penn.
Farotimi, Oluseyi O. - George Mason
Fateman, Richard J. - UC/Berkeley
Feigenbaum, Edward A. - Stanford
Feiner, Steven - Columbia
Feldman, Jerome A. - UC/Berkeley
Feldman, Julian - UC/Irvine
Ferrari, Domenico - UC/Berkeley
Ferris, Michael C. - Univ. Wisconsin
Fischer, Charles N. - Univ. Wisconsin
Fischer, Michael J. - Yale
Fisher, Allan L. - CMU
Fitzwater, Donald R. - Univ. Wisconsin
Floyd, Robert W. - Stanford
Flynn, Michael J. - Stanford
Foley, James D. - GeorgiaTech
Forbus, Kenneth - Northwestern
Fowler, Robert J. - Rochester
Fox, David W. - Univ. Minnesota
Fox, Geoffrey - Syracuse
Fox, Mark S. - CMU
Frankowski, K.S. - Univ. Minnesota
Fredman, Michael L. - Rutgers
Freeman, Peter - UC/Irvine
Freeman, Peter A. - GeorgiaTech
Freyd, Peter - Univ. Penn.
Friedberg, Stuart A. - Univ. Wisconsin
Frieder, Gideon - Syracuse
Frieder, Ophir - George Mason
Friedman, Daniel P. - Indiana
Friedman, H.G., Jr. - Univ. Ill.
Friedman, Joel - Princeton
Frisch, A.M. - Univ. Ill.
Fuchs, Henry - UNC/Chapel Hill
Fujimoto, Richard M. - GeorgiaTech
Fujimura, Kikuo - Ohio
Fulk, Mark A. - Rochester
Furst, Merrick L. - CMU
Furuta, Richard - Univ. Maryland
Fussell, Donald S. - Univ. Texas
Fürer, Martin - Penn State
Gafni, Eleizer - UCLA
Gajski, Daniel D. - UC/Irvine
Galil, Zvi - Columbia
Gallier, Jean - Univ. Penn.

Gannon, Dennis - Indiana
Gannon, John - Univ. Maryland
Garcia-Molina, Hector - Princeton
Gardiner, Judith D. - Ohio
Gardner, Carl L. - Duke
Gasarch, William I. - Univ. Maryland
Gasser, Les - USC
Gasser, Michael - Indiana
Gazit, Hillel - Duke
Gelernter, David - Yale
Gelernter, Herbert - SUNY Stony Brook
Gelsey, Andrew - Rutgers
Genesereth, Michael R. - Stanford
Gerber, Richard - Univ. Maryland
Gerla, Mario - UCLA
Ghandeharizadeh, Shahram - USC
Giacalone, Alessandro - SUNY Stony Brook
Gifford, David K. - MIT
Gini, Maria - Univ. Minnesota
Ginosar, Ran - Univ. Utah
Ginsburg, Seymour - USC
Goda, John J., Jr. - GeorgiaTech
Goel, Ashok K. - GeorgiaTech
Goldberg, Andrew V. - Stanford
Goldberg, Benjamin - NYU
Goldberg, Kenneth - USC
Golde, Hellmut - Univ. Wash.
Goldman, Ron - Rice
Goldstein, Max - NYU
Goldstine, Jonathan - Penn State
Goldwasser, Shafrira - MIT
Golin, Eric J. - Univ. Ill.
Golub, Gene H. - Stanford
Gonzalez, Teofilo F. - UC/Santa Barbara
Goodman, James R. - Univ. Wisconsin
Gopalakrishnan, Ganesh C. - Univ. Utah
Gottlieb, Allan - NYU
Gouda, Mohamed G. - Univ. Texas
Graham, Susan L. - UC/Berkeley
Granger, Richard H. - UC/Irvine
Greenberg, Donald P. - Cornell
Greenside, Henry S. - Duke
Greibach, Sheila A. - UCLA
Gries, David - Cornell
Grigoriadis, Michael D. - Rutgers
Grimson, William E.L. - MIT
Grishman, Ralph - NYU
Griswold, Ralph E. - Univ. Arizona

Gross, Jonathan L. - Columbia
Gross, Thomas R. - CMU
Guenter, Brian K. - GeorgiaTech
Guibas, Leonidas J. - Stanford
Gunter, Carl - Univ. Penn.
Gupta, Anoop - Stanford
Gupta, Rajiv - Univ. Pittsb.
Gurari, Eitan M. - Ohio
Guttag, John V. - MIT
Habermann, A. Nico - CMU
Haddad, Abraham H. - Northwestern
Hagstrom, Stanley - Indiana
Halton, John H. - UNC/Chapel Hill
Hamburger, Henry J. - George Mason
Hammer, Peter L. - Rutgers
Hanks, Steve - Univ. Wash.
Hanrahan, Patrick - Princeton
Hansen, Per Brinch - Syracuse
Hanson, Andrew J. - Indiana
Hanson, David - Princeton
Harandi, Mehdi T. - Univ. Ill.
Harrison, Malcolm - NYU
Harrison, Michael A. - UC/Berkeley
Hartmanis, Juris - Cornell
Hartmann, Carlos R.P. - Syracuse
Hayes, C.C. - Univ. Ill.
Haynes, Christopher T. - Indiana
He, Xin (Roger) - SUNY Buffalo
Hedlund, Kye S. - UNC/Chapel Hill
Held, James - Univ. Minnesota
Heller, Jack - SUNY Stony Brook
Hellerstein, Lisa - Northwestern
Hemachandra, Lane A. - Rochester
Henderson, Peter B. - SUNY Stony Brook
Henderson, Thomas C. - Univ. Utah
Hendler, James A. - Univ. Maryland
Hennessy, John L. - Stanford
Hennie, Frederick C. III - MIT
Henschen, Lawrence J. - Northwestern
Herlihy, Maurice P. - CMU
Herrera, Jorge L. Diaz - George Mason
Hewitt, Carl E. - MIT
Hilfinger, Paul N. - UC/Berkeley
Hill, Mark D. - Univ. Wisconsin
Hirschberg, Daniel - UC/Irvine
Hirsh, Haym - Rutgers
Hoare, Charles Anthony Richard - Univ. Texas
Hodges, Larry F. - GeorgiaTech
Hoffman, Donald - UC/Irvine

Hofstadter, Douglas R. - Indiana
Holden, Alistair D. C. - Univ. Wash.
Hollaar, Lee A. - Univ. Utah
Holliday, Mark A. - Duke
Hopcroft, John E. - Cornell
Horn, Berthold K.P. - MIT
Horowitz, Ellis - USC
Horwitz, Susan - Univ. Wisconsin
Howden, William E. - UC/San Diego
Howe, Douglas J. - Cornell
Hsiang, Jieh - SUNY Stony Brook
Hu, T.C. - UC/San Diego
Huang, Chua-Huang - Ohio
Huang, Ming-Deh - USC
Hudak, Paul - Yale
Hudson, Scott - Univ. Arizona
Hughes, John F. - Brown
Hull, Jonathan J. - SUNY Buffalo
Hull, Richard - USC
Hummel, Robert - NYU
Hurley, William D. - Univ. Pittsb.
Huttenlocher, Daniel P. - Cornell
Hwang, Kai - USC
Ibarra, Oscar H. - UC/Santa Barbara
Ierardi, Douglas - USC
Ioannidis, Yannis E. - Univ. Wisconsin
Ipsen, Ilse - Yale
Irwin, Mary Jane - Penn State
Jacobs, Dean - USC
Janardan, Ravi - Univ. Minnesota
Jayaraman, Bharadwaj - SUNY Buffalo
Jayasimha, Doddaballapur N. - Ohio
Jeffay, Kevin - UNC/Chapel Hill
Jefferson, David - UCLA
Jensen, Alton P. - GeorgiaTech
Johnson, Gerald G., Jr. - Penn State
Johnson, Ralph E. - Univ. Ill.
Johnson, Robert R. - Univ. Utah
Johnson, Steven D. - Indiana
Johnsson, Lennart - Yale
Jones, L.G. - Univ. Ill.
Jordan, Scott - Northwestern
Joseph, Deborah A. - Univ. Wisconsin
Joshi, Aravind K. - Univ. Penn.
Kaelbling, Leslie P. - Brown
Kahan, William M. - UC/Berkeley
Kahn, Jeffry, - Rutgers
Kahng, Andrew B. - UCLA
Kaiser, Frances E. - GeorgiaTech

Kaiser, Gail E. - Columbia
Kalay, Jehuda - SUNY Buffalo
Kale, L.V. - Univ. Ill.
Kalyanasundaram, Bala - Univ. Pittsb.
Kamin, S.N. - Univ. Ill.
Kanade, Takeo - CMU
Kanal, Laveen N. - Univ. Maryland
Kanellakis, Paris C. - Brown
Kannan, Ravindran - CMU
Kannan, Sampath - Univ. Arizona
Kannwurf, Carl R. - Northwestern
Kant, Krishna - Penn State
Kao, Ming-Yang - Duke
Kaplan, Kenneth - Rutgers
Kaplan, S.M. - Univ. Ill.
Karin, Sidney - UC/San Diego
Karp, Richard M. - UC/Berkeley
Karplus, Walter J. - UCLA
Katsaggelos, Aggelos K. - Northwestern
Katz, Randy H. - UC/Berkeley
Kaufman, Arie - SUNY Stony Brook
Kedem, Gershon - Duke
Kedem, Zvi - NYU
Kehl, Theodore H. - Univ. Wash.
Kemmer, Richard A. - UC/Santa Barbara
Kender, John - Columbia
Kennedy, Ken, - Rice
Kerkhoven, T. - Univ. Ill.
Kerr, Douglas S. - Ohio
Kessler, Robert - Univ. Utah
Khachiyan, Leonid - Rutgers
Kibler, Dennis - UC/Irvine
Kifer, Michael - SUNY Stony Brook
Kim, Hyoung-Joo - GeorgiaTech
Kim, K.H. (Kane) - UC/Irvine
King, John Leslie - UC/Irvine
Kjell, Bradley - George Mason
Klein, Philip N. - Brown
Klein, Sheldon - Univ. Wisconsin
Kleinrock, Leonard - UCLA
Kling, Rob - UC/Irvine
Klinger, Allen - UCLA
Knapp, D.W. - Univ. Ill.
Knuth, Donald E. - Stanford
Ko, Ker-I - SUNY Stony Brook
Kolodner, Janet L. - GeorgiaTech
Konheim, Allan G. - UC/Santa Barbara
Korf, Richard E. - UCLA
Korner, Kim - USC
Korth, Henry F. - Univ. Texas

Kozen, Dexter - Cornell
Kraemer, Kenneth L. - UC/Irvine
Krentel, Mark - Rice
Krizanc, Danny D. - Rochester
Krueger, Phillip E. - Ohio
Krulee, Gilbert K. - Northwestern
Kruskal, Clyde P. - Univ. Maryland
Kube, Paul R. - UC/San Diego
Kubitz, W. J. - Univ. Ill.
Kuck, David J. - Univ. Ill.
Kuechlin, Wolfgang W. - Ohio
Kuipers, Benjamin J. - Univ. Texas
Kulikowski, Casimir - Rutgers
Kumar, Srikanta - Northwestern
Kumar, Vipin - Univ. Minnesota
Kunen, Kenneth - Univ. Wisconsin
Kung, H. T. - CMU
Kurdahi, Fadi - UC/Irvine
Kyburg, Jr., Henry E. - Rochester
Ladner, Richard - Univ. Wash.
Lai, Ten-Hwang - Ohio
Lam, Monica S. - Stanford
Lam, Simon S. - Univ. Texas
Lambert, Joseph M. - Penn State
Landweber, Lawrence H. - Univ. Wisconsin
Langley, Patrick - UC/Irvine
Lanka, Sitaram - Penn State
Lapaugh, Andrea - Princeton
Larmore, Lawrence - UC/Irvine
Larus, James R. - Univ. Wisconsin
Lasowska, Edward D. - Univ. Wash.
Lastra, Anselmo A. - Duke
Latombe, Jean-Claude - Stanford
Lawler, Eugene - UC/Berkeley
Lawrie, Duncan H. - Univ. Ill.
Lawton, Daryl T. - GeorgiaTech
Leake, David - Indiana
LeBlanc, Richard J., Jr. - GeorgiaTech
LeBlanc, Thomas J. - Rochester
Lee, Chung-Chieh - Northwestern
Lee, Der-Tsai - Northwestern
Lee, Dik Lun - Ohio
Lee, Insup - Univ. Penn.
Lee, Peter - CMU
Leiserson, Charles E. - MIT
Leivant, Daniel - Indiana
Lenat, Douglas B. - Stanford
Leveson, Nancy - UC/Irvine
Levoy, Mark - Stanford

Levy, Henry M. - Univ. Wash.
Levy, Saul - Rutgers
Lewis, Philip M. - SUNY Stony Brook
Li, Ching-Chung - Univ. Pittsb.
Li, Kai - Princeton
Li, Zexiang - NYU
Lifschitz, Vladimir - Univ. Texas
Lin, K.-J. - Univ. Ill.
Lin, Wei-Chung - Northwestern
Lindstrom, Gary E. - Univ. Utah
Lipton, Richard - Princeton
Liskov, Barbara H. - MIT
Litman, Diane - Columbia
Littman, David C. - George Mason
Liu, Chung L. - Univ. Ill.
Liu, J.W.-S. - Univ. Ill.
Liu, Ming T. - Ohio
Livny, Miron - Univ. Wisconsin
Long, Timothy J. - Ohio
Lopresti, Daniel - Brown
Loranzo-Pérez, Tomás - MIT
Lovász, László - Princeton
Loveland, Donald W. - Duke
Lueker, George S. - UC/Irvine
Lynch, Gary S. - UC/Irvine
Lynch, Nancy A. - MIT
Magó, Gyula A. - UNC/Chapel Hill
Maguire, Gerald Q., Jr. - Columbia
Mahaney, Stephen R. - Univ. Arizona
Malik, Jitendra - UC/Berkeley
Mallat, Stephane - NYU
Mamrak, Sandra A. - Ohio
Manber, Udi - Univ. Arizona
Mangasarian, Olvi L. - Univ. Wisconsin
Manna, Zohar - Stanford
Marcus, Marvin - UC/Santa Barbara
Marcus, Mitch - Univ. Penn.
Marhic, Michael E. - Northwestern
Mark, Leo - Univ. Maryland
Marshall, Jonathan A. - UNC/Chapel Hill
Martin, David F. - UCLA
Marzullo, Keith - Cornell
Mason, Matthew T. - CMU
Mattson, Harold F., Jr. - Syracuse
McAllester, David A. - MIT
McCarthy, John - Stanford
McCarty, L. Thorne - Rutgers
McClelland, James L. - CMU
McCluskey, Edward J. - Stanford

McCurley, E. Robert - GeorgiaTech
McDermott, Drew V. - Yale
McHugh, John - UNC/Chapel Hill
McKeown, Kathleen - Columbia
McLeod, Dennis - USC
McNamee, Lawrence - UCLA
Medioni, Gerard G. - USC
Mehrotra, Kishan G. - Syracuse
Melhem, Rami - Univ. Pittsb.
Melkanoff, Michel A. - UCLA
Meyer, Albert R. - MIT
Micali, Silvio - MIT
Michalski, Ryszard S. - George Mason
Mickunas, M.D. - Univ. Ill.
Miikkulainen, Risto - Univ. Texas
Miller, Barton P. - Univ. Wisconsin
Miller, Dale - Univ. Penn.
Miller, Raymond E. - Univ. Maryland
Miller, Russ - SUNY Buffalo
Miller, Webb C. - Penn State
Miller, William F. - Stanford
Mills, Jonathan W. - Indiana
Minker, Jack - Univ. Maryland
Minsky, Marvin L. - MIT
Minsky, Naftaly - Rutgers
Mintz, Max - Univ. Penn.
Miranker, Daniel P. - Univ. Texas
Miranker, Willard - Yale
Mishra, Bhubaneswar - NYU
Mishra, Prateek - SUNY Stony Brook
Misra, Jayadev - Univ. Texas
Mitchell, John C. - Stanford
Mitchell, Tom M. - CMU
Mjolsness, Eric - Yale
Mohan, Chilukuri K. - Syracuse
Mok, Aloysius K. - Univ. Texas
Mooney, Raymond J. - Univ. Texas
Moore, Johanna D. - Univ. Pittsb.
Moore, Ramon E. - Ohio
Morris, F. Lockwood - Syracuse
Morris, James H. - CMU
Moses, Joel - MIT
Moss, Lawrence S. - Indiana
Motwani, Rajeev - Stanford
Mount, David M. - Univ. Maryland
Mukherjee, Amarnath - Univ. Penn.
Muller, Mervin E. - Ohio
Muntz, Richard R. - UCLA

Muroga, Saburo - Univ. Ill.
Murphy, Gordon J. - Northwestern
Myer, Robert R. - Univ. Wisconsin
Myers, Eugene W., Jr. - Univ. Arizona
Nadathur, Gopalan - Duke
Nau, Dana S. - Univ. Maryland
Naughton, Jeffrey F. - Univ. Wisconsin
Navathe, Sham - GeorgiaTech
Nayar, Shree K. - Columbia
Neal, Jeannette G. - SUNY Buffalo
Neiger, Gil - GeorgiaTech
Nelson, Randal C. - Rochester
Nevatia, Ramakant - USC
Newell, Allen - CMU
Ng, P. - Univ. Ill.
Nicolau, Alexandru - UC/Irvine
Nilsson, Nils J. - Stanford
Nocedal, Jorge - Northwestern
Norberg, Arthur - Univ. Minnesota
Norordewier, Michiel - Rutgers
Norris, Eugene M. - George Mason
Notkin, David - Univ. Wash.
Novacky, George A., Jr. - Univ. Pittsb.
Novak, Gordon S., Jr. - Univ. Texas
O'Hearn, Peter William - Syracuse
O'Leary, Dianne P. - Univ. Maryland
O'Malley, Sean William - Univ. Texas
O'Rorke, Paul - UC/Irvine
Ogden, William F. - Ohio
Oliger, Joseph - Stanford
Omiecinski, Edward R. - GeorgiaTech
Orailoglu, Alex - UC/San Diego
Osterweil, Leon J. - UC/Irvine
Ousterhout, John K. - UC/Berkeley
Overton, Michael - NYU
Owens, Robert M. - Penn State
Pachowicz, Piotr - George Mason
Padua, David A. - Univ. Ill.
Paige, Robert - NYU
Painter, Jamie - Univ. Utah
Palis, Michael - Univ. Penn.
Panda, D. - Ohio
Pangrie, Barry M. - Penn State
Papadimitriou, Christos H. - UC/San Diego
Papadopoulos, Gregory M. - MIT
Pardalos, Panayote - Penn State
Parent, Richard E. - Ohio
Park, Haesun - Univ. Minnesota

Park, Nohbyung - UC/Irvine
Parker, D. Scott - UCLA
Parlett, Beresford N. - UC/Berkeley
Parter, Seymour V. - Univ. Wisconsin
Pasquale, Joseph C. - UC/San Diego
Patrick, Merrell L. - Duke
Patten, Terry - Ohio
Patterson, David A. - UC/Berkeley
Paturi, Ramamohan - UC/San Diego
Pauli, Marvin C. - Rutgers
Pavlidis, Theo - SUNY Stony Brook
Pawagi, Shaunak - SUNY Stony Brook
Pazzani, Michael J. - UC/Irvine
Pearl, Judea - UCLA
Perlin, Kenneth - NYU
Perlis, Donald - Univ. Maryland
Perlman, Gary - Ohio
Peterson, Gary L. - GeorgiaTech
Peterson, Larry L. - Univ. Arizona
Petrarca, Anthony E. - Ohio
Pingali, Keshav - Cornell
Pitt, L.B. - Univ. Ill.
Pizer, Stephen M. - UNC/Chapel Hill
Plaisted, David A. - UNC/Chapel Hill
Plantinga, Harry - Univ. Pittsb.
Plaxton, Greg - Univ. Texas
Plonus, Martin A. - Northwestern
Plotkin, Serge A. - Stanford
Pollack, Jordan B. - Ohio
Pollack, Richard - NYU
Polyzos, George C. - UC/San Diego
Ponce, Jean - Univ. Ill.
Pong, Ting-Chuen - Univ. Minnesota
Port, Robert F. - Indiana
Porter, Adam - Univ. Maryland
Porter, Bruce W. - Univ. Texas
Pothen, Alex - Penn State
Powell, Patrick - Univ. Minnesota
Pratt, Vaughan - Stanford
Preparata, Franco P. - Brown
Prins, Jan F. - UNC/Chapel Hill
Prosser, Franklin - Indiana
Pruhs, Kirk - Univ. Pittsb.
Pu, Calton - Columbia
Pugh, William W. - Univ. Maryland
Purdom, Paul W. - Indiana
Purtilo, James M. - Univ. Maryland
Purushothaman, S. - Penn State

Qadah, Ghassan Z. - Northwestern
Quammen, Donna J. - George Mason
Raatz, Stan - Rutgers
Rabinowitz, Irving N. - Rutgers
Raibert, Marc H. - MIT
Rajamoney, Shankar A. - USC
Ralston, Anthony - SUNY Buffalo
Ram, Ashwin - GeorgiaTech
Ramachandran, Umakishore - GeorgiaTech
Ramachandran, Vijaya - Univ. Texas
Ramakrishnan, I.V. - SUNY Stony Brook
Ramakrishnan, Raghu - Univ. Wisconsin
Ramamoorthy, Chittoor V. - UC/Berkeley
Ramanan, Prakash - UC/Santa Barbara
Ramm, Dietolf - Duke
Ranade, Abhiram - UC/Berkeley
Rangan, Venkat P. - UC/San Diego
Ranka, Sanjay - Syracuse
Rapaport, William J. - SUNY Buffalo
Rashid, Richard F. - CMU
Rawlins, Gregory J.E. - Indiana
Ray, S. R. - Univ. Ill.
Reddy, Raj - CMU
Reddy, U.S. - Univ. Ill.
Reed, Daniel A. - Univ. Ill.
Reed, Irving S. - USC
Regan, Kenneth W. - SUNY Buffalo
Reggia, James A. - Univ. Maryland
Reif, John H. - Duke
Reiss, Steven P. - Brown
Rekasius, Zenonas V. - Northwestern
Rendell, Larry A. - Univ. Ill.
Rennels, David - UCLA
Reps, Thomas - Univ. Wisconsin
Requicha, Aristides A. G. - USC
Reynolds, John C. - CMU
Rheingold, Edward M. - Univ. Ill.
Richardson, Debra J. - UC/Irvine
Richardson, Jane S. - UNC/Chapel Hill
Richter, Gerard - Rutgers
Ridsdale, Gary - Univ. Utah
Riedl, John - Univ. Minnesota
Riesbeck, Christopher K. - Northwestern
Riesenfeld, Richard F. - Univ. Utah
Rine, David - George Mason
Ristad, Eric Sven - Princeton
Rivest, Ronald L. - MIT
Robertson, Edward L. - Indiana
Robinson, J. Alan - Syracuse

Robinson, Stephen M. - Univ. Wisconsin
Rogers, Anne - Princeton
Rokhlin, Vladimir - Yale
Rombach, H. Dieter - Univ. Maryland
Ron, Amos - Univ. Wisconsin
Rose, Donald J. - Duke
Rosen, J. Ben - Univ. Minnesota
Rosenbloom, Paul - USC
Rosier, Louis E. - Univ. Texas
Roussopoulos, Nicholas - Univ. Maryland
Rowe, Lawrence A. - UC/Berkeley
Royer, James S. - Syracuse
Rudich, Steven - CMU
Rudolph, Luther D. - Syracuse
Russell, Stuart J. - UC/Berkeley
Rutenbar, Rob A. - CMU
Rutledge, Janet C. - Northwestern
Ruzzo, Walter L. - Univ. Wash.
Saad, Youcef - Univ. Minnesota
Saavedia-Barrera, Rafael - USC
Sacks, Elisha - Princeton
Sadayappan, P. - Ohio
Sahakian, Alan V. - Northwestern
Sahni, Sartaj K.- Univ. Minnesota
Saied, Faisal - Univ. Ill.
Saks, Michael - Rutgers
Saks, Michael E. - UC/San Diego
Salem, Kenneth R. - Univ. Maryland
Salton, Gerald - Cornell
Saltzer, Jerome H. - MIT
Samet, Hanan - Univ. Maryland
Sanchis, Luis - Syracuse
Sarrafzadeh, Majid - Northwestern
Satyanarayanan, M. - CMU
Savage, John E. - Brown
Savitch, Walter J. - UC/San Diego
Saylor, Paul E. - Univ. Ill.
Schank, Roger C. - Northwestern
Schäffer, Alejandro - Rice
Scherlis, William L. - CMU
Scheuermann, Peter - Northwestern
Schlichting, Richard D. - Univ. Arizona
Schmidt, Charles - Rutgers
Schneider, Fred B. - Cornell
Schnitger, Georg - Penn State
Schonberg, Edmond - NYU
Schubert, Lenhart K. - Rochester
Schultz, Martin H. - Yale
Schwan, Karsten - GeorgiaTech

Schwartz, Jacob - NYU
Scott, Dana S. - CMU
Scott, Michael L. - Rochester
Sedgewick, Robert - Princeton
Segall, Zary - CMU
Segre, Alberto M. - Cornell
Seidel, Raimund - UC/Berkeley
Seiferas, Joel I. - Rochester
Selby, Richard W. - UC/Irvine
Sellis, Timos K. - Univ. Maryland
Selman, Alan L. - SUNY Buffalo
Séquin, Carlo H. - UC/Berkeley
Shankar, A. Udaya - Univ. Maryland
Shannon, Gregory E. - Indiana
Shapiro, Linda - Univ. Wash.
Shapiro, Stuart C. - SUNY Buffalo
Shasha, Dennis - NYU
Shavlik, Jude W. - Univ. Wisconsin
Shaw, Alan C. - Univ. Wash.
Shaw, Mary - CMU
Shekhar, Shashi - Univ. Minnesota
Shelly, Anne - Syracuse
Sher, David B. - SUNY Buffalo
Shilling, John J. - GeorgiaTech
Shirley, Peter - Indiana
Shneiderman, Ben - Univ. Maryland
Shoham, Yoav - Stanford
Shragowitz, Eugene - Univ. Minnesota
Shu, Wennie Wei - SUNY Buffalo
Siegel, Alan - NYU
Siewiorek, Daniel P. - CMU
Sikorski, Kris - Univ. Utah
Silberschatz, Abraham - Univ. Texas
Simmons, Robert F. - Univ. Texas
Simon, Herbert A. - CMU
Singh, Ambuj - UC/Santa Barbara
Singhal, Mukesh - Ohio
Skeel, R. D. - Univ. Ill.
Skiena, Steven - SUNY Stony Brook
Skrzypek, Josef - UCLA
Slagle, James - Univ. Minnesota
Sleator, Daniel D. - CMU
Smith, Carl H. - Univ. Maryland
Smith, David R. - SUNY Stony Brook
Smith, F. Donelson - UNC/Chapel Hill
Smith, John B. - UNC/Chapel Hill
Smith, Kent F. - Univ. Utah
Smolka, Scott A. - SUNY Stony Brook
Snodgrass, Richard T. - Univ. Arizona

Snyder, Lawrence - Univ. Wash.
Soffa, Mary Louise - Univ. Pittsb.
Sohi, Gurindar S. - Univ. Wisconsin
Solomon, Marvin H. - Univ. Wisconsin
Somani, Arun - Univ. Wash.
Sontag, Eduardo D. - Rutgers
Sood, Arun K. - George Mason
Soundararajan, Neelamegam - Ohio
Spector, Alfred Z. - CMU
Spencer, Joel - NYU
Springer, George - Indiana
Srihari, Sargur N. - SUNY Buffalo
Srinivasan, Chitoor V. - Rutgers
Srivastava, Jaideep - Univ. Minnesota
Stanat, Donald F. - UNC/Chapel Hill
Standish, Thomas A. - UC/Irvine
Star, Susan Leigh - UC/Irvine
Stark, Eugene - SUNY Stony Brook
Starmer, C. Frank - Duke
Stasko, John T. - GeorgiaTech
Statman, Richard - CMU
Steiger, William - Rutgers
Steiglitz, Kenneth - Princeton
Stein, Lynn A. - MIT
Stein, Marvin L. - Univ. Minnesota
Stenger, Frank - Univ. Utah
Stern, Richard M. - CMU
Stewart, G.W. - Univ. Maryland
Stolfo, Salvatore - Columbia
Stonebraker, Michael R. - UC/Berkeley
Storm, Edward F. - Syracuse
Stotts, P. David - Univ. Maryland
Strikwerda, John C. - Univ. Wisconsin
Strzalkowski, Tomasz - NYU
Su, Jianwen - UC/Santa Barbara
Subrahmanian, V.S. - Univ. Maryland
Subramanian, Devika - Cornell
Suda, Tatsuya - UC/Irvine
Sullivan, Barry J. - Northwestern
Supowit, Kenneth J. - Ohio
Szemeredi, Endre, - Rutgers
Szolovits, Peter - MIT
Taflove, Allen - Northwestern
Tamassia, Roberto - Brown
Tamir, Yuval - UCLA
Tanimoto, Steven L. - Univ. Wash.
Tanner, Michael C. - George Mason
Tarjan, Robert - Princeton
Taylor, Richard - UC/Irvine

Tecuci, Gheorge - George Mason
Teitelbaum, Tim - Cornell
Tennenhouse, David L. - MIT
Thompson, William - Univ. Minnesota
Tiwari, Prasoon - Univ. Wisconsin
Tomita, Masaru - CMU
Tompa, Martin - Univ. Wash.
Toueg, Sam - Cornell
Traub, Joseph F. - Columbia
Travis, Larry E. - Univ. Wisconsin
Trefethen, Lloyd N. - Cornell
Tripathi, Anand - Univ. Minnesota
Tripathi, Satish K. - Univ. Maryland
Trivedi, Kishor S. - Duke
Tsai, Wei-Tek - Univ. Minnesota
Tyagi, Akhilesh - UNC/Chapel Hill
Tygar, Doug - CMU
Uhr, Leonard M. - Univ. Wisconsin
Uht, Augustus K. - UC/San Diego
Ullman, Jeffrey D. - Stanford
Unger, Stephen H. - Columbia
Upadhyaya, Shambu - SUNY Buffalo
Vaidya, Pravin - Univ. Ill.
Van Gucht, Dirk - Indiana
Van Hentenryck, Pascal - Brown
Van Ness, James A. - Northwestern
van Dam, Andries - Brown
van de Geijn, Robert A. - Univ. Texas
van Loan, Charles - Cornell
VanLehn, Kurt - CMU
VanLehn, Kurt - Univ. Pittsb.
VanVerth, Patricia - SUNY Buffalo
Vavasis, Stephen - Cornell
Vazirani, Umesh - UC/Berkeley
Venkatesan, Shankar - Univ. Minnesota
Venkateswaran, H. - GeorgiaTech
Vergis, Anastasios - Univ. Minnesota
Vernon, Mary K. - Univ. Wisconsin
Vianu, Victor - UC/San Diego
Vichnevetsky, Robert - Rutgers
Vidal, Jacques J. - UCLA
Vishnubhotla, Prasad - Ohio
Viswanathan, Chand R. - UCLA
Vitalari, Nicholas P. - UC/Irvine
Vitter, Jeffrey S. - Brown
von der Malsburg, Christoph - USC
Wagner, Robert A. - Duke
Walters, Deborah K.W. - SUNY Buffalo

Wang, DeLiang - Ohio
Wang, Pearl Y. - George Mason
Wang, Yuan-Fang - UC/Santa Barbara
Ward, Stephen A. - MIT
Warren, David S. - SUNY Stony Brook
Warren, Joe - Rice
Wasilewska, Anita - SUNY Stony Brook
Watanabe, Hiroyuki - UNC/Chapel Hill
Wawrzynek, John - UC/Berkeley
Wechsler, Harry - George Mason
Wegner, Peter - Brown
Weide, Bruce W. - Ohio
Weihl, William E. - MIT
Weir, David - Northwestern
Weiss, Stephen F. - UNC/Chapel Hill
Welch, Jennifer L. - UNC/Chapel Hill
Weld, Dan - Univ. Wash.
Wessels, Bruce - Northwestern
Westbrook, Jeffery R. - Yale
Weyuker, Elaine - NYU
Widlund, Olof - NYU
Wiederhold, Gio - Stanford
Wigderson, Avi - Princeton
Wilensky, Robert - UC/Berkeley
Wilkins, David C. - Univ. Ill.
Wing, Jeannette M. - CMU
Winkel, David E. - Indiana
Winograd, Terry - Stanford
Winsborough, William H. - Penn State
Winslett, Marianne S. - Univ. Ill.
Winston, Patrick H. - MIT
Wise, David S. - Indiana
Witkin, Andrew P. - CMU
Wittie, Larry D. - SUNY Stony Brook
Woll, S. Heather - UC/San Diego
Wong, Martin D.F. - Univ. Texas
Wood, David A. - Univ. Wisconsin
Wood, Roger C. - UC/Santa Barbara
Wozniakowski, Henryk - Columbia
Wright, Paul - NYU
Wu, Chi-haur - Northwestern
Yagel, Roni - Ohio
Yao, Andrew - Princeton
Yap, Chee - NYU
Yasuhara, Ann - Rutgers
Yelick, Katherine - UC/Berkeley
Yemini, Yechiam - Columbia
Yip, Kenneth Man-kam - Yale
Young, David M. - Univ. Texas

Young, Paul - Univ. Wash.
Yuen, Horace P. - Northwestern
Zachary, Joseph - Univ. Utah
Zadeck, F. Kenneth - Brown
Zadeh, Lotfi A. - UC/Berkeley
Zahorjan, John - Univ. Wash.
Zdonik, Stanley B. - Brown
Zelkowitz, Marvin V. - Univ. Maryland
Zmijewski, Earl - UC/Santa Barbara
Znati, Taieb - Univ. Pittsb.
Zuck, Lenore - Yale
Zunde, Pranas - GeorgiaTech
Zwaenepoel, Willy E. - Rice
Zweben, Stuart H. - Ohio

3D medical imaging - Fuchs, Henry
Abstract programming and specification languages - Cartwright, Robert S.
Advanced automation - Horn, Berthold K.P.
Algebraic computations - Reif, John H.
Algebraic logic - Dunn, J. Michael
Algebraic manipulation systems - Moses, Joel
Algorithm design and analysis - Cole, Richard
Algorithm design and analysis - Stanat, Donald F.
Algorithm visualization - Sedgewick, Robert
Algorithm-structured multicomputer architectures - Uhr, Leonard M.
Algorithmically-driven programming constructs - Kedem, Zvi
Algorithms - Dijkstra, Edsger Wybe
Algorithms - Fredman, Michael L.
Algorithms - Galil, Zvi
Algorithms - Greibach, Sheila A.
Algorithms - Hopcroft, John E.
Algorithms - Kahan, William M.
Algorithms - Miller, Webb C.
Algorithms - Papadimitriou, Christos H.
Algorithms - Saks, Michael E.
Algorithms - Stein, Marvin L.
Algorithms - Stenger, Frank
Algorithms - Yap, Chee
Algorithms and complexity - Carlyle, Jack W.
Algorithms and logic programming - Plaisted, David A.
Algorithms for polynomial and piecewise polynomial curves and surfaces - Goldman, Ron
Algorithms for spatial reasoning - Lozano-Pérez, Tomás
Algorithms for storing, retrieving and manipulating information - Elias, Peter
Amortized analysis - Cole, Richard
Analogical reasoning - Carbonell, Jaime G.
Analogy-based reasoning - Winston, Patrick H.
Analysis of algorithms - Chvatal, Vaclav
Analysis of algorithms - Dobkin, David
Analysis of algorithms - Eberlein, Patricia James
Analysis of algorithms - Fox, David W.
Analysis of algorithms - Hagstrom, Stanley
Analysis of algorithms - Hirschberg, Daniel
Analysis of algorithms - Knuth, Donald E.
Analysis of algorithms - Mehrotra, Kishan G.
Analysis of algorithms - Purdom, Paul W.
Analysis of algorithms - Rivest, Ronald L.
Analysis of algorithms - Schonberg, Edmond
Analysis of algorithms - Sedgewick, Robert

Analysis of algorithms - Steiger, William
Analysis of algorithms - Yao, Andrew
Analysis of empirical data in socio-economic areas - Aoki, Masanao
Analysis of large-scale systems - Rekasius, Zenonas V.
Animation - Riesenfeld, Richard F.
Application development tools - Rowe, Lawrence A.
Application of computers and concepts from computer science to education - Dwyer, Thomas A.
Application of knowledge-based systems - Moses, Joel
Application of parallelism to scientific computing - Schultz, Martin H.
Application of queueing theory - Kleinrock, Leonard
Application of technology and computer systems to health care - Estrin, Thelma
Applications of digital systems to engineering problems - Bruno, John L.
Applications of discrete mathematics - Hennie, Frederick C. III
Applications of formal methods to program and system design - Hoare, Charles Anthony Richard
Applications of information-based complexity - Traub, Joseph F.
Applications of universal algebra and category theory - Pratt, Vaughan
Applications to communications and control - Haddad, Abraham H.
Applications to psychology, education and industry - Minsky, Marvin L.
Applicative architectures - Winkel, David E.
Applicative programming - Wise, David S.
Applied algebra - Sontag, Eduardo D.
Applied analysis - Bareiss, Erwin H.
Applied linear algebra - Bareiss, Erwin H.
Applying combinatorial, probabilistic, and analytic methods to computational, scientific and
        engineering problems - Halton, John H.
Approximation theory - de Boor, Carl
Archaeology of cognition - Klein, Sheldon
Architecture - Lipton, Richard
Architecture - Steiglitz, Kenneth
Architecture for large-scale scientific computing - Patrick, Merrell L.
Artificial intelligence - Abelson, Harold
Artificial intelligence - Allen, James F.
Artificial intelligence - Amarel, Saul
Artificial intelligence - Ballard, Dana H.
Artificial intelligence - Bekey, George A.
Artificial intelligence - Bledsoe, W. W.
Artificial intelligence - Boyer, Robert S.
Artificial intelligence - Brown, Christopher M.
Artificial intelligence - Buchanan, Bruce
Artificial intelligence - Buchanan, Bruce G.
Artificial intelligence - Carbonell, Jaime G.
Artificial intelligence - Chandrasekaran, Balakrishnan
Artificial intelligence - Charniak, Eugene
Artificial intelligence - Davis, Larry S.
Artificial intelligence - Davis, Randall
Artificial intelligence - Dershowitz, Nachum
Artificial intelligence - Dyer, Charles R.

Automata - Scott, Dana S.
Automata and formal languages - Greibach, Sheila A.
Automata theory - Hennie, Frederick C. III
Automata theory - Lewis, Philip M.
Automated deduction - Gallier, Jean
Automated deduction - Kunen, Kenneth
Automated deduction - Manna, Zohar
Automated manufacturing - Wright, Paul
Automated reasoning - Constable, Robert L.
Automated reasoning - Feigenbaum, Edward A.
Automated reasoning - Nilsson, Nils J.
Automated reasoning - Pearl, Judea
Automated theorem proving - Loveland, Donald W.
Automatic code generation - Fischer, Charles N.
Automatic detection and processing of radar data - Reed, Irving S.
Automatic planning - Schubert, Lenhart K.
Automatic programming - Biermann, Alan W.
Automatic programming - Cardenas, Alfonso F.
Automatic target recognition - Wechsler, Harry
Automatic theorem proving - Bledsoe, W. W.
Automatic theorem proving - Boyer, Robert S.
Behavior synthesis - Simmons, Robert F.
Biological computation - Feldman, Jerome A.
Biological modeling - Starmer, C. Frank
Biological motor systems - Raibert, Marc H.
Biomedical computing - Bajcsy, Ruzena
Biomedical computing - Ray, S. R.
Biomedical research data management - Starmer, C. Frank
Boolean methods in operations research and related areas - Hammer, Peter L.
Brain theory in artificial intelligence - Arbib, Michael
Built-in self-test designs - McCluskey, Edward J.
CAD - Breuer, Melvin A.
CAD - Greenberg, Donald P.
CAD - Melkanoff, Michel A.
CAD design - Gonzalez, Teofilo F.
CAD design - Hu, T.C.
CAD design - Kulikowski, Casimir
CAD design of VLSI circuits - Séquin, Carlo H.
CAD for VLSI circuits - Director, Stephen W.
CAD of digital systems - Faiman, M.
CAD of digital systems - Kubitz, W. J.
CAD of digital systems - Liu, Chung L.
CAD of digital systems - Muroga, Saburo
CAD of digital systems - Unger, Stephen H.
CAD tools - Allen, Jonathan
CAD tools - Irwin, Mary Jane
Capacity planning of computer systems - McNamee, Lawrence

Case-based reasoning - Kolodner, Janet L.
Category theory - Freyd, Peter
Category theory - Meyer, Albert R.
Causal reasoning about designed artifacts - Davis, Randall
Cellular communication - Starmer, C. Frank
Charge-coupled devices - Viswanathan, Chand R.
Circuit complexity - Saks, Michael E.
Clustering - Michalski, Ryszard S.
Coding theory - Mehrotra, Kishan G.
Cognition - Newell, Allen
Cognitive mapping - McDermott, Drew V.
Cognitive science - Hofstadter, Douglas R.
Cognitive science - Joshi, Aravind K.
Cognitive science - Kolodner, Janet L.
Cognitive science - Kyburg, Henry E., Jr.
Cognitive science - Schank, Roger C.
Cognitive science - Shapiro, Stuart C.
Cognitive science and multiple-valued logic - Michalski, Ryszard S.
Collaboration support systems - Weiss, Stephen F.
Combinatorial algorithms - Hu, T.C.
Combinatorial algorithms - Lawler, Eugene
Combinatorial and discrete mathematics - Ralston, Anthony
Combinatorial database theory - Papadimitriou, Christos H.
Combinatorial mathematics - Dantzig, George B.
Combinatorial mathematics - Knuth, Donald E.
Combinatorial optimization - Kanellakis, Paris C.
Combinatorial optimization - Lovász, László
Combinatorial optimization - Steiglitz, Kenneth
Combinatorial, parallel and randomized algorithms - Karp, Richard M.
Combinatorics - Chvatal, Vaclav
Combinatorics - Edelsbrunner, Herbert
Combinatorics - Fredman, Michael L.
Combinatorics - Kahn, Jeffry
Combinatorics - Osterweil, Leon J.
Combinatorics - Rheingold, Edward M.
Combinatorics - Saks, Michael E.
Combinatorics - Spencer, Joel
Combinatorics and graph theory - Statman, Richard
Communication networks - Campbell, Roy H.
Communication networks - Faiman, M.
Communication networks - Liu, J.W.-S.
Communication protocols - Lam, Simon S.
Communication, control, translator, application software systems - Calingaert, Peter
Communications - Murphy, Gordon J.
Communications and distributed systems - Weiss, Stephen F.
Communications networks - Hollaar, Lee A.
Compacting PLA and Weinberger's array - Hu, T.C.

Compiler design - Schonberg, Edmond
Compiler optimization - Schwartz, Jacob
Compiler technology - Hennessy, John L.
Compiler theory and design - Fischer, Charles N.
Compilers - Dewar, Robert
Compilers - Gallier, Jean
Compilers - Golde, Hellmut
Compilers - LeBlanc, Richard J., Jr.
Compilers - Lewis, Philip M.
Compilers - Purdom, Paul W.
Compilers - Rabinowitz, Irving N.
Compilers - Reiss, Steven P.
Compilers - Stein, Marvin L.
Compilers of parallel systems - Soffa, Mary Louise
Complex analysis - Springer, George
Complexity - Lipton, Richard
Complexity - Papadimitriou, Christos H.
Complexity - Smith, Kent F.
Complexity - Tarjan, Robert
Complexity - Yap, Chee
Complexity of dynamic data structures - Saks, Michael E.
Complexity theory - Adleman, Leonard
Complexity theory - Fredman, Michael L.
Complexity theory - Greibach, Sheila A.
Complexity theory - Lynch, Nancy A.
Complexity theory - Savitch, Walter J.
Computability, and connections with mathematical logic - Young, Paul
Computational analysis of spoken language - Marcus, Mitch
Computational biology - Lawler, Eugene
Computational complexity - Bareiss, Erwin H.
Computational complexity - Blum, Manuel
Computational complexity - Daley, Robert
Computational complexity - Fischer, Michael J.
Computational complexity - Hartmanis, Juris
Computational complexity - Ibarra, Oscar H.
Computational complexity - Khachiyan, Leonid
Computational complexity - Ko, Ker-I
Computational complexity - Kozen, Dexter
Computational complexity - Ladner, Richard
Computational complexity - Lee, Chung-Chieh
Computational complexity - Lee, Der-Tsai
Computational complexity - Lewis, Philip M.
Computational complexity - Lueker, George S.
Computational complexity - Meyer, Albert R.
Computational complexity - Robertson, Edward L.
Computational complexity - Ruzzo, Walter L.
Computational complexity - Saks, Michael E.

Computer architecture - Kuck, David J.
Computer architecture - Kung, H. T.
Computer architecture - Lawrie, Duncan H.
Computer architecture - Magó, Gyula A.
Computer architecture - Ramamoorthy, Chittoor V.
Computer architecture - Séquin, Carlo H.
Computer architecture - Smith, David R.
Computer architecture - Srihari, Sargur N.
Computer architecture - Ward, Stephen A.
Computer architecture - Wittie, Larry D.
Computer architecture - Wood, Roger C.
Computer architecture and organization - Flynn, Michael J.
Computer architecture and organization - Liu, Ming T.
Computer architecture systems - Reed, Daniel A.
Computer architectures - Tripathi, Satish K.
Computer arithmetic - Avizienis, Algirdas
Computer arithmetics - Irwin, Mary Jane
Computer arithmetics - Kahan, William M.
Computer arithmetics - Preparata, Franco P.
Computer communication - Chu, Wesley W.
Computer communication - Konheim, Allan G.
Computer communication theory - Ladner, Richard
Computer communications and networking - Liu, Ming T.
Computer conferencing - Unger, Stephen H.
Computer design - Kehl, Theodore H.
Computer design - Schwartz, Jacob
Computer design: reliable computers and manufacturing test - McCluskey, Edward J.
Computer graphics - Badler, Norman I.
Computer graphics - Barsky, Brian A.
Computer graphics - Bork, Alfred M.
Computer graphics - Campbell, Roy H.
Computer graphics - Dyer, Charles R.
Computer graphics - Fuchs, Henry
Computer graphics - Greenberg, Donald P.
Computer graphics - Guibas, Leonidas J.
Computer graphics - Hagstrom, Stanley
Computer graphics - Hanrahan, Patrick
Computer graphics - Kaufman, Arie
Computer graphics - Klinger, Allen
Computer graphics - Kubitz, W. J.
Computer graphics - Pavlidis, Theo
Computer graphics - Raibert, Marc H.
Computer graphics - Riesenfeld, Richard F.
Computer graphics - Tanimoto, Steven L.
Computer graphics - van Dam, Andries
Computer graphics and geometric modeling - Séquin, Carlo H.
Computer hardware - Hagstrom, Stanley

Computer methods for partial differential equations - Vichnevetsky, Robert
Computer methods in neuroscience - Estrin, Thelma
Computer modeling - McNamee, Lawrence
Computer networking and distributed systems - Ramamoorthy, Chittoor V.
Computer networks - Enslow, Philip H., Jr.
Computer networks - Ferrari, Domenico
Computer networks - Golde, Hellmut
Computer networks - Lam, Simon S.
Computer networks - Lee, Chung-Chieh
Computer networks - Manber, Udi
Computer networks - Miller, Raymond E.
Computer networks - Saltzer, Jerome H.
Computer networks - Solomon, Marvin H.
Computer networks - Sood, Arun K.
Computer networks - Tripathi, Satish K.
Computer networks and interconnection topologies - Wittie, Larry D.
Computer networks and protocols - Landweber, Lawrence
Computer processing of natural language - Krulee, Gilbert K.
Computer productivity - Dertouzos, Michael L.
Computer program testing - Chandrasekaran, Balakrishnan
Computer programming theory - Blum, Edward K.
Computer science education - Prosser, Franklin
Computer science theory - Blum, Lenore C.
Computer security - Harrison, Michael A.
Computer software - Harrison, Michael A.
Computer software diagnosis - Kahan, William M.
Computer supported cooperative work - Winograd, Terry
Computer system architecture - Avizienis, Algirdas
Computer system modeling - Wood, Roger C.
Computer system performance and performance evaluation - Muntz, Richard R.
Computer system security and reliability - Kemmer, Richard A.
Computer systems - Enslow, Philip H., Jr.
Computer systems - Ferrari, Domenico
Computer systems - Konheim, Allan G.
Computer systems - Saltzer, Jerome H.
Computer systems - Zahorjan, John
Computer systems design - Miller, William F.
Computer systems: modeling and analysis - Lasowska, Edward D.
Computer technology and public policy - Kling, Rob
Computer version - Bajcsy, Ruzena
Computer vision - Brown, Christopher M.
Computer vision - Davis, Larry S.
Computer vision - Dyer, Charles R.
Computer vision - Kanade, Takeo
Computer vision - Kanal, Laveen N.
Computer vision - Kaufman, Arie
Computer vision - Klinger, Allen

Computer vision - Li, Ching-Chung
Computer vision - Sahni, Sartaj K.
Computer vision - Shapiro, Linda
Computer vision - Sood, Arun K.
Computer vision and robotics - Ballard, Dana H.
Computer-aided geometric design - Riesenfeld, Richard F.
Computer-aided geometric design and modeling - Barsky, Brian A.
Computer-aided learning - Jensen, Alton P.
Computer-assisted collaboration - Estrin, Gerald
Computer-based learning - Bork, Alfred M.
Computer-integrated manufacturing - Melkanoff, Michel A.
Computer-integrated manufacturing - Rowe, Lawrence A.
Computer-supported cooperative work - Calingaert, Peter
Computer-supported instruction - Chiaraviglio, Lucio
Computers and education - Schank, Roger C.
Computers to aid the handicapped - Ladner, Richard
Computing management - Travis, Larry E.
Computing with symbolic expressions - McCarthy, John
Conceptual clustering - Michalski, Ryszard S.
Conceptual database models - Wiederhold, Gio
Concrete complexity - Hirschberg, Daniel
Concrete computational complexity - Eisenstat, Stanley
Concurrent algorithms - Fox, Geoffrey
Concurrent programming - Bernstein, Arthur J.
Concurrent programming - Hansen, Per Brinch
Concurrent programming - Manna, Zohar
Concurrent programs - Meyer, Albert R.
Concurrent systems - Lewis, Philip M.
Configuration management - Davis, Alan Mark
Constructive induction - Michalski, Ryszard S.
Consultation systems - Kulikowski, Casimir
Control of distributed networks and distributed processing systems - Gerla, Mario
Control systems - Van Ness, James A.
Control theory - Demmel, James
Control theory - Saad, Youcef
Control theory - Sontag, Eduardo D.
Convex analysis and geometry - Khachiyan, Leonid
Coordination theory - Lawler, Eugene
Correctness of abstract data type implementation - Martin, David F.
Covering radius - Mattson, Harold F., Jr.
Cryptographic protocols - Fischer, Michael J.
Cryptography - Blum, Manuel
Cryptography - Galil, Zvi
Cryptography - Konheim, Allan G.
Cryptography - Micali, Silvio
Cryptography - Rivest, Ronald L.
Cryptography and data security - Rudolph, Luther D.

Cultural factors in computing environments - Gross, Jonathan L.
Data communication and computer methodology - Carlyle, Jack W.
Data communications - Aagaard, James S.
Data communications - Enslow, Philip H., Jr.
Data compression - Reif, John H.
Data compression - Rudolph, Luther D.
Data management systems - Aagaard, James S.
Data modeling and database design - Su, Jianwen
Data networks - Kleinrock, Leonard
Data structures - Chazelle, Bernard
Data structures - Fredman, Michael L.
Data structures - Hirschberg, Daniel
Data structures - Klinger, Allen
Data structures - Lee, Der-Tsai
Data structures - Lueker, George S.
Data structures - Melkanoff, Michel A.
Data structures - Saks, Michael E.
Data structures - Samet, Hanan
Data structures - Stanat, Donald F.
Data structures - Standish, Thomas A.
Data structures - Tarjan, Robert
Data structures for persistent storage - Burkhard, Walter A.
Database and knowledge-based systems - Kedem, Zvi
Database architecture - Dale, A.G.,
Database design - Melkanoff, Michel A.
Database engineering applications - Navathe, Sham
Database machines - Sood, Arun K.
Database management systems - Cardenas, Alfonso F.
Database management systems - Dale, A.G.,
Database management systems - DeWitt, David J.
Database management systems - Katz, Randy H.
Database management systems - Reiss, Steven P.
Database management systems - Stonebraker, Michael R.
Database methodology for software engineering - Su, Jianwen
Database modeling and design - Navathe, Sham
Database support for software engineering - Rine, David
Database systems - Buneman, Peter
Database systems - Burkhard, Walter A.
Database systems - Garcia-Molina, Hector
Database systems - Heller, Jack
Database systems - Robertson, Edward L.
Database systems - Roussopoulos, Nicholas
Database systems - Silberschatz, Abraham
Database systems - Warren, David S.
Database theory - Ginsburg, Seymour
Databases - Kanellakis, Paris C.
Databases - Kulikowski, Casimir

Databases - Minker, Jack
Databases and information systems - Belford, Geneva G.
Databases and information systems - Campbell, Roy H.
Databases and information systems - Liu, J.W.-S.
Databases and parallel computation - Ullman, Jeffrey D.
Dataflow and functional languages and architectures - Ercegovac, Milos D.
Dataflow systems - Arvind
Declarative languages - Stanat, Donald F.
Deductive databases - Henschen, Lawrence J.
Dependable computing and fault-tolerance - Avizienis, Algirdas
Design and analysis - Wood, Roger C.
Design and analysis of algorithms - Floyd, Robert W.
Design and analysis of algorithms - Gonzalez, Teofilo F.
Design and analysis of algorithms - Horowitz, Ellis
Design and analysis of algorithms - Ibarra, Oscar H.
Design and analysis of algorithms - Ladner, Richard
Design and analysis of algorithms - Larmore, Lawrence
Design and analysis of algorithms - Lee, Der-Tsai
Design and analysis of algorithms - Loveland, Donald W.
Design and analysis of algorithms - Pauli, Marvin C.
Design and analysis of algorithms - Preparata, Franco P.
Design and analysis of algorithms - Savage, John E.
Design and correctness of operating systems - Bernstein, Arthur J.
Design and evaluation of systems and networks- Agrawala, Ashkok K.
Design and implementation - Lasowska, Edward D.
Design and implementation of concurrent programming languages - Andrews, Gregory R.
Design and implementation of programming languages - Soffa, Mary Louise
Design automation - Despain, Alvin M.
Design automation - Siewiorek, Daniel P.
Design diversity in software and hardware - Avizienis, Algirdas
Design of algorithms - Kaplan, Kenneth
Design of algorithms - Manber, Udi
Design of centralized, distributed, & antonomous databases - Wiederhold, Gio
Design of computer networks - Grigoriadis, Michael D.
Design of computing systems - Murphy, Gordon J.
Design of custom integrated circuits - Allen, Jonathan
Design of imperative, nonfunctional programming facilities - Storm, Edward F.
Design of information systems - Estrin, Gerald
Design techniques - Davis, Alan Mark
Designer-computer interfaces - Estrin, Gerald
Development environments - Graham, Susan L.
Device-based computability theory - Floyd, Robert W.
Digital communications - Lee, Chung-Chieh
Digital design - Winkel, David E.
Digital hardware - Prosser, Franklin
Digital image processing - Wechsler, Harry
Digital signal processing - Sahni, Sartaj K.

Digital systems design - Smith, David R.
Discrete mathematics - Eisenstat, Stanley
Discrete optimization - Khachiyan, Leonid
Discrete-state and stochastic systems - Carlyle, Jack W.
Distributed algorithms - Bernstein, Arthur J.
Distributed algorithms - Kleinrock, Leonard
Distributed and parallel systems - Lasowska, Edward D.
Distributed and parallel systems research - Kleinrock, Leonard
Distributed architecture - Frieder, Gideon
Distributed artificial intelligence systems and robots - Nilsson, Nils J.
Distributed collaboration - Farber, David
Distributed communications - Kleinrock, Leonard
Distributed computation - Burkhard, Walter A.
Distributed computation - Micali, Silvio
Distributed computer systems - Farber, David
Distributed computer systems for human communication - Morris, James H.
Distributed computing - Garcia-Molina, Hector
Distributed computing - Kanellakis, Paris C.
Distributed computing - Liskov, Barbara H.
Distributed computing - Lynch, Nancy A.
Distributed computing - Manber, Udi
Distributed computing - Saks, Michael E.
Distributed computing protocols - Saks, Michael E.
Distributed control - Kleinrock, Leonard
Distributed data and information systems - Muller, Mervin E.
Distributed data management - Cardenas, Alfonso F.
Distributed data management - Lynch, Nancy A.
Distributed database algorithms and modeling - Muntz, Richard R.
Distributed databases - Chu, Wesley W.
Distributed databases - Su, Jianwen
Distributed databases and knowledge-based systems - Navathe, Sham
Distributed operating systems - Solomon, Marvin H.
Distributed operating systems - Wittie, Larry D.
Distributed processing - Arvind
Distributed processing - Chu, Wesley W.
Distributed processing - Enslow, Philip H., Jr.
Distributed processing - LeBlanc, Richard J., Jr.
Distributed processing - Mamrak, Sandra A.
Distributed processing - Muntz, Richard R.
Distributed real-time computer systems - Kim, K.H. (Kane)
Distributed systems - Bruno, John L.
Distributed systems - Ferrari, Domenico
Distributed systems - Gannon, John
Distributed systems - Hollaar, Lee A.
Distributed systems - Miller, Raymond E.
Distributed systems - Ousterhout, John K.
Distributed systems - Silberschatz, Abraham

Distributed systems - Tripathi, Satish K.
Distributed systems and networks - Belford, Geneva G.
Distributed systems and networks - Campbell, Roy H.
Distributed systems and networks - Faiman, M.
Distributed systems and networks - Liu, J.W.-S.
Distributed systems instrumentation and measurement - Muntz, Richard R.
Document preparation systems - Harrison, Michael A.
Dynamic systems - Rekasius, Zenonas V.
Dynamic voting algorithms - Burkhard, Walter A.
Economic technological development - Miller, William F.
Economics and management of computing - Kraemer, Kenneth L.
Economics of computing - King, John Leslie
Educational computing - Abelson, Harold
Electronic CAD - Sahni, Sartaj K.
Electronic mail - Landweber, Lawrence
Electronic publishing - Scott, Dana S.
Elliptic partial differential equations - Rokhlin, Vladimir
Empirical studies of programming - Morris, James H.
Engineering education - Estrin, Thelma
Environmental systems - Vichnevetsky, Robert
Environments - Buneman, Peter
Error analysis - Kahan, William M.
Error-correcting codes - Mattson, Harold F., Jr.
Expert systems - Chandrasekaran, Balakrishnan
Expert systems - Slagle, James
Expert systems - Stonebraker, Michael R.
Expert systems - Travis, Larry E.
Expert systems - Vidal, Jacques J.
Expert systems - Wechsler, Harry
Expert systems development and applications in physiology and medicine - DiStefano, Joseph J., III
Expert systems for clinical decision making - Estrin, Thelma
Expert systems for design - Gajski, Daniel D.
Expert systems for designing testable circuits - McCluskey, Edward J.
Expert systems with learning capabilities - Michalski, Ryszard S.
External graph theory - Szemeredi, Endre
Fault detection in digital systems - Hartmann, Carlos R.P.
Fault tolerance in distributed databases - Chu, Wesley W.
Fault-tolerance - Tripathi, Satish K.
Fault-tolerant computer systems - Kim, K.H. (Kane)
Fault-tolerant systems - Breuer, Melvin A.
Financial computations - Kahan, William M.
Financial systems - Muller, Mervin E.
Floor-planning, placement and routing - Hu, T.C.
Formal bases for document representation and processing - Brown, Allen, Jr.
Formal definitions of programming languages - Rabinowitz, Irving N.
Formal languages - Ginsburg, Seymour
Formal languages - Savitch, Walter J.

Formal methods in programming languages - Gries, David
Formal specifications - Guttag, John V.
Foundations of geometry - Kahn, Jeffry
Foundations of logic programming - Brown, Allen, Jr.
Functional and logic languages - Arvind
Functional and logic programming - Berkling, Klaus J.
Functional program testing and analysis of real time systems - Howden, William E.
Functional programming languages - Morris, James H.
Game playing - Purdom, Paul W.
General and specialized inference methods - Schubert, Lenhart K.
Geometric modeling - Brown, Christopher M.
Geometric modeling - Requicha, Aristides A. G.
Geometry - Dobkin, David
Grammar forms - Ginsburg, Seymour
Grammars and generating systems - Greibach, Sheila A.
Graph algorithms - Greibach, Sheila A.
Graph algorithms - Reif, John H.
Graph algorithms - Tarjan, Robert
Graph and network optimization - Grigoriadis, Michael D.
Graph theory - Chvatal, Vaclav
Graph theory - Lovász, László
Graph theory - Sahni, Sartaj K.
Graphical programming - Reiss, Steven P.
Graphics - Brown, Christopher M.
Graphics - Dobkin, David
Graphics - Foley, James D.
Graphics - Kulikowski, Casimir
Graphics - Pizer, Stephen M.
Graphics and image processing - Vidal, Jacques J.
Graphs - Cantor, David G.
Heterogeneous inference - Barwise, K. Jon
High energy physics phenomenology - Fox, Geoffrey
High speed computer networks - Farber, David
High-level "new generation" architecture - Berkling, Klaus J.
High-level programming languages - Robinson, J. Alan
High-performance I/O - Patterson, David A.
High-speed scientific computing - Karplus, Walter J.
Holography - Marhic, Michael E.
Human and computer vision - Pizer, Stephen M.
Human and machine planning and plan recognition - Schmidt, Charles
Human movement simulation - Badler, Norman I.
Human-computer interaction - Foley, James D.
Human-computer interaction - Schmidt, Charles
Human-computer interaction - Shneiderman, Ben
Human-computer interfaces - Rowe, Lawrence A.
Human-machine interaction - Vidal, Jacques J.

Hybrid digital/analogue computing - Miranker, Willard
Hypertext and user interfaces - Klinger, Allen
Image analysis - Pavlidis, Theo
Image analysis - Tanimoto, Steven L.
Image indexing - Klinger, Allen
Image processing - Greenberg, Donald P.
Image processing - Samet, Hanan
Image processing and display - Pizer, Stephen M.
Image synthesis and rendering - Hanrahan, Patrick
Implementation and correctness of programming language translators - Martin, David F.
Implementation-oriented semantics - Morris, F. Lockwood
Incremental compilers - Soffa, Mary Louise
Inductive inference (learning algorithms) - Daley, Robert
Information efficiency of representations - Elias, Peter
Information exchange theory - Chang, Shi-Kuo
Information organization and retrieval - Salton, Gerald
Information processing in biological systems - Bekey, George A.
Information retrieval - Scott, Dana S.
Information retrieval systems - Hollaar, Lee A.
Information science - Zunde, Pranas
Information storage and retrieval - Weiss, Stephen F.
Information systems - Zunde, Pranas
Information technology and public policy - Kraemer, Kenneth L.
Information theory - Elias, Peter
Information theory - Rudolph, Luther D.
Information-based complexity - Wozniakowski, Henryk
Information-theoretic approaches to semantics - Barwise, K. Jon
Integrated architectures planning and learning - Carbonell, Jaime G.
Integrated circuit of devices - Viswanathan, Chand R.
Integrated wholistic systems - Uhr, Leonard M.
Intelligent information systems - Shapiro, Linda
Interactive graphics - Chandrasekaran, Balakrishnan
Interactive program development environments - Fischer, Charles N.
Interactive software - Graham, Susan L.
Interactive systems - Pavlidis, Theo
Interactive systems - Warren, David S.
Interpretation problems - Amarel, Saul
Knowledge acquisition for expert systems - Carbonell, Jaime G.
Knowledge base systems - Buneman, Peter
Knowledge evaluation - Loveland, Donald W.
Knowledge representation - Carbonell, Jaime G.
Knowledge representation - Feigenbaum, Edward A.
Knowledge representation - McDermott, Drew V.
Knowledge representation - Schubert, Lenhart K.
Knowledge representation - Shapiro, Stuart C.
Knowledge representation - Wilensky, Robert
Knowledge-based distributed systems - Chu, Wesley W.

Knowledge-based heuristic problem-solving systems - Gelertner, Herbert
Knowledge-based image processing - Li, Ching-Chung
Knowledge-based machine translation - Carbonell, Jaime G.
Knowledge-based systems - Holden, Alistair D.C.
Knowledge-based systems - Zadeh, Lotfi A.
Knowledge-based techniques in database management, query and update - Wiederhold, Gio
Knowledge-directed databases - Chandrasekaran, Balakrishnan
Lambda calculus - Meyer, Albert R.
Language and vision - Bajcsy, Ruzena
Language data processing - Simmons, Robert F.
Language design - Schwartz, Jacob
Language generation in the context of knowledge structures - Klein, Sheldon
Language specifications - Rine, David
Language understanding in the context of knowledge structures - Klein, Sheldon
Languages - Berkling, Klaus J.
Large-scale computing - Goodman, James R.
Large-scale dynamic systems - Van Ness, James A.
Large-scale particle simulations - Rokhlin, Vladimir'
Large-scale scientific computing - Bayliss, Alvin
Large-scale structured problems - Grigoriadis, Michael D.
Learning and inference - Biermann, Alan W.
Learning and memory - Lynch, Gary S.
Learning and problem solving - Kolodner, Janet L.
Learning theories - Carr, John W. III
Learning theory - Ibarra, Oscar H.
Learning theory - Schank, Roger C.
Learning theory - Winston, Patrick H.
Legal issues concerning computers - Hollaar, Lee A.
Legal reasoning - McCarty, L. Thorne
Legged locomotion - Raibert, Marc H.
Linear algebra - Stenger, Frank
Linear and integer programming - Hu, T.C.
Linear and multilinear algebra - Marcus, Marvin
Linear and nonlinear network optimization - Myer, Robert R.
Linear and nonlinear programming - Overton, Michael
Linear numerical analysis - Marcus, Marvin
Linear programming - Chvatal, Vaclav
Load leveling - Muntz, Richard R.
Logic - Barwise, K. Jon
Logic - Freyd, Peter
Logic design - Ercegovac, Milos D.
Logic of programs - Manna, Zohar
Logic of programs - Meyer, Albert R.
Logic programming - Davis, Martin
Logic programming - Despain, Alvin M.
Logic programming - Gallier, Jean
Logic programming - Kanellakis, Paris C.

Mathematical programming - Golub, Gene H.

Mathematical programming - Grigoriadis, Michael D.

Mathematical programming - Khachiyan, Leonid

Mathematical programming - Mangasarian, Olvi L.

Mathematical programming algorithms - Rosen, J. Ben

Mathematical representation, manipulation, and analysis of shape using computers - Goldman, Ron

Mathematical software - Cline, Alan K.

Mathematical software - Skeel, R. D.

Mathematical theory of computation - Manna, Zohar

Mathematical typography - Knuth, Donald E.

Mathematics - Goldstein, Max

Mathematics - Novacky, George A., Jr.

Matrix algebra - Sahni, Sartaj K.

Matrix computations - Kahan, William M.

Measurement and modeling - Ferrari, Domenico

Measurement theory - Kyburg, Henry E., Jr.

Mechanical theorem proving - Plaisted, David A.

Mechanization of deduction - Travis, Larry E.

Medical graphics - Frieder, Gideon

Medical imaging - Pizer, Stephen M.

Medically-motivated computing - Frieder, Gideon

Memory hierarchy design - Flynn, Michael J.

Methodology for modeling and control of dynamic data sources - Aoki, Masanao

Microcomputer applications - Carlyle, Jack W.

Microprocessor architectures - Dewar, Robert

Microprocessors - Murphy, Gordon J.

Mobile robots - Kanade, Takeo

Model theory - Scott, Dana S.

Model-based reasoning - Davis, Randall

Modeling - Haddad, Abraham H.

Modeling and analysis - Konheim, Allan G.

Modeling and analysis of concurrent systems - Estrin, Gerald

Modeling and analysis of fault-tolerant multiple processor systems - Trivedi, Kishor S.

Modeling and optimization of large-scale energy systems - Dantzig, George B.

Modeling and simulation - Hopcroft, John E.

Modeling and simulation of systems - Karplus, Walter J.

Modeling and simulation of systems - Vichnevetsky, Robert

Modeling program behavior - Flynn, Michael J.

Modeling theory and methodology in the life sciences - DiStefano, Joseph J., III

Models for parallel and distributed computation - Greibach, Sheila A.

Models for task partition and allocation - Chu, Wesley W.

Models of computation - Hirschberg, Daniel

Models of computation - Traub, Joseph F.

Models of human reasoning and human memory - Schank, Roger C.

Models of intelligence - Uhr, Leonard M.

Multicomputers - Hwang, Kai

Multimedia applications and databases - Rowe, Lawrence A.

Multimedia document preparation systems - van Dam, Andries
Multiple error-correcting communication codes - Reed, Irving S.
Multiple representation - Harrison, Michael A.
Multiprocessing architectures and algorithms - Wise, David S.
Multiprocessor and multicomputer systems - Despain, Alvin M.
Multiprocessor systems - Dertouzos, Michael L.
Multiprocessors - Hwang, Kai
Multiprocessors - Siewiorek, Daniel P.
Musical concepts - Minsky, Marvin L.
Natural and synthetic languages - Zadeh, Lotfi A.
Natural language and logic - Warren, David S.
Natural language interfaces - Joshi, Aravind K.
Natural language processing - Allen, James F.
Natural language processing - Allen, Jonathan
Natural language processing - Carbonell, Jaime G.
Natural language processing - Charniak, Eugene
Natural language processing - Grishman, Ralph
Natural language processing - Joshi, Aravind K.
Natural language processing - Marcus, Mitch
Natural language processing - Savitch, Walter J.
Natural language processing - Schank, Roger C.
Natural language processing - Weiss, Stephen F.
Natural language understanding - Schubert, Lenhart K.
Natural language understanding - Shapiro, Stuart C.
Networks - Cantor, David G.
Networks - Corbato, Fernando J.
Networks and graphs - Bruno, John L.
Neural architecture - von der Malsburg, Christoph
Neural networks - Holden, Alistair D.C.
Neural networks - Mehrotra, Kishan G.
Neural networks - Pearl, Judea
Neural networks - Wechsler, Harry
Neural networks - Wittie, Larry D.
Neural networks for system simulation - Karplus, Walter J.
Neurocybernetics and neural models - Vidal, Jacques J.
Non-deterministic computation - Sanchis, Luis
Non-monotonic reasoning - Brown, Allen, Jr.
Non-procedural knowledge representation - Travis, Larry E.
Non-standard logics - Dunn, J. Michael
Nonlinear equations - Saad, Youcef
Nonmonotonic reasoning - McCarthy, John
Nonmonotonic reasoning - Minker, Jack
Nonnumerical computation - Schwartz, Jacob
Number theory - Szemeredi, Endre
Numerical analysis - Bareiss, Erwin H.
Numerical analysis - Bayliss, Alvin
Numerical analysis - Blum, Edward K.

Numerical analysis - Cline, Alan K.
Numerical analysis - de Boor, Carl
Numerical analysis - Demmel, James
Numerical analysis - Eisenstat, Stanley
Numerical analysis - Golub, Gene H.
Numerical analysis - Kahan, William M.
Numerical analysis - Miranker, Willard
Numerical analysis - O'Leary, Dianne P.
Numerical analysis - Oliger, Joseph
Numerical analysis - Overton, Michael
Numerical analysis - Parlett, Beresford N.
Numerical analysis - Schultz, Martin H.
Numerical analysis - Springer, George
Numerical analysis - Stenger, Frank
Numerical analysis - Van Ness, James A.
Numerical analysis - van Loan, Charles
Numerical analysis - Vichnevetsky, Robert
Numerical analysis - Widlund, Olof
Numerical analysis - Young, David M.
Numerical analysis and interval analysis - Moore, Ramon E.
Numerical and scientific computing - Saylor, Paul E.
Numerical and scientific computing: linear algebra - Skeel, R. D.
Numerical computing - Pizer, Stephen M.
Numerical control machining - Melkanoff, Michel A.
Numerical linear algebra - Eberlein, Patricia James
Numerical linear algebra - Rokhlin, Vladimir
Numerical linear algebra - Rose, Donald J.
Numerical linear algebra - Stewart, G.W.
Numerical methods for partial differential equations - Oliger, Joseph
Numerical methods for partial differential equations - Parter, Seymour V.
Numerical scattering theory - Rokhlin, Vladimir
Numerical software - Overton, Michael
Numerical software - Widlund, Olof
Numerical solution of differential equations - Rose, Donald J.
Numerical solution of integral equations - Rokhlin, Vladimir
Numerical stability - Wozniakowski, Henryk
Object models for multi-user database query and update processing interfaces - Wiederhold, Gio
Office automation - Heller, Jack
Office automation - Unger, Stephen H.
Office information systems - Horowitz, Ellis
Operating systems - Aagaard, James S.
Operating systems - Andrews, Gregory R.
Operating systems - Campbell, Roy H.
Operating systems - Corbato, Fernando J.
Operating systems - Dewar, Robert
Operating systems - Enslow, Philip H., Jr.
Operating systems - Ferrari, Domenico

Operating systems - Gottlieb, Allan
Operating systems - Habermann, A. Nico
Operating systems - Hagstrom, Stanley
Operating systems - Hansen, Per Brinch
Operating systems - Harrison, Malcolm
Operating systems - Lawrie, Duncan H.
Operating systems - Liu, J.W.-S.
Operating systems - Liu, Ming T.
Operating systems - Mamrak, Sandra A.
Operating systems - Ousterhout, John K.
Operating systems - Reed, Daniel A.
Operating systems - Schwartz, Jacob
Operating systems - Shaw, Alan C.
Operating systems - Silberschatz, Abraham
Operating systems - Stonebraker, Michael R.
Operating systems - Ward, Stephen A.
Operations research - Chvatal, Vaclav
Operations research - Hu, T.C.
Operations research - Robinson, Stephen M.
Optical communication - Plonus, Martin A.
Optical communication - Yuen, Horace P.
Optical computation - Reif, John H.
Optical fibers - Plonus, Martin A.
Optical materials - Wessels, Bruce
Optical networks - Marhic, Michael E.
Optical phenomena - Kannwurf, Carl R.
Optical phenomena - Taflove, Allen
Optical processing - Marhic, Michael E.
Optimal coding - Larmore, Lawrence
Optimal experiment design methodology - DiStefano, Joseph J., III
Optimization - Overton, Michael
Optimization - Papadimitriou, Christos H.
Optimization - Sood, Arun K.
Optimization of compiled code - Kennedy, Ken
Optimization theory - Steiger, William
Optimization theory - Vichnevetsky, Robert
Optoelectronic device applications - Chang, Robert
Ordinary differential equations - Skeel, R. D.
Organization of large scale systems - Moses, Joel
Organizational and social impacts of computing - Kraemer, Kenneth L.
Parallel algorithms - Cole, Richard
Parallel algorithms - Gottlieb, Allan
Parallel algorithms - Lee, Der-Tsai
Parallel algorithms - O'Leary, Dianne P.
Parallel algorithms - Papadimitriou, Christos H.
Parallel algorithms - Patrick, Merrell L.
Parallel algorithms - Reif, John H.

Parallel machines including sparse memory - Flynn, Michael J.
Parallel processing - Arvind
Parallel processing - Baer, Jean-Loup
Parallel processing - Hwang, Kai
Parallel programming - Misra, Jayadev
Parallel programming environments - LeBlanc, Thomas J.
Parallelizing compilers - Soffa, Mary Louise
Parametrically and implicitly represented geometry - Goldman, Ron
Partial differential equations - Saad, Youcef
Partial differential equations - Widlund, Olof
Partial differential equations - Young, David M.
Pattern perception - Uhr, Leonard M.
Pattern recognition - Chandrasekaran, Balakrishnan
Pattern recognition - Kanal, Laveen N.
Pattern recognition - Klinger, Allen
Pattern recognition - Li, Ching-Chung
Pattern recognition - Mangasarian, Olvi L.
Pattern recognition - Michalski, Ryszard S.
Pattern recognition - Sahni, Sartaj K.
Pattern recognition - Shapiro, Linda
Pattern recognition - Srihari, Sargur N.
Pattern recognition - Zunde, Pranas
Performance analysis - Lam, Simon S.
Performance analysis and graph algorithms - Kennedy, Ken
Performance and scheduling issues in parallel and distributed systems - Zahorjan, John
Performance evaluation - Ferrari, Domenico
Performance evaluation - Gerla, Mario
Performance evaluation - Liu, Ming T.
Performance evaluation - Mamrak, Sandra A.
Performance evaluation - Tripathi, Satish K.
Performance evaluation and design - Kleinrock, Leonard
Performance limits of parallel processors - Flynn, Michael J.
Performance modeling - Sood, Arun K.
Performance modeling and evaluation - Zahorjan, John
Personal computer systems and applications - Desautels, Edouard J.
Perturbation theory - Stewart, G.W.
Philosophical aspects of computer science - Daley, Robert
Philosophical foundations of artificial intelligence - Travis, Larry E.
Philosophy of mind - Hofstadter, Douglas R.
Philosophy of science - Kyburg, Henry E., Jr.
Photogrammetry - Horn, Berthold K.P.
Pictorial data management - Cardenas, Alfonso F.
Pictorial information systems - Chang, Shi-Kuo
Planning, representation of beliefs, goals and action - Allen, James F.
Policies for computer management and use in organizations - King, John Leslie
Practical decoding algorithms - Hartmann, Carlos R.P.
Principles and theory of databases - Su, Jianwen

Probabilistic algorithms for graph isomorphism and topological invariants - Gross, Jonathan L.
Probabilistic analysis of algorithms - Lueker, George S.
Probabilistic methods - Spencer, Joel
Problem solving - Carr, John W. III
Problems involved in managing the computer resources of an organization - Feldman, Julian
Problems of representation and modeling in problem solving - Amarel, Saul
Procedural logic - Simmons, Robert F.
Process specification languages - Pratt, Vaughan
Production systems for computer-based learning - Bork, Alfred M.
Productivity technology - Winston, Patrick H.
Program complexity - Zelkowitz, Marvin V.
Program correctness - Dijkstra, Edsger Wybe
Program development - Zelkowitz, Marvin V.
Program development systems - Solomon, Marvin H.
Program logic and semantics - Kozen, Dexter
Program portability - Griswold, Ralph E.
Program semantics - Cartwright, Robert S.
Program transformations - Schonberg, Edmond
Program validation - Cartwright, Robert S.
Program verification - Boyer, Robert S.
Program verification - Martin, David F.
Program verification - Stanat, Donald F.
Programming - Zelkowitz, Marvin V.
Programming and specification language design - Kemmer, Richard A.
Programming as mathematical exposition - Morris, F. Lockwood
Programming aspects of parallel computers - Lindstrom, Gary E.
Programming environments - Fateman, Richard J.
Programming environments - Gallier, Jean
Programming environments - Standish, Thomas A.
Programming language design - Lindstrom, Gary E.
Programming language design and implementation - Graham, Susan L.
Programming language design and implementation - Griswold, Ralph E.
Programming language design and implementation - Harrison, Malcolm
Programming language semantics - Stanat, Donald F.
Programming languages - Arvind
Programming languages - Berry, Daniel M.
Programming languages - Buneman, Peter
Programming languages - Campbell, Roy H.
Programming languages - Carr, John W. III
Programming languages - Dershowitz, Nachum
Programming languages - Dewar, Robert
Programming languages - Friedman, Daniel P.
Programming languages - Gannon, John
Programming languages - Gries, David
Programming languages - Habermann, A. Nico
Programming languages - Hansen, Per Brinch
Programming languages - Hanson, David

Programming languages - Knuth, Donald E.
Programming languages - Liskov, Barbara H.
Programming languages - Liu, J.W.-S.
Programming languages - Magó, Gyula A.
Programming languages - Melkanoff, Michel A.
Programming languages - Minsky, Naftaly
Programming languages - Rabinowitz, Irving N.
Programming languages - Reynolds, John C.
Programming languages - Schonberg, Edmond
Programming languages - Solomon, Marvin H.
Programming languages - Springer, George
Programming languages - Wegner, Peter
Programming languages and compilers - Fateman, Richard J.
Programming languages and data structures - Burkhard, Walter A.
Programming languages and environments - LeBlanc, Richard J., Jr.
Programming languages and systems - Reiss, Steven P.
Programming logic - Rine, David
Programming logics - Constable, Robert L.
Programming methodology - Gries, David
Programming methodology - Guttag, John V.
Programming methodology - Liskov, Barbara H.
Programming multiprocessors - Guttag, John V.
Programming theory - Hoare, Charles Anthony Richard
Proof theory - Dunn, J. Michael
Proof theory - Gallier, Jean
Pseudo-random numbers - Traub, Joseph F.
Psycholinguistics - Simmons, Robert F.
Public key cryptosystems - Adleman, Leonard
Public policy and social impact aspects of computer use - King, John Leslie
Quadrature formulae for singular functions - Rokhlin, Vladimir
Quality and production concepts - Muller, Mervin E.
Query optimization for distributed database systems - Muntz, Richard R.
Query, transaction, and programming languages for databases - Su, Jianwen
Question-and-answer systems - Melkanoff, Michel A.
Randomization - Traub, Joseph F.
Randomized algorithms - Reif, John H.
Randomness and complexity - Blum, Lenore C.
Randomness and computational complexity - Micali, Silvio
Real-time 3D computer graphics - Brooks, Frederick P., Jr.
Real-time computation - Karplus, Walter J.
Real-time computing systems - Campbell, Roy H.
Real-time computing systems - Liu, Chung L.
Real-time computing systems - Liu, J.W.-S.
Real-time hardware and software systems - Kehl, Theodore H.
Real-time information retrieval - Aagaard, James S.
Real-time learning systems - Kim, K.H. (Kane)

Real-time systems - Shaw, Alan C.
Real-time systems - Tripathi, Satish K.
Reasoning - Shapiro, Stuart C.
Reflexive structures - Sanchis, Luis
Relation algebras - Pratt, Vaughan
Relational database applications - Hennie, Frederick C. III
Relations between logic and computer science - Dunn, J. Michael
Reliable computing - Siewiorek, Daniel P.
Representation and manipulation of geometric objects - Guibas, Leonidas J.
Requirements analysis and specification - Davis, Alan Mark
Resource management for parallel systems - Browne, J.C.
Rewriting systems - Purdom, Paul W.
Robot architecture - Nilsson, Nils J.
Robot motion planning - Reif, John H.
Robotics - Bajcsy, Ruzena
Robotics - Bekey, George A.
Robotics - Brown, Christopher M.
Robotics - Dyer, Charles R.
Robotics - Guibas, Leonidas J.
Robotics - Hopcroft, John E.
Robotics - Lozano-Pérez, Tomás
Robotics - Minsky, Marvin L.
Robotics - Mitchell, Tom M.
Robotics - Nevatia, Ramakant
Robotics - Raibert, Marc H.
Robotics - Reddy, Raj
Robotics - Shapiro, Linda
Robotics - Sontag, Eduardo D.
Robotics - Wright, Paul
Robotics - Yap, Chee
Robotics and computer vision - Schwartz, Jacob
Scheduling theory - Bruno, John L.
Scheduling theory - Gonzalez, Teofilo F.
Science for design - Gajski, Daniel D.
Scientific applications - Gelertner, Herbert
Scientific computation - Abelson, Harold
Scientific computation - Fateman, Richard J.
Scientific computation - Marcus, Marvin
Scientific computing - Demmel, James
Scientific computing - Klinger, Allen
Scientific computing - Rose, Donald J.
Scientific computing - Schultz, Martin H.
Scientific computing in the life sciences - DiStefano, Joseph J., III
Scientific programming environments - Kennedy, Ken
Screen design - Bork, Alfred M.
Secure protocols - Micali, Silvio
Selector properties - Sanchis, Luis

Semantics - Buneman, Peter
Semantics - Gries, David
Semantics - Reiss, Steven P.
Semantics of computation, theory - Martin, David F.
Semantics of programming languages - Freyd, Peter
Semantics of programming languages - Martin, David F.
Semantics of programming languages - Meyer, Albert R.
Semantics prototyping systems - Martin, David F.
Semiconductor devices - Wessels, Bruce
Sensing - Binford, Thomas O.
Sequential logic circuits - Unger, Stephen H.
Set theory - Scott, Dana S.
Shared-memory multiprocessors - Goodman, James R.
Signal processing - Sood, Arun K.
Silicon compilation - Gajski, Daniel D.
Simulation - Bork, Alfred M.
Simulation - Carlyle, Jack W.
Simulation - McNamee, Lawrence
Simulation and modeling - Sood, Arun K.
Simulation and modeling of physical and conceptual processors - Flynn, Michael J.
Simulation and numerical analysis of large dynamic phenomena - Aoki, Masanao
Simulation designs and analyses - Muller, Mervin E.
Simulation of language transmission and language change - Klein, Sheldon
Simulation via computer - Simmons, Robert F.
Small-scale systems in instructional environments - Jensen, Alton P.
Social analysis of computing - Kling, Rob
Social implications of computer technology - Estrin, Thelma
Social implications of computing - Travis, Larry E.
Sociology of computing - Kling, Rob
Software engineering - Basili, Victor R.
Software engineering - Berry, Daniel M.
Software engineering - Chu, Yaohan
Software engineering - Dershowitz, Nachum
Software engineering - Freeman, Peter A.
Software engineering - Hagstrom, Stanley
Software engineering - Horowitz, Ellis
Software engineering - Howden, William E.
Software engineering - Kemmer, Richard A.
Software engineering - LeBlanc, Richard J., Jr.
Software engineering - Minsky, Naftaly
Software engineering - Muller, Mervin E.
Software engineering - Rabinowitz, Irving N.
Software engineering - Ramamoorthy, Chittoor V.
Software engineering - Robertson, Edward L.
Software engineering - Shaw, Mary
Software engineering - Wegner, Peter

Software engineering - Weyuker, Elaine
Software engineering - Zelkowitz, Marvin V.
Software environments - Osterweil, Leon J.
Software metrics - Weyuker, Elaine
Software process - Osterweil, Leon J.
Software productivity - Farber, David
Software project management - Davis, Alan Mark
Software quality assurance - Basili, Victor R.
Software quality measurement - Ralston, Anthony
Software reliability - Mehrotra, Kishan G.
Software specifications - Shaw, Alan C.
Software systems - Miller, William F.
Software systems design and optimization - Vitter, Jeffrey S.
Software testing - Weyuker, Elaine
Software testing and analysis - Osterweil, Leon J.
Software testing and validation - Howden, William E.
Solid-state electronics - Viswanathan, Chand R.
Sorting and searching - Cantor, David G.
Sparse matrix computations - Saad, Youcef
Spatial and temporal reasoning - McDermott, Drew V.
Special-purpose architectures for arithmetic-intensive computations - Ercegovac, Milos D.
Specification and verification of systems - Kemmer, Richard A.
Specification and verification techniques - Lam, Simon S.
Specification of VLSI algorithms and structures - Ercegovac, Milos D.
Speech analysis - Klinger, Allen
Speech generation - Allen, Jonathan
Speech recognition - Allen, Jonathan
Speech understanding - Allen, Jonathan
Speech understanding - Holden, Alistair D.C.
Static analysis techniques and their utilization - Soffa, Mary Louise
Statistical computations - Muller, Mervin E.
Statistical computations - Stewart, G.W.
Statistical computing - Golub, Gene H.
Statistical computing - Steiger, William
Statistical inference - Mehrotra, Kishan G.
Stochastic realization theory - Aoki, Masanao
Stochastic systems - Haddad, Abraham H.
Strategic planning and management - Miller, William F.
String and list processing - Griswold, Ralph E.
String manipulating languages - Unger, Stephen H.
Structured logic circuits - Smith, Kent F.
Subnanosecond arithmetic processors - Flynn, Michael J.
Supercomputer architectures (hypercube) - Fox, Geoffrey
Supercomputers - Ercegovac, Milos D.
Supercomputers - Hwang, Kai
Supercomputers - Karin, Sidney
Supercomputing - Taflove, Allen

Superconductors - Kannwurf, Carl R.
Switching networks for parallel processors - Unger, Stephen H.
Symbolic mathematical computation - Fateman, Richard J.
Symbolic methods of inductive inference - Michalski, Ryszard S.
Synaptic change - Lynch, Gary S.
System architecture - Baer, Jean-Loup
System design - Howden, William E.
System design - Johnson, Robert R.
System performance analysis - Muller, Mervin E.
System theory - Zunde, Pranas
Systems programming - Desautels, Edouard J.
Task allocation - Muntz, Richard R.
Task force scheduling - Muntz, Richard R.
Teaching of programming - Feldman, Julian
Techniques for proving Lower Bounds - Galil, Zvi
Technology-society issues - Unger, Stephen H.
Telecommunication systems - Enslow, Philip H., Jr.
Term rewriting systems - Plaisted, David A.
Text processing - Berry, Daniel M.
Text processing - Salton, Gerald
Theorem proving - Guttag, John V.
Theorem proving - Harrison, Malcolm
Theorem proving - Henschen, Lawrence J.
Theoretical computer science - Statman, Richard
Theoretical computer science - Szemeredi, Endre
Theoretical computing - Dershowitz, Nachum
Theoretical computing - Liu, Chung L.
Theoretical computing: analysis of algorithms and data structures - Edelsbrunner, Herbert
Theoretical computing: analysis of algorithms and data structures - Rheingold, Edward M.
Theoretical foundations of computer science - Daley, Robert
Theory - Selman, Alan L.
Theory and practice of fast computer arithmetic - Ercegovac, Milos D.
Theory of algorithms - Amarel, Saul
Theory of algorithms - Hennie, Frederick C. III
Theory of algorithms - Spencer, Joel
Theory of computation - Constable, Robert L.
Theory of computation - Davis, Martin
Theory of computation - Gallier, Jean
Theory of computation - Hartmanis, Juris
Theory of computation - Hennie, Frederick C. III
Theory of computation - Ibarra, Oscar H.
Theory of computation - Kanellakis, Paris C.
Theory of computation - Ko, Ker-I
Theory of computation - Kozen, Dexter
Theory of computation - Ladner, Richard
Theory of computation - Robertson, Edward L.
Theory of computation - Statman, Richard
Theory of computation - Weyuker, Elaine

References

The following publications have been helpful while preparing this guide. Not mentioned in this list are hundreds of books, booklets, brochures, etc., the departments sent to us.

American Society for Engineering Education:
Engineering Education: Engineering College Research & Graduate Study,
Washington, D.C., March, 1991.

Association for Computing Machinery:
GAD - Graduate Assistantship Directory in the Computer Sciences,
ACM Press, 1991.

Brauer, W.; Haacke, W.; Münch, S.:
Studien- und Forschungsführer Informatik, Zweite neubearbeitete und erweiterte Auflage,
Springer-Verlag, Berlin, Heidelberg, New York, Tokyo, 1990.

The Computing Research Association:
The Forsythe List of Ph.D. Granting Departments of Computer Science and Computer Engineering,
Washington, D.C., March, 1991.

Connors, Martin (editor):
Computers and Computing Information Resources Directory, First Edition,
Gale Research Co., Michigan, 1987.

Peterson's Guides, Inc.:
Graduate Programs in Engineering & Applied Sciences 1991, Peterson's Guide to Graduate Study: Book 5, Twenty-fifth Edition,
Princeton, 1990.

U.S. News & World Report:
America's Best Graduate Schools, Vol. 110, #16,
April 29, 1991.

GPSR Compliance

The European Union's (EU) General Product Safety Regulation (GPSR)
is a set of rules that requires consumer products to be safe and our
obligations to ensure this.

If you have any concerns about our products, you can contact us on
ProductSafety@springernature.com

In case Publisher is established outside the EU, the EU authorized
representative is:

Springer Nature Customer Service Center GmbH
Europaplatz 3
69115 Heidelberg, Germany

Batch number: 09624501

Printed by Printforce, the Netherlands